AF361324

THE CATHOLIC UNIVERSITY OF AMERICA
CANON LAW STUDIES
No. 228

Religious Superioresses

A HISTORICAL SYNOPSIS AND A COMMENTARY

BY

Thomas J. Bowe, A.B., J.C.L.
Priest of the Archdiocese of San Francisco

A DISSERTATION

*Submitted to the Faculty of the School of Canon Law of the
Catholic University of America in Partial Fulfillment
of the Requirements for the Degree of
Doctor of Canon Law*

THE CATHOLIC UNIVERSITY OF AMERICA PRESS
WASHINGTON, D. C.
1 9 4 6

COPYRIGHT, 1947

THE CATHOLIC UNIVERSITY OF AMERICA PRESS, INC.

Printed by

THE PAULIST PRESS

401 WEST 59TH STREET

NEW YORK 19, N. Y.

51

TABLE OF CONTENTS

PART II

CANONICAL COMMENTARY

CHAPTER IV

CHAPTER V

CHAPTER VI

CHAPTER VII

CHAPTER VIII

CHAPTER IX

FOREWORD

It is of the essence of the religious state that members of the community subject themselves to the direction of a higher authority. The consequence of this necessity has been the development of a canonical institute which provides stable offices in every religious community. Those elected or appointed to these offices are invested with the power necessary for governing the members of the community. The aim of this work is to discuss the canonical regulations affecting the offices of the local superioress, the provincial, and the superioress general in communities of women religious.

From its very nature the office of superioress penetrates every aspect of religious life. It has been necessary therefore to limit the field of this study. The prescriptions governing the elections of superioresses have been omitted; those matters in which it becomes necessary for the superioress to approach authorities external to the religious institute have been discussed only when the functions of the superioress form a principal part. For this reason the erection of a religious institute, the process of obtaining papal approval for an institute, and the erection of a province, have not been treated in detail. The subject of administration in schools, hospitals, and like institutions has not been considered, and finally, no attempt has been made to comment on the procedures requisite for exclaustration and secularization.

By way of explanation it may be noted that throughout this work the term superioress has been used in preference to the term superior, in order to leave no doubt that the particular legislation discussed applies to the moderators of women religious. In citing the opinions of authors, even if they have used the masculine gender, provided the matter embraces women religious, their statements have been transposed to the feminine gender.

The writer wishes to express his sincere gratitude to the Most Reverend John J. Mitty, D.D., Archbishop of San Francisco, for the opportunity of pursuing a course of advanced study in Canon Law; to the faculty of the School of Canon Law of the Catholic University of America for their direction and assistance in the preparation of this work, and to all others who have given their aid and encouragement toward its completion.

Part I

Historical Synopsis

CHAPTER I

THE FIRST SUPERIORESSES OF WOMEN RELIGIOUS

Canon 487 of the Code of Canon Law declares that the religious state is to be held in honor by all. What is set down there in the form of law has from early times been evidenced in the hearts of men. Prior to Christ it was so even among pagan nations, manifest, for example, in the honor that was paid to the Vestal Virgins. With Christ its nobility and its consequent acceptableness to Almighty God were specifically proclaimed.[1]

History offers ample evidence that these counsels of Christ were at once put into practice, and that the number of ascetics and virgins grew rapidly.[2] Some remained in their homes; others gathered in communities, that they might better practice the austerities of the religious state.[3] Of interest especially is the fact that such formations were embraced by women prior to the time that the same steps were taken by groups of men. One reads in the life of St. Anthony (251-356), as it is related by St. Athanasius (296-373), that hearing the call of God, this father of the cenobitic life placed his sister with known and trusty virgins in a sisterhood.[4] This dates back to approximately the year 270.

---

[1] Matthew, xix, 21.

[2] Alzog, *Manual of Universal Church History* (4 vols., Dublin: M. H. Gill & Son, 1879), I, 524.

[3] Montalembert, *The Monks of the West* (2 vols., New York: P. J. Kenedy & Sons, 1905), I, 170.

[4] Migne, *Patrologiae Cursus Completus, Series Latina* (221 vols., Parisiis, 1844-1864), LXXIII, 128, cap. 3 (hereafter referred to as *MPL*); Migne, *Patrologiae Cursus Completus, Series Graeca* (162 vols., Parisiis, 1857-1866), XXVI, 843, cap. 3.

The story of St. Anthony, and of how, though he left the world to find solitude, his life became a great force of attraction to others, is familiar history. Hundreds gathered about him to imitate him and to follow the rules he enacted for a community life dedicated to the service of God. Women were no less inspired than men. Virgins and widows gathered together. From Palladius (ca. 365-ca. 430) one learns that by the end of the fourth century there were numerous nunneries in all parts of monastic Egypt.[5]

In these first communities one finds definite mention of one of their members as the head. This is not at all surprising in view of the very nature of the life that they had chosen. Besides the direction that was necessary for beginners, the religious state called for submission and obedience. Many authors feel that the sister of St. Anthony guided the group of which she was a member.[6] St. Pachomius (ca. 292-346) founded two nunneries, one under his sister at Tabennisi.[7] Palladius makes mention of one Dorotheus,[8] in spiritual charge of a nunnery, and of another, Mother Talis, superioress of a convent at Antinoë.[9] St. Augustine (354-430) founded for women at Hippo a monastery of which he made his sister the superioress.[10]

With the coming of St. Athanasius (ca. 297-373) to Rome in 340, and of St. Jerome (ca. 342-420) in 382, the West showed a zeal for the religious life parallel to that of the East. Many holy women gathered about St. Jerome, seeing in him an able spiritual director. Marcella, a young widow of an illustrious family, placed herself at the head of a select number of matrons. Paula, directly descended from the younger Scipio (185-129 B. C.), followed Jerome to the Holy Land, and established a monastery for women in Beth-

---

[5] Butler, *The Lausiac History of Palladius* (Texts and Studies, VI, 2 vols., Cambridge, 1898-1904), II, 151.

[6] Thomassinus, *Vetus et Nova Ecclesiae Disciplina circa Beneficia et Beneficiarios* (10 vols., Moguntiae, 1787), Pars I, lib. III, cap. 44, n. 1; Alzog, *Manual of Universal Church History*, I, 529.

[7] Butler, "Monasticism," *The Cambridge Medieval History* (8 vols., Reprint, New York: The Macmillan Company, 1936), I, 530.

[8] Butler, *The Lausiac History of Palladius*, II, 151.

[9] *Ibidem*, p. 153.

[10] Montalembert, *The Monks of the West*, II, 262.

lehem. Melania, the elder daughter of a consul, instituted another monastery in Jerusalem.[11]

These great women are the early founders of communities of women religious. They are also the first to hold what may be called the office of superioress, the institute with whose development the present study is concerned. Today the one holding such an office is known by a title fixed in the constitutions of her respective community. In the early ages of the Church formal titles, like the institute itself, had to pass through a process of development. The first superioresses were referred to under the title *mater monasterii, mater monacharum,* or simply *praeposita.*[12] In his *Regula Monacharum* St. Jerome (ca. 342-420) commanded obedience to the *praeposita* as to a mother.[13] St. Augustine (354-430) mentioned that the monastery was ruled by a *praeposita* and a priest.[14] In the *Regula ad Virgines* of St. Caesarius of Arles (470-543) one reads of the *mater* and the *praeposita.*[15]

It need hardly be said that at this early date one does not find specific legislation of the Church defining the powers and duties of these superioresses. That their office gave to them rights and duties and the power to carry these out is quite evident. Each of these communities was subject to a rule written by its founder, or adopted from one prepared by the fathers of the spiritual life. In each of these it is pointed out that the superioress has charge of the members. St. Jerome stated that the superioress has a heavy burden on her shoulders and is responsible before God for the souls, the bodies, the words, and the conduct of her subjects.[16] St. Augustine indicated that the superioress is to be obeyed and honored, lest God be of-

---

[11] Montalembert, *op. cit.,* I, 229-248; Butler, "Monasticism," *The Cambridge Medieval History,* I, 531, 532.

[12] Besse, "Abbesse," *Dictionnaire d'Archéologie Chrétienne et de Liturgie* (16 vols., Paris: Libraire Letouzey et Ané, 1907-1939), I, 42 (hereafter referred to as *DACL*).

[13] *MPL,* XXX, 400, n. 8.

[14] *Epistola CCXI—Corpus Scriptorum Ecclesiasticorum Latinorum* (Vindobonae, 1866—), LVII, 369 (hereafter referred to as *CSEL*).

[15] *MPL,* LXVII, 1109, n. 16.

[16] *MPL,* XXX, 399, n. 7.

fended in her.[17]   St. Caesarius wrote that those who are in charge
are to be zealous in seeing that the rule is carried out, acting with
charity, piety, and discretion.   They should correct the unruly, con-
sole the young, and take care of the sick.[18]

By the beginning of the sixth century one notes that the communities of women religious were numerous, that they were quite
well organized, and that there existed in them an office which gave
right to precedence over others and necessitated obedience from
others.   The holder of this office was a representative of Almighty
God to the group in her charge, and was responsible to Him for
their spiritual and temporal welfare.

[17] *Epistola CCXI—CSEL*, LVII, 369.
[18] *MPL*, LXVII, 1115, n. 32.

CHAPTER II

SUPERIORESSES OF ORDERS

ARTICLE 1. THE INFLUENCE OF ST. BENEDICT

PRIOR to the Rule of St. Benedict (480-553) the office of superior
was well established, but with this Rule it took on a new dignity and
an added definiteness. The official title became abbot, and upon
the abbot depended the whole government of the religious house.[1]
Any other officers of the community were assistants to him.[2] This
Rule with its specific norms was not only to influence all monasticism in the West, but it was to become its general law, if not completely, at least in spirit.[3] Not only men but also women religious
followed the Rule of St. Benedict, and in their communities the
superioress held a post of importance like to that of the abbot.

The term to become recognized as the regular title of a superioress of nuns was that of *abbatissa* or abbess. St. Benedict in his
Rule pointed out that the abbot holds the place of Christ. He is
the father of the monks.[4] The abbess was the mother of the nuns.
At what date women religious actually adopted this title is not clear.

---

[1] Gasquet, *English Monastic Life* (2. ed. rev., New York, 1904), p. 50.

[2] Butler, *Benedictine Monasticism* (2. ed., London: Longmans, Green &
Co., 1924), p. 216.

[3] Council of Autun (670), c. 15—Hardouin, *Acta Conciliorum et Epistolae
Decretales ac Constitutiones Summorum Pontificum* (12 vols., Parisiis, 1714-
1715), III, 1015 (hereafter referred to as Hardouin); c. 15—Mansi, *Sacrorum
Conciliorum Nova et Amplissima Collectio* (53 vols. in 60, Paris-Leipzig-Arnhem,
1901-1927), XI, 124 (hereafter referred to as Mansi); Council of Lobbes (743),
c. 1—*Monumenta Germaniae Historica*, Legum Sectio III, *Concilia Aevi Karolini I*, Tom. II, Pars 1 (ed. A. Werminghoff, Hannoverae et Lipsiae, 1904), p. 6
(hereafter referred to as *MGH*); Mansi, XII, 370; Hardouin, III, 1921; Council
of Tours (813), c. 25—*MGH, ibid.*, p. 290; Mansi, XIV, 87; II General Council
of the Lateran (1139), c. 26—Mansi, XXI, 532.

[4] Montalembert, *The Monks of the West*, I, 334.

5

In all probability this occurred shortly after it was established among men. The first record of its use is found in an inscription on a tombstone dated 569 in the Christian Era.[5] Evidence of its general use appears more and more as the office of superioress took on a canonical character and became the subject of ecclesiastical legislation. Other names from time to time were used, such as *priorissa* and *antistita*, but these were employed rather for particular groups or lesser officials, to whom, as will be seen, the same legislation applied.

Before turning to this legislation one will properly note that, although women seem to have embraced the religious state earlier than men, the first law in the Church on monastic life did not have them as its object. It was when abuses began to appear that Synods and Councils became definite in their prescriptions for the activities of religious communities. It was for the most part the monks who were making these encroachments, and it was they who were checked. Again, perhaps legislation for women religious would have come sooner, and would also have been more detailed, but for the practice of following, wherever possible, what was regulated for men. The nuns imitated the monks, and looked at their laws as binding on themselves. Legislation by the Church for women religious was throughout the centuries sparser than for men, arising mainly when abuse called for it, or when questions arose that could not be adequately handled by the current laws for men. Honorius III (1216-1227) advised nuns to observe the laws enacted for men whenever

---

[5]
>Hic Requiescit in Somno Pacis
>Justina Abbatissa
>Fundatrix Sancti Loci Hujus
>Quae Vixit Plus Minus
>Deposita Sub Die Kalarum Novembrium
>Imp. DN. N. Justino PP. Aug.
>Ann. IIII. PC Ejusdem
>Indictione Tertia.

Ferraris, *Prompta Bibliotheca Canonica, Iuridica, Moralis, Theologica, nec non Ascetica, Polemica, Rubricistica Historica* (8 vols., Romae, 1885-1892, Supplementum ed. I. Bucceroni, Romae, 1899), "Abbatissa," n. 91 (hereafter referred to as Ferraris); Besse, "Abbesse," *DACL* I, 42.

these laws could be applied to themselves.[6] In the present law the situation has not changed. The same practice continues.[7]

Besides those women religious whose institutes, one might say, were an outgrowth from the Order of St. Benedict, other orders of women religious likewise came into being. For the superioresses of all of these the law of the Church had its regulations. A conspectus of them will be offered in the four remaining articles of this chapter. These articles will discuss the qualifications for the office of superioress, her investiture, her power (with emphasis on the much discussed problem of jurisdiction), and finally her rights and duties.

ARTICLE 2. QUALIFICATIONS

The first superioresses of women religious were those who took the initiative to gather around themselves others who had aspirations like their own, and to form with them a community or a monastery. Or, again, they were those who had been selected by one of the early fathers of the spiritual life. At their death others took their places, at times appointed by their predecessor or by a bishop, at times selected by the members of the community.[8]

1. *Age*

In the course of time the Church demanded that the candidate for the office of superioress possess certain requisites. Gregory the Great (590-604) issued the first law regarding a specified requisite

---

[6] "Haec autem etiam in monasteriis, quae non habent abbates proprios, sed priores, nec non in monasteriis monialium, quo ad articulos abbatissis et monialibus congruentes, praecipimus observari."—c. 8, X, *de statu monachorum et canonicorum regularium*, III, 35; Potthast, *Regesta Pontificum Romanorum inde ab anno post Christum natum MCXCVIII (1198) ad annum MCCCIV (1304)*, (2 vols., Berolini, 1874-1875), n. 7817 (hereafter referred to as Potthast).

[7] "Quae de religiosis statuuntur, etsi masculino vocabulo expressa, valent etiam pari iure de mulieribus, nisi ex contextu sermonis vel ex rei natura aliud constet."—Can. 490.

[8] Parsons, *Canonical Elections*, The Catholic University of America Canon Law Studies, n. 118 (Washington, D. C.: The Catholic University of America Press, 1939), pp. 27-28.

age. The abbess, he said, must be sixty years old.[9] This remained
the law down through the centuries. Gratian (+ ca. 1157) included
it without change, and Ioannes Teutonicus (+1245) assumed as
a basis for it the words of St. Paul: "Let a widow who is selected
be not less than sixty years old." [10]

The next change in the law seems to have come with Boniface
VIII (1294-1303). Thenceforth no one was to become an abbess or
a prioress until she had completed her thirtieth year, and had moreover been expressly professed in a regular order.[11] In the *Glossa
Ordinaria* to this text one learns however that, although the old law
required the age of sixty years it had not been used for some time,
having been replaced by another, which was enacted in the III
General Council of the Lateran (1179), and then was repeated in
the Decretals of Gregory IX.[12]

This law of the Council and of the Decretals of Gregory IX did
not mention the abbess explicitly, but referred to officers in the
Church who were inferior in dignity to the bishop. The age to be
attained by one before he could receive a dignity or an office below a
bishopric was the twenty-fifth year.[13] To what extent this law was
considered by women religious as applicable to themselves, and to
what number communities followed it in preference to that of Gregory the Great, one is not able to say. The available commentators
on the Decretals before the Council of Trent (1545-1563) do not
mention women religious in their treatment of this law.[14]

---

[9] C. 12, C. XX, 2. 1; Jaffé, *Regesta Pontificum Romanorum ab condita
Ecclesia ad annum post Christum natum MCXCVIII (1198)*, (2. ed. [cura
Wattenbach, Kaltenbrunner (ad annum 590), Ewald (590-882), and Löwenfeld
(882-1198), and so cited as: JK, JE, JL], 2 vols. in 1, Lipsiae, 1885-1888), JE,
n. 1236; Mansi, X, 1164.

[10] *Glossa Ordinaria*, ad c. 12, C. XX, q. 1, s.v. *invenculas*; I Tim., v: 9.

[11] C. 43, *de electione et electi potestate*, I, 6, in VI°.

[12] Ioannes Andreae, ad c. 43, *de electione et electi potestate*, I, 6, in VI°,
s.v. *tricesimum*.

[13] III General Council of the Lateran (1179), c. 3—Mansi, XXII, 219; c. 7,
X, *de electione et electi potestate*, I, 6.

[14] Hostiensis, *Commentaria in Quinque Decretalium Libros* (5 vols. in 3,
Venetiis, 1581), lib. I, tit. 6, cap. 7; Panormitanus, *Commentaria in Quinque
Libros Decretalium* (5 vols. in 7, Venetiis, 1588), lib. I, tit. 6, cap. 7.

The law of Boniface VIII which regulated the requisite age of religious superioresses continued as the canonical norm until the Council of Trent. Treating the questions concerning the reform of regulars the Council stated:

> No one shall be elected abbess or prioress, or by whatever other name the one appointed or the superioress is known, who is less than forty years of age and who has not lived commendably during the eight years after having made her profession. If no one is found in a monastery possessing these qualifications, then one may be chosen from another of the same order. But if the superior who presides over the election should judge even this inconvenient, with the consent of the bishop or other superior one of those in the same monastery who is beyond her thirtieth year and has lived commendably at least five years since her profession may be chosen.[15]

There was no further change in age requirements prior to the Code. Authors merely cited the Council of Trent as the current law.[16]

2. Legitimacy

A second qualification that requires investigation is that of legitimacy. The requirement of legitimacy has to be regarded as a disputed point. First, it must be said that in pre-Code law there was no canon which stated that to be a candidate for the office of superioress in a community of women religious a person had to be of legitimate birth. The question, then, is whether or not there was at least an implicit requisite for such legitimate status.

Legislation to distinguish the rights of legitimate children as against illegitimate children appears early in the Church, but the restrictions fell on the children of men in sacred orders.[17] "It can be said that in general the Church did not legislate against illegiti-

---

[15] Sess. XXV, *de regularibus*, c. 7—Schroeder, *Canons and Decrees of the Council of Trent* (St. Louis: Herder, 1941), p. 222.

[16] Fagnanus, *Commentaria in Librum Decretalium* (5 vols., Venetiis, 1696), lib. I, tit. 6, cap. 7, n. 114; Ferraris, "Abbatissa," n. 1; Bouix, *Tractatus de Jure Regularium* (3. ed., 2 vols., Parisiis, 1882), II, 389.

[17] IX Provincial Council of Toledo (655), c. 10—Hardouin, III, 975; Mansi, XI, 29.

mate children with respect to the reception of sacred orders during the first ten centuries, even though the ordination of such children was looked upon as unbecoming."[18]

The same view can be taken with reference to the office of superioress, since any claim for legitimacy as a requisite is quite naturally based on the law which deals with the requisites for the reception of orders. The Council of Poitiers (1078) enacted that illegitimate children could not be promoted to sacred orders unless they became monks, or unless they joined a canonical congregation whose members lived in accordance with some set Rule. But under no condition could they receive a prelacy.[19] This law appears in the Decretals of Gregory IX (1227-1241). It denied sacred orders to those who were illegitimate, with the exception of those who had become monks. But this latter exception did not apply when there was a question of a prelacy.[20]

A further development occurred under Boniface VIII (1294-1303). In treating the case of the removal of an abbess he mentioned two points that later authors found applicable.[21] With reference to the election of an abbess he stated that she was to receive her official confirmation in office *"si alias inventa fuerit canonica."* Ioannes Andreae (1272-1348) explained that the term *canonica* envisioned both the proper electoral procedure and the requisite personal fitness for the office. Hence, if the person was of illegitimate status, the requisite personal fitness for the office was wanting.[22]

The pope furthermore declared under what conditions it was allowable for nuns to submit a plea after the election of an abbess *"ut a dignitate deiiciatur,"* for the recognized rule of the law existed: *"Infamibus portae non pateant dignitatum."*[23] Thus Boniface VIII spoke of the office of superioress as a dignity, and at the same time

[18] McDevitt, *Legitimacy and Legitimation*, The Catholic University of America Canon Law Studies, n. 138 (Washington, D. C.: The Catholic University of America Press, 1941), p. 37.

[19] C. 8—Mansi, XX, 498-499.

[20] C. 1, X, *de filiis presbyterorum ordinandis vel non*, I, 17.

[21] C. 43, *de electione et electi potestate*, I, 6, in VI°.

[22] *Glossa Ordinaria* ad c. 43, *de electione et electi potestate*, I, 6, in VI°, s.v. *canonica*.

[23] Reg. 87, R. J., in VI°.

enunciated in his *Regula Iuris* that all rightful accession to dignities was to be denied to those who were of blemished character. More than this is not evident on the face of the law. It seems to have been the practice of the Church to require a status of legitimacy in all candidates for an electoral office. This in all probability came as a result of the extension of the laws just cited to make them applicable to the honors which were held in the Church by women. But from the text of the law, as then current, there is not a sufficient deducible evidence to enable one to judge with apodictic certainty.

The Council of Trent was equally silent on this point. Corroboration again must come, if at all, from laws on similar subjects. For example, in dealing with benefices the Council required legitimacy of status in those who were to govern cathedral churches.[24]

Of the authors who wrote after the Council of Trent, Fagnanus (1598-1678) held that an illegitimate person could not be elected as abbess or prioress without a dispensation from the pope. This, he added, was the view of almost all the *doctores*. His argument was based on the Decretals already cited. The abbess enjoyed a dignity. Those who were born of an illegitimate union could not rightfully obtain a prelacy. The office of an abbess, although it was not a prelacy in the strict sense, constituted a quasi-prelacy, and therefore similar qualifications were postulated for it in the law.[25] This view was maintained by practically all the authors up to the time of the present Code.[26]

This opinion seemed fully justified in the light of the general attitude of the Church's laws relative to that point, especially when

---

[24] Sess. VII, *de ref.*, c. 1—*Concilium Tridentinum, Diariorum, Actorum, Epistolarum, Tractatuum, Nova Collectio* (Edidit Societas Goerresiana, 13 vols., Friburgi Brisgoviae: B. Herder, 1901-1938), V, 997 (citations of the acts of the Council will hereafter be taken from this edition).

[25] Fagnanus, *Commentaria in Librum Decretalium*, lib. I, tit. 17, cap. 1, n. 38.

[26] Cf. Pellizzarius (1596-1651), *Tractatio de Monialibus* (3. ed., Venetiis, 1631), cap. VIII, q. 32, n. 43; Ferraris, "Abbatissa," n. 8; Bouix (1808-1870), *Tractatus de Jure Regularium*, II, 392.

coupled with the common tendency and practice of extending to women religious the legislation which had been enacted for men religious.[27]

ARTICLE 3. INVESTITURE

1. *Confirmation in Office*

In the first centuries of monasticism superiors attained their office either through their founding of a community or through their appointment to it, the members exercising little if any influence. The Rule of St. Benedict shows clearly that it was his mind to have the monks choose their own superior. In time this became the accepted method and the decisive one. In general it may be said that in some places the abbess was elected by the nuns of the community, in others for a long time she was appointed. Any further detailed explanation of the method whereby an abbess gained her office lies outside the purpose of the present study.[28]

On the assumption, then, that the abbess was elected, one may proceed to consider who had the right of granting confirmation in office. From the beginning of legislation for religious the local bishop was recognized as having authority over those who resided in his territory.[29] St. Benedict made no pretense to exclude this authority. Various councils spoke of the consent of the bishop in matters of election.[30]

With the gradual development of exemption new conditions arose. At times secular princes exercised great influence over the Church. They were proprietors of the monasteries and could nominate the

---

[27] Rodericus (+ 1613), who held the opposite view, remarked that even if this impediment were applicable to superioresses, the superiors of mendicant orders by privilege could dispense nuns subject to them, and by a mutual sharing of privileges all regulars could do so.—*Resolutiones Questionum Regularium* (Lugduni, 1634), Resolutio II, n. 4.

[28] Cf. Parsons, *Canonical Elections*, pp. 27 ff.

[29] Council of Chalcedon (451), c. 4—Mansi, VI, 1226.

[30] Council of Frankfort (794), c. 16—*MGH*, Legum Sectio II, *Capitula Regum Francorum*, Tom. I (ed. A. Boretius), p. 76; c. 10—*MGH*, Legum Sectio III, *Concilia Aevi Karolini I*, Tom. II, Pars 1 (ed. Werminghoff), p. 591.

superior.[31] While the royality or other proprietors dominated, or at times also bishops, elections were held by way of special privilege rather than by way of strict right.[32] This privilege was also granted to specific monasteries by various proprietors, or also by the pope himself, as was done by Leo IX (1049-1054).[33]

The external authority that existed for so many centuries over monasteries, whether it was papal, episcopal, religious, or lay, gave rise to the practice of granting confirmation in office. The right to exercise this practice belonged to the one to whom the monastery was subject. In the Decretal law one observes that usage. Innocent III (1198-1216) declared that before confirmation by the proper superior the elected person should not exercise any administration.[34] Alexander III (1159-1181) had referred to a case in which he himself confirmed an abbess.[35] Further evidence appears in a decretal of Clement V (1305-1314).[36] Although he made mention of it only incidentally, the pope spoke of confirmation as the accepted thing. By the common law of the Decretals, then, there existed the requirement of confirmation in office before the elected person could exercise his or her office. The practice of granting confirmation in office to an elected candidate was a general one even prior to the time of the Decretal law. It seems warranted to assume that the consistency of that widespread practice reflected at the same time a note of legal necessity through the medium of customary law.

The Council of Trent dealt with the matter of the election of abbesses, but its main concern was the enforcement of the use of, the secret ballot.[37] Regarding the confirmation of the election by the one in whom this right rested, the earlier law still continued to assert its force subsequent to the Council of Trent. Until the appearance of the present Code the situation remained the same as it

[31] Levy-Bruhl, *Études sur les Élections Abbatiales en France* (Paris, 1913), p. 190.

[32] Parsons, *Canonical Elections*, p. 35.

[33] Mansi, XIX, 683, 685, 698.

[34] C. 7, X, *de consuetudine*, I, 4—Potthast, n. 3397; c. 18, X, *de praebendis et dignitatibus*, III, 5; c. 1, X, *de electionibus et electi potestate*, I, 6.

[35] C. 13, X, *de accusationibus*, V, 1—JL, n. 8903.

[36] C. 2, *de statu monachorum vel canonicorum regularium*, III, 10, in Clem.

[37] Sess. XXV, *de regularibus*, c. 6.

had been under the pre-Tridentine law. A clarification was introduced by the authors, who based their doctrine on a response of the Sacred Congregation of the Council.

The occasion for the response derived from a doubt which had arisen regarding the proper interpretation of a Constitution of Gregory XV (1621-1623). In this Constitution the pope had stated that the bishop could preside either personally, or by means of a delegate, together with the regular superior at the elections of superioresses of women religious.[38] Upon being questioned the Sacred Congregation answered that this Constitution by no means reserved to the bishop the right of granting confirmation, since that right belonged to the regular prelate who was the immediate superior.[39]

It may be stated, then, that prior to the Code the law on the granting of confirmation in office was as follows: the right belonged to the regular superior, unless the monastery was subject to the bishop; in the latter event the right belonged to the bishop. If the monastery was subject immediately to the Holy See, then the act of confirmation was to be granted by the pope through a procurator.[40]

2. *Blessing*

Thus far it has been seen that by way of preliminary requirement for the capacity of gaining office the prospective abbess had to be in possession of certain qualifications. Further, it was necessary that she be appointed or elected, and that her election be confirmed. But there was still another important step. She had to receive the special blessing. One finds that as early as. the time of Gregory the Great (590-604) a papal letter was written in which instruction was given to a bishop to "ordain" the abbess of Marseilles.[41]

[38] Const. *"Inscrutabuli,"* 5 febr. 1622—*Fontes,* n. 199.

[39] S. C. C., 17 dec. 1622—Fagnanus, *Commentaria in Librum Decretalium,* lib. V, tit. 7, cap. 16.

[40] Tamburini (+ 1666), *De Jure Abbatum et Aliorum Praelatorum* (3 vols. in 2, Coloniae Agrippinae, 1691), tom. I, disp. 22, q. 16, n. 5; Pellizzarius, *Tractatio de Monialibus,* cap. X, sect. 1, q. 17, n. 110; Ferraris, "Abbatissa," n. 37; Bouix, *Tractatus de Jure Regularium,* II, 396; Bachofen (1872-1943), *Compendium Juris Regularium* (New York: Benziger Bros., 1903), p. 213, n. 3.

[41] Mansi, X, 56; Martène (1654-1739), *De Antiquis Ecclesiae Ritibus* (4 vols., Rotomagi, 1700), III, 2.

Evidence of the ancient practice of this rite is found in pontifical and sacramentary manuscripts. · In that of the Church of Besançon, dating from the year 600,[42] side by side with the blessing of an abbot, there is a special blessing of the newly elected abbess.[43] Another example is that which is found for the consecration of an abbess in a very old pontifical of the Church of Arles. The elected abbess is examined as a part of the ceremony. There is a prostration before the altar, and the presentation of the staff by the bishop.[44]

In 688, in a council held under Theodore, Archbishop of Canterbury (668-690), it was mentioned that among the Greeks the bishop said the Mass of the election of an abbot or abbess, but it was also declared that locally a priest was authorized to consecrate an abbess with the celebration of Mass.[45] Finally, in the Missal of the Monastery of Gellone (St. Guilhem du Desert in the diocese of Lodève), written before 900, there are contained three forms of orations for the blessing of abbots and abbesses.[46]

Turning to the Decretal law one reads that Alexander III (1159-1181) instructed the bishop to impart the blessing to the abbess of the Monastery of St. Zachary.[47] Boniface VIII declared that, when an abbess was elected and her election was confirmed, she was also to receive the blessing.[48] Clement V (1305-1314) added new legislation which ruled that if the custom of her monastery called for it, the abbess was to receive her blessing within a year from the time she had been granted confirmation in her office, or otherwise forfeit that office.[49]

A few further points appear in the *Glossa Ordinaria*. First, inasmuch as the blessing of an abbess was regarded as a quasi-sacrament,

---

[42] Martène, *Tractatus de Antiqua Ecclesiae Disciplina in Divinis Celebrandis Officiis* (Lugduni, 1706), p. iv.

[43] Martène, *De Antiquis Ecclesiae Ritibus*, III, 26.

[44] Martène, *De Antiquis Ecclesiae Ritibus*, III, 42.

[45] C. 1—Hardouin, III, 1771; Mansi, XII, 25.

[46] Martène, *De Antiquis Ecclesiae Ritibus*, III, 5.

[47] C. 13, X, *de accusationibus*, V, 1; JL, 8903.

[48] C. 43, *de electione et electi potestate*, I, 6, in VI°.

[49] C. 2, *de statu monachorum vel canonicorum regularium*, III, 10, in Clem.

the possibility of its repetition was seriously questioned.[50]   This point, however, was not commonly elaborated among the authors. Secondly, no price was to be exacted for this blessing. Finally, the ceremony of the blessing could be performed on any day.[51]

With Clement V the laws regarding the blessing of abbesses became fixed. Since he spoke of custom as the norm which determined which abbesses had the right, or also the obligation, to receive the blessing, it seems that the practice of bestowing the ceremonial blessing had in his day become less common. The Council of Trent did not speak of it at all. The post-Tridentine authors merely summarized the legislative enactments contained in the Decretals. Tamburini (+1666), for example, stated that a custom of forty years' duration gave rise to the obligation of receiving the blessing. He added that the right of performing the ceremonial blessing belonged to the one who enjoyed the right of granting confirmation for the election: to the pope or to his delegate with reference to exempt nuns; to the bishop with regard to non-exempt nuns; to the abbot in the event that he enjoyed the right or privilege to confirm the election of the abbess.[52]

The authors were in agreement that, if the receiving of the blessing was required by custom, then the elected abbess forfeited her office if she did not receive the blessing within a year.[53] Bachofen (1872-1943) noted that not all abbesses were under the obligation to receive the blessing, but only those who were elected for a lifetime incumbency in their office. This was the usage as it continued up to the time of the present Code.[54]

3. *Term of Office*

Closely allied with the subject of entering upon office is that of its duration. The first centuries of monasticism were generally silent

---

[50] Ioannes Andreae, ad c. 2, *de statu monachorum vel canonicorum regularium*, III, 10, in Clem., s.v. *benedici.*

[51] *Loc. cit.*

[52] *De Jure Abbatum et Aliorum Praelatorum,* tom. I, disp. 22, q. 8, nn. 1-2.

[53] Rodericus, *Resolutiones Questionum Regularium, Resolutio* II, n. 3; Pellizzarius, *Tractatio de Monialibus,* cap. VIII, q. 44, n. 62.

[54] *Compendium Juris Regularium,* p. 213, n. 4.

on this question, but it is in this silence that one finds the key to the accepted practice. When superioresses took up the task of governing their community, they did so for life. It was natural for the founders to do this; their successors, in turn, followed the same practice. The Code of Justinian gives evidence that formerly the oldest monk was the one who was appointed by the bishop to the office of superior, thus indicating that the appointment implied a lifetime incumbency in the office.[55]

St. Benedict was very clear on this matter. He was thoroughly convinced that the superior's lifetime term of office provided the way in which the best interests of religious community life were to be promoted. The abbot governed the monastery with full authority, and was chosen by the monks for life.[56] It has been mentioned before that the Rule of St. Benedict was widely adopted and followed by both men and women religious. The lifetime office for superioresses or abbesses was thus accepted. No change in this practice appeared for many centuries. In the Decree of Gratian the same practice was still implied. It was there pointed out, in reliance upon a letter of Pope Pelagius II (578-590), that monks could not expel their abbots or choose others at will.[57]

In the Decretals of Gregory IX it was stated that priors, once they were canonically elected, should not be changed. Bernard of Parma (+1266) commented that this was to be understood of those who were perpetually instituted in consequence of a canonical election along with the due confirmation granted by the proper superior.[58]

A Decretal of Innocent III seemed for a long time to furnish occasion for possible misunderstanding. In speaking of the officers of monasteries, the pope declared that a perpetual obedience was not due to them. But it seems fully warranted to assume that he was speaking of assistants or lesser superiors who held office through an appointment, and not through a canonical election which had received its proper confirmation from authority. It was to this distinction

---

[55] C. (1, 3) 46.

[56] Butler, "Monasticism," *The Cambridge Medieval History*, I, 539.

[57] C. 9, C. XVIII, q. 2; JK, n. 696.

[58] *Glossa Ordinaria*, ad c. 2, X, *de statu monachorum et canonicorum regularium*, III, 35, s.v. *non mutentur*.

that the glossator adverted in his doctrine regarding the uniform and general application of the traditional law.[59]

Permanence in office, then, was the general rule. Still one finds in the Decretals that not all types of superiors held office for life. The mendicant orders at the beginning of the thirteenth century, in view of the foundation of many houses in various places, found temporary superiors more convenient. Thus the Franciscans in a general chapter could remove their minister general from office by a unanimous vote.[60]

The Council of Trent simply gave recognition to the two types of superiors, namely, permanent and temporary. It mentioned that all superiors were to be chosen by secret ballot, but the question regarding how long they were to remain in office it left untouched, intimating that no change was demanded from what each community had in the past been accustomed to follow as its norm.[61]

Gregory XIII (1572-1585) provided the first specific legislation on the subject. In view of the many difficulties that had arisen through the permanent tenure of office on the part of women superioresses, he ordered that for the future in Italy and Sicily the tenure of office should extend for a period of only three years. Furthermore, after this three-year tenure of office had expired, a superioress could not again hold office for a second term until three more years had elapsed. The binding force of these rules was sanctioned with the issue of nullity for any contrary procedure, and the new law was to be accepted regardless of any constitutions, customs, or privileges to the contrary.[62]

This decree of the pope was explicit and clear in what it demanded, but left room for speculation regarding the extent of its

---

[59] Bernard of Parma, *Glossa Ordinaria*, ad c. 6, X, *de statu monachorum et canonicorum regularium*, III, 35, s.v. *perpetuo*; Potthast, n. 1734.

[60] Augustine, *A Commentary on the New Code of Canon Law* (8 vols., Vol. III, 5. ed., 1938; Vol. VI, 3. ed., 1931, St. Louis: Herder), III, 11 (hereafter referred to as *Commentary*).

[61] Sess. XXV, *de regularibus*, c. 6.

[62] Const. *"Exposcit debitum,"* 1 ian. 1583—*Bullarum Diplomatum et Privilegiorum Sanctorum Romanorum Pontificum Tauriensis Editio* (25 vols., Augustae Taurinorum, 1857-1885), VIII, 404 (hereafter referred to as *Bull. Rom. Taur.*).

application, inasmuch as only Italy and Sicily were specifically mentioned. The question arose whether the pope, while simply mentioning Italy and Sicily, really intended to include other countries as well. It certainly can be said that it was the preference of the Holy See in this matter that the law be followed throughout the universal Church.

Some authors indicated that this law of Gregory XIII was soon afterwards extended to all communities of women religious throughout the world.[63]   Rodericus (+1613) asserted that the Constitution did not bind outside of Italy.[64]   Cardinal De Luca (1614-1683) related that in his time the perpetual tenure of office on the part of abbesses existed especially *"ultra montes,"* and that this practice was tolerated, but that when confirmation was granted to incumbents of these offices, the Holy See was to be consulted, whereupon it would act as the circumstances required.[65]

Further evidence of the Holy See's desire for the temporary tenure of office on the part of superioresses appeared from time to time in decrees that either demanded it or at least expressed the hope for the adoption of it.[66]   Thus the situation from the time of the Constitution of Gregory XIII was one in which the tenure of office on the part of women superioresses throughout the world by custom gradually came to be of a temporary character. Some institutes very definitely held to a permanent tenure of office. The decrees that

---

[63] Cf. Barbosa (1589-1649) cited to this effect a decree of the S. C. Ep. et Reg., 22 maii 1604, but did not give the text of it himself—*Collectanea eorum Doctorum qui in suis operibus Concilii Tridentini loca referentes illorum materiam incidenter tractarunt* (Lugduni, 1657), Sess. XXV, *de Reg. et Monial.*, c. 7, nn. 10-11.

[64] *Resolutiones Questionum Regularium*, Resolutio II, n. 6.

[65] *Theatrum Veritatis et Justitiae* (15 vols. in 8, Coloniae Agrippinae, 1706), tom. III, disc. 1, n. 142.

[66] S. C. Ep. et Reg., 18 mart. 1700, *in causa Mazarien.*—Bizzarri, *Collectanea in Usum Secretariae Sacrae Congregationis Episcoporum et Regularium* (2. ed., Bizzarri, Romae, 1885), p. 283 (hereafter referred to as *Coll. S. C. Ep et Reg.*); "Sed extra Italiam incongrua etiam videtur et regulari disciplinae repugnans in Leodien. Visitationis die Ianuarii 22, 1763."—Pallottini, *Collectio omnium conclusionum et resolutionum quae in causis propositis apud S. Cong. Cardinalium S. Concilii Tridentini Interpretum prodierunt ab anno 1564 ad annum 1860* (18 vols., Romae, 1868-1895), I, p. 76, n. 87.

appeared did not become completely effective by means of a universal adoption. Some authors, however, maintained that there was an obligation by law that superioresses be elected for a limited time only.[67]

On June 4, 1910, the Sacred Congregation of Religious finally settled the matter by a declaration. Outside of Italy the rules and constitutions as approved by the Holy See were to be followed, and the preservation of immemorial customs in this matter was also sanctioned.[68]

ARTICLE 4. THE POWER OF THE SUPERIORESS

The regular power exercised by the superioress is that power which is designated as being of a dominative character. Because of the nature of this question it has seemed more advisable to deal with it in one treatment in the commentary section of this work.[69]

The question raised in this article is the problem of jurisdiction in relation to the superioress. Did the superioresses actually exercise jurisdictional power by virtue of the common law, or, if not in this way, did they ever hold or exercise it by way of delegation granted by ecclesiastical authority?

In answer to the first part of this question it can be said that by common law women did not possess ecclesiastical jurisdiction. The whole attitude of the early Church and of law, both civil and ecclesiastical, points to this fact. St. Paul set the norm in his directive: "Let women keep silence in the churches. . . ." [70] Again he said: "For I do not allow a woman to teach or to exercise authority over men; but she is to keep quiet." [71] Evidence of the

---

[67] Ferraris, "Abbatissa," nn. 53-57; Bachofen, *Compendium Juris Regularium*, p. 214, n. 4.

[68] "Cum adhuc perdurent dubia circa extensionem Constitutionis *Exposcit debitum,* diei 1 ian. 1583 extra Italiam. . . . Eṁi ac Rṁi Patres Cardinales declarandum censuerunt:

"Servandas esse hac in re extra Italiam regulas et constitutiones a Sancta Sede approbatas et consuetudines immemorabiles; facto verbo cum Sanctissimo."
—*Fontes,* n. 4403.

[69] Cf. *infra,* pp. 76 ff.

[70] I Cor. xxiv, 34.

[71] I Tim., ii, 12.

mind of the Fathers is found in St. John Chrysostom (c. 344-407), when he spoke of it as a perversion in things if women seek to rule.[72]

The same spirit was reflected in the IV Council of Carthage (398), where it was stated that a woman, though she be learned and holy, may not baptize or teach.[73] Sharing a like view the civil law prescribed that women were to be kept from all civil and public offices, that they could not be judges or advocates.[74]

In the First Capitularies issued at Aix-la-Chapelle (789) it was declared to be against the custom of the Church for abbesses to perform blessings or to veil virgins, and therefore these practices were to be discontinued.[75] The VI Council of Paris (819) in legislating on the same subject threatened punishment for future offenses. "We find," it stated, "that some abbesses and nuns are accustomed to veil not only widows and virgins, but also young girls. Such a practice on the part of women is illicit." [76] Gratian incorporated this conciliar enactment in his *Decretum,* and furthermore stated that women were to be subject to men in all things.[77]

The laws which have been mentioned here, although they are not explicit in denying jurisdiction to women, nevertheless furnish good reasons for such a deduction. In the IV General Council of the Lateran (1215) the law was more specific. To the laity, even though they were religious, no power was acknowledged in matters ecclesiastical.[78]

This law was repeated in the Decretals.[79] A decretal of Innocent III (1198-1216) stated that it is preposterous and absurd for women to exercise the power of the keys, when Christ Himself did

[72] *On the Priesthood* (English Translation by Boyle, Westminster, Md.: The Newman Book Shop, 1943), p. 50.

[73] Cc. 99-100—Mansi, III, 959.

[74] D. (50, 17) 2.

[75] C. 74—Mansi, XVII B, 238.

[76] C. 43—Mansi, XIV, 564.

[77] "Mulierem constat subiectam dominio viri esse, et nullam auctoritatem habere; nec docere potest, nec testis esse, neque fidem dare, nec iudicare."—c. 17, C. XXXIII, q. 5.

[78] "Quum laicis, quamvis religiosis, disponendi de rebus ecclesiae nulla sit attributa potestas, quos obsequendi manet necessitas, non auctoritas imperandi." —Mansi, XXII, 1027.

[79] C. 12, X, *de rebus ecclesiae aliendis vel non,* III, 13.

not give such power to His own Blessed Mother, who was greater in dignity and in excellence than even the Apostles on whom He did bestow it.[80]

From the evidence cited it seems safe to say that from the beginning of the Church her common law, as expressed either in her tradition or in her actual legislation, forbade women to exercise ecclesiastical jurisdiction. It is true that in the early days of the Church, and even for many centuries, the exact notion of jurisdiction as it is known today had not received a clarified expression, but in matters that involved the use of legislative, judicial, or coercive power women were generally not to have part.

Again, in the legislation on this matter there was an apparent confusion between the power of orders and the power of jurisdiction. Regarding orders the fact that women were barred from that power is clear, as for example from the words of Innocent III which have just been quoted. But also regarding jurisdiction it may be said that women by law did not possess it, for such a possession would have implied official power in the Church, concerning which, however, the IV General Council of the Lateran declared that it belonged only to clerics.

Having arrived at the conclusion that in law women were barred from sharing ecclesiastical jurisdiction, one comes to the second question of this problem, namely, did superioresses ever by special delegation actually receive this power and exercise it? The matter is one about which a great deal has been written, both sides of the question being supported by renowned authors.

Although the controversy is concerned with Decretal and post-Decretal times, by way of introduction it should be noted that ab-

---

[80] "Nova quaedam nuper, de quibus miramur non modicum, nostris sunt auribus intimata, quod abbatissae videlicet, in Burgensi et in Palentinensi dioecesibus constitutae, moniales proprias benedicunt, ipsarum quoque confessiones in criminibus audiunt, et legentes evangelium presumunt publice praedicare. Quum igitur absonum sit pariter et absurdum, nec a nobis aliquatenus sustinendum, discretioni vestrae per apostolica scripta mandamus, quatenus, ne id de cetero fiat, auctoritate curetis apostolica firmiter inhibere, quia, licet beatissima virgo Maria dignior et excellentior fuerit Apostolis universis, non tamen illi, sed istis Dominus claves regni coelorum commisit."—c. 10, *de poenitentiis et remissionibus,* V. 38.

besses were often very important persons with great influence. Because of the extent of their monasteries, or because of their personal background and titles, they received recognition that otherwise they would never have been accorded. Thus, for example, one finds the names of abbesses among the signatures affixed to the acts of certain early synods and councils.[81]

Evidence of this kind, however, is extremely limited. What brings the question to the fore is a letter of Honorius III (1216-1227) as found in the Decretals. The text reads:

> Dilecta in Christo filia abbatissa de Bubrigen. transmissa nobis petitione monstravit, quod, quum ipsa plerumque canonicas suas et clericos suae iurisdictioni subiectos propter inobedientias et culpas eorum officio beneficioque suspendat iidem confisi ex eo, quod eadem abbatissa excommunicare eos non potest, suspensionem huiusmodi non observant, propter quod ipsorum excessus remanent incorrecti. Quo circa discretioni tuae mandamus, quatenus dictas canonicas et clericos, ut abbatissae praefatae obedientiam et reverentiam debitam impendentes, eius salubria monita et mandata observent, monitione praemissa, ecclesiastica censura appellatione remota compellas.[82]

Several things stand out plainly in this text. First, the term jurisdiction without any qualification is used to describe the power of the abbess over her subjects, both men and women.[83] It is known with certainty that from 1215 jurisdiction was understood to be the public power of ruling a perfect society, embracing accordingly a legislative, a judicial, and a coercive power.[84] However, it cannot be presumed that from that date forward the word "jurisdiction," no matter where it appeared, was always employed in that meaning.

[81] Synod of Whitby (664)—Mansi, XI, 68; Council of Becanfield (694)—Mansi, XI, 91; Council at the River Nith (705)—Mansi, XII, 172.

[82] C. 12, X, *de maioritate et obedientia*, I, 33; Potthast, n. 6857.

[83] Canonesses were not women religious in a strictly taken sense. They did not make any profession, nor did they live in common. They wore a quasi-religious habit, and gathered for the canonical hours. They lived from prebends and patrimony.—Hostiensis, *Commentaria in Quinque Decretalium Libros*, lib. I, tit. 33, cap. 12.

[84] Van der Kerckhove, "De notione jurisdictionis apud decretistas et priores decretalistas," *Jus Pontificium* (Romae, 1921—), XVIII (1938), 12-13.

It could still have been employed, as it had been employed in the past, to signify administration.[85]

Secondly, the pope stated that the subjects of this abbess owed her reverence and obedience. Her warnings and commands could be enforced by ecclesiastical censure. This censure, however, was not to be inflicted by herself, but by an abbot. The pope agreed with the abbess, as it were, that she had not the power of inflicting excommunication.

A third and final point to be made in summing up the contents of this Decretal is the remark of the pope that this abbess suspended her subjects from office and from benefice. This seems to point to what constituted a regular practice at this monastery. In view of the fact that in using the words "ecclesiastical censure" the pope at the same time restricted to the abbot the right to invoke this penalty, he appeared to regard the act of suspension as something distinct from this penalty.

Turning to the *Glossa Ordinaria*, one finds stated there that as a result of this Decretal the abbess was to be considered as having some jurisdiction, but of a kind which was not so complete as that possessed by a man. She could suspend incumbents from office and from benefice; she could confer churches and benefices, and also institute clerics in the churches of her monastery. She could do these things because she had the administration of temporal and spiritual affairs. She was not capable of inflicting excommunication or of granting absolution. Neither could she inflict a suspension or an interdict, for these functions pertained to the power of the keys, which power did not fall within the competence of the feminine sex. Christ had given that power not to His Blessed Mother, but to His Apostles. Again, a woman was not made, as was the man, in the image of God. She should be subject to man who is made to the image of God.[86]

Hostiensis ($+$1271) held the same view, and supported it with the same reasons. He added that a woman was not able to judge or to perform the offices proper to men. A woman did not fully have

---

[85] Reiffenstuel, *Ius Canonicum Universum* (5 vols. in 7, Parisiis, 1864-1870), lib. I, tit. 1, n. 29.

[86] Bernard of Parma, ad c. 12, X, *de maioritate et obedientia*, I, 33, s.v. *iurisdictionem*.

jurisdiction, since she was not able to hear confessions, could not grant absolution, and was powerless also in other things that pertained to the power of the keys.[87]

Sandeus (1444-1503), in referring to this text, contended that a woman who succeeded to a dignity was capable of receiving jurisdiction, and that she could administer it personally, as for example a queen was empowered to do.[88] Further, he referred to a decision made by the Sacred Roman Rota which held that, while the care of souls was not within the competence of a woman as to its actual exercise, the *ius curae* could be committed to an abbess and her nuns, who could then depute its actual exercise to a man capable of that power. The decision also stated that an abbess could institute a *"vicarius temporalis in ecclesia sibi pleno iure spectante."* [89] Sandeus remarked, however, that the things which require the power of orders were not within the competence of women. Such things, he noted, included excommunication and real suspension, namely, the type which entailed an irregularity.[90]

Prior to the Council of Trent, as has been seen, superioresses were at times permitted to perform acts which implied the possession of broad powers. But whether these were such as flowed necessarily from the possession of ecclesiastical jurisdiction it is difficult to say. The Council of Trent did not clarify the situation. Some general legislation was indeed enacted, as, for example, that the monasteries of nuns immediately subject to the Holy See should be supervised by the bishops as its delegates. An exception was made in the cases of those which were supervised by persons delegated in general chapters or by other regulars.[91]

Again, it was decreed that, when the care of souls for people distinct from those who belonged to the monastic household was annexed to a monastery of men or of women, the person who exercised

---

[87] *Commentaria in Quinque Decretalium Libros,* lib. I, tit. 33, cap. 12.

[88] *Commentaria Iuris Canonici in Quinque Libros Decretalium* (3 vols., Venetiis, 1570), lib. I, tit. 33, cap. 12, nn. 1-5.

[89] De Praebendis, Decisio XXI—*Rotae Auditorum Decisiones Novae, Antiquae, et Antiquiores* (Venetiis, 1570), p. 486.

[90] *Loc. cit.*

[91] Sess. XXV, *de regularibus,* c. 9.

that care was to be under the jurisdiction of the bishop in all that pertained to the pastoral care and to the administration of the sacraments.[92] Regarding benefices the Council declared that the local ordinary was to visit each year the benefices which, while the care of souls was attached to them, were annexed to monasteries, and that he was to see to it that such benefices had competent and perpetual vicars as incumbents.[93] Furthermore, all nominees for benefices, no matter by whom they were nominated, had to submit to an examination as directed by the local ordinary. The only exception in this regard existed for those who were presented, elected, or nominated, by universities or colleges for general studies.[94]

If one turns to the post-Tridentine authors who treated this question of jurisdiction, one finds strong differences of opinion. For convenience of arrangement one may classify these authors in two groups, namely, those who held that women did not have spiritual jurisdiction, and those who favored the opposite view.

Suarez (1548-1617) admitted that the abbess could appoint to and suspend from office and benefice, and that she had, so to speak, ecclesiastical censure at her beck and call. However, her power in these two instances, so he contended, did not derive from her own ordinary or delegated jurisdiction. When she removed a cleric from office, the jurisdiction involved in her acts was that of the pope. She herself served simply as an agent for the removal when the proper conditions were present to call for such an act. In regard to censures, it was the abbot through whom she acted.[95]

Rodericus (+1613) stated more definitely that the abbess was incapable of the power of the keys and of spiritual jurisdiction in a strict sense, since that kind of power pertained to the power of orders. Her acts of instituting clerics in office were merely similar to acts of the exercise of spiritual jurisdiction.[96]

Pirhing (1606-1679) also held that women were incapable of

---

[92] Sess. XXV, *de regularibus*, c. 11.

[93] Sess. VII, *de ref.*, c. 7.

[94] Sess. VII, *de ref.*, c. 13.

[95] *Opera Omnia* (26 vols., Parisiis, 1856-1878), tom. XVI, *De Religiosis Quatenus Praelati Sunt*, tract. 8, lib. 2, cap. 9, nn. 13, 15.

[96] *Resolutiones Questionum Regularium*, Resolutio II, n. 2.

receiving the power of the keys. The abbess, however, could act through a superior to enforce her commands by censure. She could forbid her subjects to celebrate Mass, and she could likewise deprive them of the fruits of their benefice, but such a prohibition was simply of a preceptive character.[97]

Reiffenstuel (1642-1703) repeated the view of Pirhing by emphasizing again that what pertained to the power of the keys was not within the competence of women. He admitted, though, that by privilege or also by special law an abbess could become qualified to remove incumbents from their benefices, or to order her subjects not to celebrate Mass.[98]

Ferraris (+ ca. 1763) held that an abbess was incapable of becoming the bearer of jurisdiction. He stated, however, that she was capable of conferring parishes and of naming and instituting pastors, in the event that the prospective incumbents had been approved by the ordinary as suited for undertaking the care of souls. She could likewise deprive these incumbents of their benefices, since she was merely taking away what she had given, namely, title and possession. She could not dispense from the regular ecclesiastical observances. If at times she seemed to do this, her act was to be regarded simply as a declaration that an obligation had ceased.[99]

All of the aforementioned authors were united in their opinion that the superioress did not and could not exercise spiritual jurisdiction. They insisted on the point that what pertained to the power of the keys was beyond the competence of women. Any acts which a superioress was permitted by the Church to perform, though they wore the appearance of jurisdictional power, were merely acts of government or administration.

Opposed to this view was an equally large number of authors. Navarrus (1493-1586) insisted that a woman in religion was capable of being the bearer of ecclesiastical jurisdiction through a special commission from the pope.[100]

---

[97] *Jus Canonicum Nova Methodo Explicatum* (5 vols. in 4, Dillingae, 1674-1678), lib. I, tit. 33, sec. 1, n. 18.

[98] *Ius Canonicum Universum*, lib. I, tit. 33, n. 36.

[99] "Abbatissa," nn. 63-69.

[100] *Opera Omnia* (6 vols., Venetiis, 1618-1621), tom. IV, comment. 3, *de judiciis*, n. 143.

Barbosa (1589-1649) declared that a distinction was in order. Women were incapable of all that pertained to the power of orders and the sacramental power, but for that which pertained to jurisdiction, even though Christ did not Himself grant it to women, they were not inherently incompetent. Regularly the exercise of the power of jurisdiction was forbidden to them by the Church's traditional canons. But in view of the evident moral danger that could or would accompany the residence of men in the monasteries of nuns, the Church by special commission granted the exercise of jurisdictional power to abbesses in their monasteries.[101]

A third author, Laymann (1574-1635), invoked a twofold distinction in the power of the keys, namely, the power of orders and the power of jurisdiction. Women were capable of sharing in the second, at least by way of a special commission of that power to them. They had never been granted the power of inflicting censures, and it did not appear expedient or fitting that it ever should be granted; still, the granting of power in this manner was not essentially repugnant to the divine law. However, by Apostolic privilege superioresses could be given the capacity to confer benefices and to institute clerics in the churches attached to their monasteries, and could bestow possession of title to the benefices.[102]

One of the most favorable in his support of the opinion that abbesses could hold and exercise ecclesiastical jurisdiction was Cardinal Petra (1662-1747). He maintained the view that by privilege or by prescription abbesses acquired full jurisdiction in their territories *nullius*, exercising it through a vicar in matters in which they themselves lacked capacity. They did not merely depute their vicars, who in turn received jurisdiction from the pope; the jurisdiction was vested in the monastery itself which the abbess, as its head, was the qualified person to share with the vicars.[103]

In support of his opinion Petra cited many Rota decisions. In

---

[101] *Collectanea Doctorum in Ius Pontificium Universum* (3 vols. in 6, Lugduni, 1656), lib. I, tit. 33, cap. 12, nn. 1-3.

[102] *Theologia Moralis in Quinque Libros Partita* (Venetiis, 1719), lib. I, tract. 5, pars 1, cap. 3, n. 4.

[103] *Commentaria ad Constitutiones Apostolicas* (5 vols. in 2, Venetiis, 1729), III, 199, n. 20 ff.

one, dated in 1638, it was stated, first of all, that an abbess had the right of conferring benefices in the churches of her monastery, and that these acts partook of the nature of spiritual jurisdiction, and not of the power of orders. Secondly, it was declared that the institution of clerics in their benefices by the abbess bestowed title and possession, but did not confer the power of exercising the actual care of souls, since it was not within the competence of women to confer such a power.[104]

In another decision, dated in 1698, the case before the Rota hinged on the question whether a certain abbess had acquired ordinary jurisdiction in a town near her monastery. The Rota indeed solved the case in favor of the bishop's possession of the local jurisdiction, but the reason for so deciding was that the possession of jurisdiction on the part of the ruling abbess at that monastery was not evinced as a factor which had existed from time immemorial.[105] It was not demonstrated that the abbesses of that monastery had gained possession of jurisdictional power through immemorial custom, and therefore the present abbess could not claim the right to this power.

Another document to which Petra pointed in confirmation of his doctrine was a response of the Sacred Congregation of Bishops and Regulars, given in the year 1708. In this case the Sacred Congregation was asked whether at a certain monastery of St. Benedict the abbess had to exercise her jurisdiction through a vicar. The answer was in the affirmative. To the further question whether with reference to benefices which involved the care of souls the abbess could nominate incumbents, who then became removable at her will, the answer was in the negative. In a third question it was asked whether on the creation of a new abbess the clergy were obligated to appear in clerical habit, and then, while in kneeling posture, to kiss the hand of the abbess who sat *"sub Baldacchino cum Pastorali et Mitra."* The answer was in the negative, but it declared that some kind of homage should be shown. In the following year the Sacred

---

[104] 9 mart. 1638, Decisio 504—*Decisiones Sacrae Rotae Romanae coram Dunozati* (2 vols., Romae, 1668), I, 543.

[105] 11 apr. 1698, Decisio 549—*Decisiones Sacrae Rotae Romanae coram Molines* (5 vols., Romae, 1718), II, 580.

Congregation determined the nature of this homage. A profound inclination was to replace the genuflection. The mitre and the staff were to be placed on a table at the side of the abbess.[106] Bizzarri added in a footnote that this response was to be regarded as of historical importance, inasmuch as it finally abrogated all further exercise of jurisdiction of this kind.

Having noted these official decisions and responses, one may lastly look to the representative doctrine of the 18th and 19th century authors. Schmalzgrueber (1663-1735) stated that through privilege, by way of special commission of power, the right to exercise some acts of spiritual jurisdiction could be communicated to the abbess, especially of that jurisdiction which, called voluntary or non-contentious, was exemplified in the act of instituting clerics in offices or benefices.[107]

And, in the past century, Bouix (1808-1870) asserted that neither Scripture nor Tradition, nor the nature of womanhood in itself necessitated the exclusion of the exercise of ecclesiastical jurisdiction in consequence of any precept of the divine law. Women, he added, never held or exercised jurisdiction in virtue of an ordinary power, but the pope could delegate to them the power and the right to exercise jurisdictional acts. Whether the pope had ever done so was, so he held, a disputed question, which was still to be solved by the authentic record of history.[108]

From this discussion it is most evident, then, that the problem of the capacity of the superioress to enjoy jurisdiction constituted a most involved question. To draw conclusions is very difficult. Keeping in mind the twofold distinction in the power of the keys, each phase being separable from the other, one may perhaps conclude that the superioress was authoritatively regarded as capable of receiving a purely ecclesiastical jurisdiction, which was totally distinct from the power of orders. The common law indeed seems al-

---

[106] S. C. Ep. et Reg., *Castellana,* 22 iun. 1708, 19 iul. 1709—*Coll. S. C. Ep. et Reg.,* p. 290.

[107] *Ius Ecclesiasticum Universum* (5 vols. in 12, Romae, 1843-1845), lib. III, tit. 7, n. 11.

[108] *Tractatus de Jure Regularium,* II, 424-426.

ways to have denied women the possession or the exercise of even this kind of jurisdiction.

At times, however, women in authoritative ecclesiastical positions enjoyed by way of special privilege what the common law did not accord to them. Inasmuch as one cannot precisely determine the nature of the acts performed by superioresses under their prerogative, or the manner in which these acts were executed, one cannot reach a fully incontestable conclusion. The evidence is clear that women superioresses were not permitted, even by privilege, to inflict ecclesiastical censures. But the evidence seems equally clear that, regarding the appointment of clerics to offices and the institution of clerical candidates in benefices which were attached to the monasteries of women religious, the same consistent authoritative refusal to share the requisite power with abbesses or superioresses did not obtain in the practice of the Church. Without access to further authentic sources and authoritative documents one cannot securely offer any more definite pronouncement in this mooted question.

ARTICLE 5. RIGHTS AND DUTIES

From the very beginning of religious communities it was the duty of the superior to take care of the many things in the course of the daily monastic life that demanded decision and direction. Secondly, when religious communities were formed a Rule was adopted which delineated the purpose of the organization, the type of life that was to be led by the members, and the general range of powers vested in the superior.

Because of this arrangement superiors had their work well defined for them. It was not necessary for the Church to draw up extensive legislation, stating point by point what rights and duties superiors of religious communities had. On the formation of new communities the Church either prescribed, as it frequently did, the simple adoption of one of the extant Rules, or approved specially prepared Rules, as in the case of the newly organized mendicant orders, as, for example, the Rule of St. Francis of Assisi (1182-1226), approved by Honorius III (1216-1227) on November 29, 1223.[109]

---

[109] Bulla *"Solet annuere"—Bull. Rom. Taur.*, III, 594.

Some legislation regarding the rights and the duties of the superioress did, however, appear. Frequently it was of a disciplinary character; at times, however, it was of a general tenor.

Of the first type were those laws, to which repeated reference has been made, which established that superioresses were forbidden by common law to exercise ecclesiastical jurisdiction. They pointed out that superioresses, inasmuch as they did not possess the power of orders, could not perform the acts for the execution of which the previous reception of orders was demanded, such as the hearing of confessions, the granting of absolution, or the bestowal of a blessing as imparted by a priest.[110]

Or, again, these laws pointed out certain other acts which at the time were either considered as pertaining to the power of orders, or were very closely allied to it, and therefore were reserved for their performance to those who had received the required orders. Such, for instance, was the law which dealt with the function of preaching. It enacted the ruling that superioresses were not to preach publicly.[111]

Another such law was that which forbade the veiling of women by superioresses. This law was stated repeatedly in a number of successive councils. One finds mention in the First Capitulary of Charlemagne (789) that the performance of this act by the abbess militated against the custom of the Church, and therefore was interdicted by the King.[112] The VI Council of Paris (819) stated that the practice of veiling virgins was still current, but indicated that it was illicit for women to conduct that ceremony. Bishops were to correct all lingering abuses in this matter. If necessary, they were to invoke penalties for accomplishing their purpose.[113] Gratian incorporated this law of the Council of Paris in his *Decretum*.[114]

Bernard of Parma (+1266), in commenting on the decretal of Innocent III regarding certain abuses as practiced by abbesses, namely, of giving absolution and of preaching to the public, noted at

---

[110] First Capitularies of Charlemagne, c. 76—*MGH*, Legum Sectio II, *Capitularia Regum Francorum*, Tom. I (ed. Boretius), p. 61; c. 74—Mansi, XVII B, 238; c. 10, X, *de poenitentiis et remissionibus*, V, 38; Potthast, n. 4143.

[111] *Loc. cit.*

[112] C. 74—Mansi, XVII B, 238.

[113] C. 43—Mansi, XIV, 564.

[114] C. 3, C. XX, q. 2.

the same time that abbesses were not permitted to veil virgins.[115]
From the time of the Decretals onward, the laws of this type touched
rather the question of jurisdiction. On that matter a sufficient conspectus is offered in the preceding article of the present chapter.

As was noted, although the greater part of the legislation that
appeared relative to the rights and duties inherent in the office of
superior was disciplinary, some legislation of a general character did
appear. In the Council of Aix-la-Chapelle (816) it was declared
that the superioress should give good example, and should teach the
subjects committed to her care the virtues of the spiritual life.[116]
Again, in the same Council it was ordered that the abbess be especially solicitous for the sick, providing a place for them to stay, and
showing herself a compassionate mother.[117] Indicating its intent
to enact legislation only if it proved necessary, the II Council of
Chalon-sur-Saône (813) stated that in matters not covered by law
the abbess was to apply to the bishop and to obey him in all things.[118]

Regarding the duty of residence and the conditioned right to
leave the monastery one finds a fuller legislation. The Council of
Verneuil-sur-Oise (755) ordered that no abbess was to superintend
more than one monastery, or to leave its precincts except once a year
when summoned by the king.[119] Again, in 813 the Council of Mainz
declared that the abbess should reside in her monastery, and that
she could lawfully depart from it only with the permission of the
bishop.[120] In the same year the II Council of Tours and the II
Council of Chalon-sur-Saône required permission from the bishop
for the abbess to leave her monastery.[121] These laws formed the
background for the stricter legislation yet to be developed, and
firmly stated by Boniface VIII.[122]

Finally, a law that is of particular interest, because of its present

---

[115] *Glossa Ordinaria,* ad c. 10, X, *de poenitentiis et remissionibus,* V, 38,
s.v. *statuimus.*

[116] C. 14—Mansi, XIV, 270.

[117] C. 23—Mansi, XIV, 275.

[118] C. 65—Mansi, XIV, 106.

[119] C. 6—Hardouin, III, 1995; Mansi, XII, 758.

[120] C. 13—Mansi, XIV, 68.

[121] C. 30—Mansi, XIII, 88; c. 47—Mansi, XIV, 105.

[122] C. un., *de statu regularium,* III, 16, in VI°.

day close counterpart, provided that the abbess was to send a report of the finances of the monastery to the king or the bishop.[128]

In the centuries prior to the Council of Trent the Church did not legislate in detail regarding the rights and duties of the superioress, or make any attempt to list them. In that Council the same practice was adopted. The first decree in the session on the reform of regulars gives ample evidence of this. Speaking of superiors of religious communities, the Fathers of the Council stated that superiors should see to it that the requirements of the Rules of their respective communities be observed, as also the common life in the matters of food and clothing.[124]

For superioresses there were only two specific duties listed by the Council. The first concerned the old law of residence. No superioress, the Council stated, should be appointed with authority over two monasteries. If in any place this condition existed, the superioress had to resign from one of her two positions of authority within six months. The penalty for failure to comply with this demand was the loss of both positions of authority.[125]

The second decree placed an obligation on the superioress to notify the bishop of the time set for profession. This notice had to be intimated a month beforehand. If the superioress did not make this notification, she was to be suspended from office for as long a period as the bishop should deem fit.[126]

In the post-Tridentine period there is apparently an even greater dearth of legislation on the rights and duties of superioresses. Gregory XV (1621-1623) renewed the old law which required an annual statement regarding the temporalities to be made by the superioress to the local bishop.[127]

For the rest it was left to the particular constitutions of each religious institute to supply all necessary prescriptions, the superioress always having the obligation to preserve and promote the observance of these among the members.

[128] Council of Verneuil-sur-Oise (755), c. 20—Hardouin, III, 1998; Mansi, XII, 584.

[124] Sess. XXV, *de regularibus*, c. 1.

[125] Sess. XXV, *de regularibus*, c. 7.

[126] Sess. XXV, *de regularibus*, c. 17.

[127] Const. *"Inscrutabili,"* 5 febr. 1622—*Fontes,* n. 199.

CHAPTER III

SUPERIORESSES OF CONGREGATIONS

ARTICLE 1. EARLY DEVELOPMENT

· THE first monasteries of religious were individual units independent of one another. Each was composed of its own entire family, with its own superior having full authority over all. St. Benedict especially saw this type of organization as the best means of accomplishing the true ends of monastic life. From time to time there occurred unions of monasteries, but the real change in this practice was introduced by the ancient mendicant orders.

The nature and purpose of their work was foreign to their remaining in a single monastery. They spread far and wide, establishing many houses in many places. The government of these orders was designed to fit many houses rather than a single monastery. The supreme power was placed in a general superior who resided at Rome. Under him were provincials, to whose care were allotted certain areas. In these areas there was a local superior for each convent.[1]

Side by side with the development of these orders of men there followed with each a corresponding order of women. However, there could not be a complete parallel in government. The mind of the Church was that orders of women should be cloistered and under solemn vows. Throughout the earlier history of women religious the Church's legislation constantly sought to make this clear. Boniface VIII in his Constitution *"Periculoso"* made the strict and perpetual cloister a universal law for all women religious of every order.[2]

The Council of Trent renewed the legislation of Boniface VIII, commanding all bishops to see to it that the enclosure of nuns be enforced wherever it had been violated, and preserved where it was still in force. No nun was to leave the cloister once she had been professed, except with the permission of the bishop.[3]

On May 29, 1566, Pius V (1566-1572) in his Constitution *"Circa*

---

[1] Cf. Alzog, *Manual of Universal Church History*, II, 488 ff.

[2] C. un., *de statu regularium*, III, 16, in VI°.

[3] Sess. XXV, *de regularibus*, c. 5.

pastoralis" again made clear the mind of the Church.[4] He repeated the decrees of Boniface VIII and of the Council of Trent. In a second Constitution he became more specific.[5] Three reasons alone permitted the leaving of the cloister: leprosy, an epidemic, and an extensive fire. For the violation of this law the guilty nun incurred excommunication reserved to the pope himself. It is hardly necessary to emphasize, then, that there was only one type of superioress among women religious. She was the superioress of each cloistered group.

Despite the legislation which required solemn vows and the perpetual cloister, a new type of community of women religious came into being. It was exemplified in the congregation of members professed with simple vows, not subject to the obligation of the cloister. The works of these members included the care of hospitals, the education of children, and other charitable works.[6]

These groups were not regarded as true religious. The Holy See refused to approve them in a formal manner, and hence they lacked a recognized canonical status. However, it must be said that there was an attitude of benign toleration toward them. Their foundation and government was left to the supervision of the local bishop. They were, as other members of his flock, entirely under his jurisdiction.[7] This status lasted for over three hundred years. It was eventually a controversy between the Congregation of the English Ladies and the Bishop of Augsburg that finally induced positive action on the part of the Church. This controversy and the Church's resultant action are delineated in the famous Constitution *"Quamvis iusto"* of Benedict XIV (1740-1758).[8]

ARTICLE 2. RECOGNITION BY ROME

The case that called the attention of Benedict XIV was one regarding jurisdiction. As has been said, congregations of simple vows

---

[4] Const. *"Circa pastoralis,"* 29 maii 1566—*Fontes,* n. 112.

[5] Const. *"Decori,"* 1 febr. 1570—*Fontes,* n. 133.

[6] Alzog, *Manual of Universal Church History,* III, 460.

[7] Orth, *The Approbation of Religious Institutes,* The Catholic University of America Canon Law Studies, n. 71 (Washington, D. C.: The Catholic University of America, 1931), pp. 52, 53.

[8] Const. *"Quamvis iusto,"* 30 apr. 1749—*Fontes,* n. 398.

had been left entirely under the authority of the local bishop. The Congregation of English Ladies had originated in England, but because of persecution there had continued its work in Germany. Not bound by the cloister its members were free to travel and change their abode among the various houses of their community. As the mendicant orders of men had elected a superior general, so they elected a superioress general. Her authority was exercised over the entire congregation. The claim, as it came to Rome, declared that it was to this superioress, and not to the bishop, that the Congregation was subject.

Benedict XIV recounted this history in the first part of the Constitution *"Quamvis."* [9] In meeting the existing difficulty itself, he insisted that the office of superioress general could remain. Her authority, however, was to be limited. She was free to visit the various houses of her community to superintend its educational work, and to transfer the members of the community from one house to another, but all under the authority of the local bishop.[10]

On making her visits this superioress could inquire how the Constitutions were being observed, how the standards of discipline were being enforced, and regarding the instruction and progress of those under the care of the local community. The bishop was then to be informed of all these matters in a report made to him.[11] Any changes to be made among the members of the local houses were also to be decided by the superioress general, but permission to make these transfers had to be obtained from the local ordinary of the houses involved.[12]

---

[9] Const. *"Quamvis iusto,"* 30 apr. 1749—*Fontes*, n. 398.

[10] "Nihil innovandum quoad Superiorissam: eius tamen auctoritatem coercendam esse ad visitationem, superintendentiam in materia educationis Puellarum, translationem Virginum de uno in alium locum; accedente debita subordinatione in praedictis ab Ordinariis locorum."—*"Quamvis iusto,"* § 6.

[11] "Eidem tamen Generali Superiorissae licebit, praevio expresso Dioecesani Praesulis assensu, Conservatoria, seu Domos visitare, et an in ipsis omnia ad propriarum Constitutionum rectaeque disciplinae normam gerantur, et quomodo Puellarum institutio ac profectus promoveatur, diligenter cognoscere . . . ad quem Episcopum post visitationem, de omnibus relatio fieri debebit."—*"Quamvis iusto,"* § 19.

[12] "Eadem quoque poterit Magistras, et Virgines, de uno in aliud Conserva-

By this Constitution no official approval was given to congregations of simple vows. The Constitution was directed to one specific Institute and, at most, gave recognition. The members of this Institute did not thereby become true religious.[13] But a new attitude was shown in this Constitution by the Holy See toward such groups, and a model was given after which other congregations of simple vows could establish their government. Along with the recognition of the congregation there came also in a very special way the recognition of the office of superioress general.

This Constitution can be looked upon as a real development in the institute of superioresses in communities of women religious. The important point seemed to be that the pope had no objection to the existence of such an office. The norms he enacted showed that he held a favorable view toward it. This was a long step from the rigorous legislation respecting the cloister and the obligation of the superioress to live within it.

ARTICLE 3. FINAL APPROVAL

Benedict XIV had directed his Constitution to one institute, but many others had come and were coming into being. The lack of norms to guide them brought numerous petitions to the Holy See for approval of the rules they were following. The Sacred Congregation of Bishops and Regulars found the problem a perplexing one. On the one hand there was a clear need for some form of central government for these institutes, while on the other the tradition in the Church was against it. Many of these communities had houses in more than one diocese. The bishops objected to any authority over the groups in their dioceses when that authority resided outside the diocese.[14]

torium transferre, prout illa in uno potius, quam in alio, opportune collocandas, et utilem operam praestituras esse, prudenter existimabit; habita tamen ad huiusmodi translationes pro tempore exsequendas, licentia, et facultate illius Ordinarii Praesulis, seu illorum, in cuius, vel quorum Dioecesi ipsa Conservatoria respective sita reperiuntur."—"*Quamvis iusto,*" § 19.

[13] "Clare patet. . . . Statum Virginum Anglicanarum non esse statum verae Religionis."—"*Quamvis iusto,*" § 13.

[14] S. C. Ep. et Reg., *Lugdunen. et Taurien.*, 9 aug. 1844—*Coll. S. C. Ep. et Reg.*, p. 501.

One solution that was attempted provided that there should be a superioress general not over the whole congregation, but rather over its houses in a given diocese. This plan was a compromise in an effort to solve the question, and at the same time to offer a solution that was satisfactory to both the bishops and the community. It applied to the Sisters of St. Joseph.[15]

In some cases the Sacred Congregation instructed particular institutes to form a central government modeled after that proposed in the Constitution *"Quamvis iusto"* of Benedict XIV.[16] In the many *animadversiones* made by the Sacred Congregation one finds no uniformity of action. The merits of each institute constituted the deciding factor. There was evidence, though, in these same *animadversiones*, of a gradual growth of favor toward a superioress general for each institute, the power of which superioress would extend to the whole institute, though spread throughout a number of dioceses. A number of institutes whose constitutions were approved received permission for a superioress general, but the constitutions of each group had to be consulted for her specific rights.[17] When the constitution had this approval, no bishop could then interfere.[18]

In all the cases in which some approval had been given to the rules or constitutions, no change occurred in the status of the congregations themselves. The members were still not to be regarded as religious. Simple vows were not yet accepted as sufficient to entitle those who were professed with them to be classed as having entered the religious state. This acknowledgment came only with the pontificate of Leo XIII (1878-1903).

The long awaited approval for congregations of simple vows came on the Feast of the Immaculate Conception, 1900. In the first part of the Constitution *"Conditae a Christo,"* Leo XIII reviewed

---

[15] S. C. Ep. et Reg., *Lugdunen. et Taurien.*, 13 iun. 1845—*Coll. S. C. Ep. et Reg.*, p. 524.

[16] S. C. Ep. et Reg., *Monacen. et Frisingen.*, 1858—*Coll. S. C. Ep. et Reg.*, p. 775, note 1.

[17] S. C. Ep. et Reg., *Monacen. et Frisingen.*, 1858; *Paderbornen.*, 10 mart. 1860; *Gandaven.*, 30 apr. 1860; *Bellicen.*, 6 iun. 1860—*Coll. S. C. Ep et Reg.*, pp. 774-776, 779, 781.

[18] *Coll. S. C. Ep. et Reg.*, p. 709, note 1.

the problem of long standing, and resolved it into two cases, namely, one involving those communities which had been approved solely by bishops, and the other involving those which had received approval from the Holy See. He treated them in the same order, enacting a number of prescriptions for each.

Regarding diocesan communities the pope made it clear that their foundation and a great deal of their internal government depended on the bishop. Before they could be regularly founded, the bishop had to consent to it, and approve their constitutions. Once founded, before they could erect houses in another diocese, he had to give his permission as well as did the bishop of the diocese in which these houses were to be erected. Candidates for admission, as also for profession, had to be examined by the bishop, and it was his right to deny either of these privileges. Superioresses were to be elected by the members of the community, but the confirmation of election rested with the bishop. Finally, the bishop had the right of visitation in matters of studies, discipline, and administration.[19]

Turning to the question of communities of pontifical approval, the Constitution prescribed a greater independence from the bishops. Superioresses could admit candidates, permitting them to wear the habit and also to make profession. The bishop, however, retained the right to examine the young women who proposed to take these steps. Again, the superioresses when elected did not need the confirmation of the bishop.

With regard to the government of these congregations a twofold aspect was to be kept in mind. What pertained to the internal government of the institute was within the competence of the superioress. What pertained to the external forum, or those matters which affected one as a member of the Church rather than as a religious, were within the competence of the bishop. Temporal administration followed the same norm. No report had to be made to the bishop except in the case wherein the funds had been given for the enhancement of divine worship or for the promotion of public charitable works. In his visitation the bishop could inquire as to dis-

---

[19] Const. *"Conditae a Christo,"* 8 dec. 1900, n. 4, art. 1, 4, 7, 9, 10—*Fontes,* n. 644.

cipline, sound doctrine, and the frequency of the reception of the sacraments.[20]

This Constitution in no way offered a complete set of rules for congregations of simple vows, but it established their rights in matters of government. Details were left to the individual constitutions. It supplied a foundation in law for what previously existed without express legal authorization. As the pope himself said, there was need that both the bishops and the congregations should have their rights clearly defined and adequately preserved.[21]

ARTICLE 4. THE *"Normae of 1901"*

It was not the purpose of Leo XIII in his Constitution *"Conditae a Christo"* to furnish a complete law for religious of simple vows. Details of law were to be cared for in the individual constitutions. However, to facilitate the drawing up of these constitutions, and to illustrate what it was accustomed to approve, the Sacred Congregation of Bishops and Regulars issued a set of rules on June 28, 1901, entitled the *"Normae."* It must be remembered that these rules were not laws.[22]

The plan of government proposed by the Sacred Congregation included three types of superioresses: the superioress general, the provincials, and the local superioresses. Art. 252: The power of the superioress general, subject always to the constitutions, extended over the institute in what pertained to it as a whole and in what pertained to its individual houses. Art. 266: It was not within the competence of the superioress general to dispense from the constitutions except in particular cases. Art. 301, 302: With the authorization of the Holy See provinces could be formed and placed under the rule of a superioress, whose authority extended over the area assigned. Art. 303: Subject to the confirmation of the supe-

---

[20] Const. *"Conditae a Christo,"* 8 dec. 1900, n. 5, art. 1, 5, 9, 11—*Fontes,* n. 644.

[21] "At ideo necesse est alteros alterorum iura pernoscere atque integra custodire."—*"Conditae a Christo,"* n. 2.

[22] *Normae secundum Quas E. Cong. Ep. et Reg. procedere solet in approbandis Novis Institutis Votorum Simplicium* (Romae: Typis S. Cong. de Propaganda Fide, 1901) hereafter referred to as *"Normae of 1901."*

rioress general the provincial together with her council could admit postulants to the habit and to vows. Art. 312: The local superioress likewise had true power over the house of which she was in charge, and was not merely a vicar of the higher superioresses.

Art. 231: To be elected to the office of superioress general one had to be at least forty years of age, and professed with perpetual vows for at least five years. Art. 207: The term of office was for six or twelve years. Art. 269, 270: Abdication or removal from office required the permission of the Sacred Congregation. Art. 309: The term of office for the local superioress was for three years, which on completion could be renewed for a second term, but not beyond that in the same house.[23] Art. 265: No one could hold the office of superioress general and at the same time be the superioress of a province or of a house. Art. 253: The residence of the superioress general was to be at that house of the community which proved most convenient for the ruling of the institute. Such residence once established could not be changed without the permission of the Holy See.

With these *"Normae of 1901"* one sees the office of superioress in communities of women religious reach the fullness of its development. The *"Normae of 1901"* did not propose anything that had not existed before, but they showed what was recommended. Thenceforth the three types of superioresses reflected the customary and accepted form of government for congregations of women religious.

[23] Battandier (1850-1921) remarked that in the silence of the *"Normae of 1901"* regarding the term of office of provincials, the term or duration prescribed for the local superioress was to be followed.—*Guide canonique pour les constitutions des institues à voeux simples* (6. ed., Paris, 1923), p. 417, n. 505 (hereafter referred to as *Guide canonique*).

PART II

CANONICAL COMMENTARY

CHAPTER IV

SUPERIORESSES AND THEIR SUBJECTS

ARTICLE 1. SUPERIORESSES IN GENERAL

INSTITUTES of women religious constitute a true society of the faithful. Further, there is in each society the twofold purpose of the attainment of perfection by the members and the employment of their time in its characteristic work. It is necessary that there be within each organization persons endowed with authority to guide and direct it toward a successful accomplishment of these ends, that there be superioresses taken from the ranks of the members and by their office vested with authority over the other religious in the community. As has been seen in the historical synopsis to this work, such an institution has been realized and developed down through the ages of the Church. In the Code of Canon Law there are found in relation to the office of superioress additional juridical details which offer far more complete regulations as to its nature and duties.

Under the name superioress come all who enjoy dominative power and are able to command in virtue of obedience.[1] Such persons would be not only those who hold a principal office, but those also who have a secondary place, as for example vicars and mistresses of novices.[2] In the stricter sense those only are to be considered superioresses

---

[1] Beste, *Introductio in Codicem* (ed. altera, Collegeville, Minn.: St. John's Abbey Press, 1944), p. 326.

[2] Schaefer, *De Religiosis ad Normam Codicis Iuris Canonici* (3. ed., Romae: Typis Polyglottis Vaticanis, 1940), p. 214; n. 102 (hereafter referred to as *De Religiosis*).

who from their office have a stable authority over the institute as a whole, over a province, or over a house. By name they are most frequently called the superioress general, the provincial, and the local superioress. One exception to this rule is the office of visitatrix, which in some communities commits permanent authority. Then it too belongs to the aforementioned group. In this work considerations will be limited to superioresses understood in the stricter sense.[3]

The superioress general is superioress absolutely, that is, her authority is not circumscribed by any geographical limits. It extends over all the provinces and houses, and over all the members of the institute. Other superioresses enjoy relative authority. They administer only in a designated territory: the provincial throughout her whole province; and the local superioress over her own community.[4] This power of subordinate superioresses must, however, be understood to be personal as well as territorial. It extends over their subjects though these be for a time outside the province or house.[5]

Besides the distinctions noted above, another that holds a most important place in the law of the Church is that of major and minor superioresses. Major superioresses comprise the superioress general of the whole institute, the provincials, their vicars, and all others who have powers equivalent to those of provincials.[6] Among this group there should also be included the superioress of nuns in an independent monastery, as for example the Carmelites and the Poor Clares.[7]

The basis for this last statement is summed up by Larraona.[8]

[3] Cocchi, *Commentarium in Codicem Iuris Canonici ad Usum Scholarum* (8 vols. in 5, Vol. IV, 3. ed., Taurinorum Augustae: Marietti, 1932), IV, p. 52, n. 23 (hereafter referred to as *Commentarium*); Fanfani, *De Iure Religiosorum ad Normam Codicis Iuris Canonici* (2. ed., Taurini-Romae: Marietti, 1925), p. 56, n. 47 (hereafter referred to as *De Iure Religiosorum.*

[4] Canon 502.

[5] Beste, *Introductio in Codicem*, p. 330.

[6] Canon 488, 8°.

[7] Creusen-Garesché-Ellis, *Religious Men and Women in the Code* (5. ed., Milwaukee, Wis.: The Bruce Publishing Co., 1940), p. 14, n. 14; Schaefer, *De Religiosis*, p. 90, n. 50.

[8] "Commentarium Codicis," *Commentarium pro Religiosis* (Romae, 1920-1935), IV (1923), 42-44 (hereafter referred to as *CpR*).

Canon 490 legislates that in matters concerning religious, although the masculine gender is used, the application of the law is to be extended to women religious, except when it is obviously otherwise intended. In canon 488, 8°, one reads that the abbot of an independent monastery is listed as a major superior. Since he is the counterpart among men religious to the superioress of an independent monastery of nuns, she, too, should be recognized as a major superioress. Again, in canon 504, where the age is specified for those holding the office of superioress general, who is certainly a major superioress, that same age minimum is required for the superioress of an independent monastery. Finally, it may be said that if these superioresses are not of major rank, many duties listed in the Code would want for some one capable of fulfilling them in these monasteries. Today authors are uniform in their opinion that the superioress of an independent monastery must be considered as a major superioress.[9]

It has been already mentioned that canon 488, 8°, includes in its list of major superioresses those also who are their vicaresses. It must be made clear that they are the vicaresses of the superioress general and of the provincials, and all others who have power equivalent to those of provincials. Thus it means that these vicaresses possess from their office an actual power that is stable and permanent as long as they hold office. Were their power merely delegated, then they could not be classed as major superioresses. The question as to which vicaresses meet this requirement can be determined only by an examination of the particular law of the institute to which they belong.[10]

Often it happens that, when a superioress general is absent, impeded, or deceased (i. e., during the interval between her death and

---

[9] Fanfani, *De Iure Religiosorum,* p. 57, n. 47; Coronata, *Institutiones Iuris Canonici ad Usum Utriusque Cleri et Scholarum* (5 vols., Vol. I, 2. ed., 1939, Taurini: Marietti), I, p. 616, n. 505 (hereafter referred to as *Institutiones*); Vermeersch-Creusen, *Epitome Iuris Canonici cum Commentariis ad Scholas et ad Usum Privatum* (3 vols., Vol. I, 6. ed., 1937; Vol. II, 5. ed., 1934; Vol. III, 5. ed., 1936, Mechliniae et Romae: H. Dessain), I, p. 428, n. 594 (hereafter referred to as *Epitome*).

[10] Coronata, *Institutiones,* I, p. 617, n. 506; Schaefer, *De Religiosis,* p. 216, n. 103.

a new election), the first assistant counsellor has the powers of a major superioress.[11] In such cases the counsellor must remember not to take grave measures of a permanent character unless necessity urges.[12] The rule, "During the vacancy of the See nothing is to be changed," must always be kept in mind.[13] Needless to say, the same rule holds for those who take the place of the provincial under the same conditions.

The question may also be asked whether the visitatrix is a major superioress. Those holding the office of visitatrix, Larraona says, are major superioresses if, outside the actual time of visitation, they possess a habitual power conferred on them by their office. In other words, they are major superioresses when they have power that is ordinary and not merely delegated.[14]

Finally, it may be said briefly that minor superioresses are all those local superioresses who have ordinary power, an exception being made for superioresses of independent monasteries who, as has been seen, are to be regarded as major superioresses.[15]

ARTICLE 2. DURATION OF OFFICE

Just as there are different degrees prescribed by law for the office of superioress, so too there are variations in the length of their terms of office according to the degree of office held. Canon 505 states that the higher superioresses shall be temporary, unless the constitutions determine otherwise; the lower local superioress is not to hold office for more than three years; on the expiration of this term she can be reappointed to the same office for a second term if the constitutions permit it, but not immediately for a third term in the same house. Thus in setting down her legislation on the duration of the term of office of a superioress, the Church makes her basic norm of division that of major and minor superioresses.

In the present article, after a few general notions applicable to

---

[11] Creusen-Garesché-Ellis, *Religious Men and Women in the Code*, p. 15, n. 14.

[12] Creusen-Garesché-Ellis, *op. cit.*, p. 43, n. 52.

[13] C. 1, X, *ne sede vacante aliquid innovetur*, III, 9.

[14] "Commentarium Codicis," *CpR*, I (1920), 30-32.

[15] Schaefer, *De Religiosis*, p. 216, n. 103.

all superioresses have been presented, the same division will be followed in regard to the duration of the term of office on the part of the superioress. The article will be concluded with a treatment of the computation of these terms and a final word on the procedure requisite in removal from office.

1. *General Notions*

First, authors agree that in extraordinary circumstances, such as in the time of war, the law on the duration of the term of office would cease in virtue of *epikeia*, and that a superioress could both validly and licitly continue in office beyond the prescribed time.[16] Secondly, since there is no clause in canon 505 to reprove any contrary custom, the regulating norm as to such a custom must be canon 5, which leaves to the judgment of the proper ordinary the decision as to whether such a custom may or may not be tolerated.[17] Thirdly, this law as enunciated in canon 505 cannot be said to be a *"lex irritans."* Consequently an election contrary to its precepts, although certainly illicit, could not be held to be invalid.[18] Finally, canon 505 cannot be said to apply to others except superioresses in the strict sense. The vicaresses of superioresses bound by the law do not come under its restrictions.[19]

2. *Major Superioresses*

Canon 505 provides a clear statement of the mind of the Church and her decided preference that the office of major superioress be a temporary one. In fact, temporary tenure is made a requirement

[16] Schaefer, *De Religiosis*, p. 252, n. 120; Vermeersch-Creusen, *Epitome*, I, p. 446, n. 623; Wernz-Vidal, *Ius Canonicum ad Codicis Normam Exactum* (7 vols. in 8, Vol. III, *De Religiosis*, Romae: Universitas Gregoriana, 1933), III, p. 93, n. 102, nota 27 (hereafter referred to as *Ius Canonicum*).

[17] Schaefer, *De Religiosis*, p. 248, n. 118; Coronata, *Institutiones*, I, p. 657, n. 538.

[18] Canon 11; Larraona, "Commentarium Codicis," *CpR*, VII (1926), 380, nota 289; Coronata, *op. cit.*, I, p. 657, n. 538; Schaefer, *op. cit.*, p. 247, n. 118; Vermeersch-Creusen, *Epitome*, I, p. 446, n. 623.

[19] Larraona, "Commentarium Codicis," *CpR*, VII (1926), 377; Schaefer, *op. cit.*, p. 252, n. 121.

of law unless the constitutions provide otherwise. The constitutions, to warrant this exception, in turn must have been reviewed and accepted by the Holy See. It may be safely said that today it is the practice of the Sacred Congregation of Religious to forbid any provision for superioresses who are to hold office for life.[20] Every effort is made to keep the now general law of the Church uniform and intact, namely, that all major superioresses shall retain their offices only for limited terms.

The law states that the offices of major superioresses are to be temporary. The question may now be asked what is to be considered the proper length of a temporary term. Certainly it would not be within the spirit or the letter of the law were terms to be made of so long a duration that they would be tantamount to life terms. It is left to the particular law of each religious institute to settle this question. A jurisprudence has developed on the point, however, with the result that now the customary terms of office for major superioresses, and the ones generally found in the constitutions of women religious, are for three, six, or twelve years. These seem acceptable to the Sacred Congregation of Religious, and are the ones ordinarily approved by it.

As was said, the law leaves the determination of the terms of major superioresses to the constitutions of each institute. There is nothing contrary to the law then in constitutions that would permit the reelection of major superioresses for a second term. Furthermore, third terms would likewise be in accord with the law. Indeed, for provincials such a practice may be said to be permitted ordinarily.[21]

Special regulations prohibit the same, however, from being said for the superioress general. The *"Normae of 1901"* issued by the Sacred Congregation of Bishops and Regulars state that supreme moderators elected for six years may be reelected for a second term, provided that this action is not contrary to the constitutions, but for a third term there is need of two-thirds of all the votes cast by the electors, and confirmation by the Holy See. If the superioress general is elected the first time for a period of twelve years,

---

[20] Maroto, "Annotationes," *CpR*, II (1921), 4.

[21] Maroto, "Annotationes," *CpR*, II (1921), 3; Schaefer, *De Religiosis*, p. 254, n. 122; Beste, *Introductio in Codicem*, p. 332.

the same two conditions spoken of above must also be fulfilled for reelection to a second term.[22]

The Sacred Congregation of Religious, in reaction to the excessive number of petitions for confirmation for third terms, pointed out in a letter to the bishops of the world that when two terms of six years have been completed, there exists a real ineligibility for office, and that it must be kept in mind that a third term is made possible only by postulation in the strict sense.[23] Consequently, before any petition is made there should be grave reasons demanding the reelection of the previous incumbent. A mere desire on the part of the voters, or the natural qualities of the candidate, would not be a sufficient reason for such a petition.

Maroto (1875-1937) taught that from the mind of the Sacred Congregation as here expressed the same ineligibility had to be admitted regarding superioresses who, in accord with the constitutions, had been elected for a term of twelve years.[24] In view of the fact that the Sacred Congregation has declared ineligibility after a second term of six years, that is, after an aggregate tenure of twelve years, it certainly is obvious that the mind of the Sacred Congregation would be even more adverse to an aggregate of twenty-four years. It must be stated, though, that the above noted declaration of the Sacred Congregation of Religious does not demand any alteration of accepted constitutions which allow an indefinite number of reelections without recourse to the Holy See, inasmuch as the law provides explicitly that the office of major superioress is temporary unless the constitutions determine otherwise.

In answer to a question regarding founders the response given by the Sacred Congregation stated that they too were bound by the ruling of the constitutions of their institute, and could not hold office for life without an apostolic indult if life tenure were contrary to the constitutions.[25] In this case, however, if all the members

---

[22] Art. 207; 235; 236.

[23] *Litterae Circulares,* 9 mart. 1920—*Acta Apostolica Sedis, Commentarium Officiale* (Romae [Civitate Vaticana], 1909—), XII (1920), 365 (hereafter referred to as *AAS*).

[24] "Annotationes," *CpR,* II (1921), 5.

[25] S. C. de Rel., *De munere supremi moderatoribus ad vitam,* 6 mart. 1922—*AAS,* XIV (1922), 163.

of the society consented to ask for it, the indult would in all likelihood be granted by the Sacred Congregation. The motivating purpose would provide an adequate reason, i. e., to preserve the spirit of the founder and to alleviate the numerous trying difficulties encountered by a young community.[26]

This restriction as to the permanent tenure of founders applies also to communities of diocesan approval, for it pertains to the common law governing these as well as the communities of pontifical approval. No one has the right of ruling subjects without authority derived under the common law either from a canonical mandate issued by a competent ecclesiastical superioress or from a legitimate election.[27] The same must be said for founders of congregations living in common without vows.[28]

Much has already been said about abbesses or superioresses of independent monasteries in the historical synopsis to this work.[29] By way of summary it may be said that prior to the promulgation of the Code there was a distinction made among such superioresses, namely, those residing within Italy and the adjacent islands, and those outside of this territory. For the former by an ancient law of Gregory XIII ineligibility for office arose after a term of three years. For the latter the constitutions and legitimate customs were to be followed.

Benedict XV (1914-1922) ordered the Sacred Congregation of Religious to notify all those whom it concerned that the Constitution of Gregory XIII was still obligatory after the Code.[30] According to this notification, however, legitimate contrary customs, as acquired rights, were to be respected. Outside Italy and the other territories mentioned the constitutions and customs, it revealed, were to set the norm.[31]

---

[26] Vermeersch, "Annotatio," *Periodica de Religiosis et Missionariis*, Brugis, 1905-1919; *Periodica de Re Canonica et Morali utilia praesertim Religiosis et Missionariis*, Brugis, 1920-1927; *Periodica de Re Morali, Canonica, Liturgica*, Brugis, 1927-1936 et Romae 1937—.

[27] Schaefer, *De Religiosis*, p. 246, n. 117.

[28] Coronata, *Institutiones*, I, p. 654, u. 538.

[29] Cf. *supra*, pp. 18-20.

[30] *Litterae Circulares*, 9 mart. 1920—*AAS*, XII (1920), 366.

[31] Maroto, "Annotationes," *CpR*, II (1921), 3-8.

In regard to the supreme moderator of a congregation with a single house of which she is also the local superioress the first section of canon 505 is to be followed in its prescriptions for major superioresses.[32] The Code in this canon uses the expression "local minor superioress" in restricting the term of the latter to three years. Consequently if a superioress general in virtue of the norms of the constitutions governs the mother house herself, she may remain superioress of that house for her full term of superioress general.[33]

Treating this precise question, Larraona points out that for the above noted exceptional tenure to be permitted there should be a clear statement in the constitutions, i. e., a foundation in particular law, that the office of superioress general and local superioress are united, and that this superioress is a major superioress. Otherwise, he believes, there will be a conflict as to which section of canon 505 is rightly applied. One holding two offices, he argues, should not apply to both the rules really applicable to only one.[34] This latter qualification as to the need of precision in the constitutions as a condition for the exceptional tenure seems correct, because the very purpose of the law is to prevent a situation of long tenure of office by the same superioress, especially in a single house.

3. *Local Minor Superioresses*

In regard to the term of office of local minor superioresses the Code is far more specific in its legislation than it is for major superioresses. It states categorically that their terms should be for not more than three years. If the constitutions authorize a reappointment, then a second term of equal duration may be granted. A third term immediately in the same house is absolutely forbidden.

This law applies to all local minor superioresses whether of com-

---

[32] Schaefer, *De Religiosis*, p. 252, n. 121.

[33] Creusen-Garesché-Ellis, *Religious Men and Women in the Code*, p. 49, n. 67; Bastien, *Directoire Canonique à l'Usage des Congrégations à Voeux Simples* (3. ed., Bruges: Beyaert, 1923), p. 333, n. 536 (hereafter referred to as *Directoire*).

[34] Larraona, "Commentarium Codicis," *CpR*, VII (1926), 377, nota 280.

munities with or without vows.[35]   No matter how large or how small
the house is, as long as it is canonically erected, the precept of canon
505 must be followed.   The same must be said whether the power
of the local minor superioress is ordinary or vicarious, provided that
she lives there, and rules the entire community.[36]   Again, the law
binds local superioresses whether their appointment involves a definite or an indefinite term.   Thus, after three years in office there
must always be an expressed reappointment, and after six years
the term of the incumbent may not be prolonged.[37]

Of the points that come to light in an analysis of this section of
canon 505 it must be said first, that the law makes the maximum
term for minor local superioresses three years, and permits the various constitutions to sanction a second term for the same period. The
constitutions are in no way obliged to do this, and if they remain
silent on the subject, since the law demands a positive permission
from them, no second term may be permitted.[38]

The restriction of the law concerns tenure of office in the same
house, and it in no way forbids that a local superioress, retaining the
same prerogative, should be immediately transferred to another house.
For a third term in the same house, that is, for a continuous tenure
of office longer than six consecutive years, a papal dispensation is
necessary.   The same must be said in the case in which three years
have passed since the appointment of the local superioress, and the
constitutions either specifically prohibit or are silent in regard to a
second term.

4. *Computation of Terms of Office*

Terms of office are to be reckoned in accord with the laws, as
found in the Code on the computation of the duration of time pe-

---

[35] Pontifical Commission of Interpretation, 25 iul. 1926—*AAS*, XVIII
(1926), 393 (hereafter referred to as P. C. I.).

[36] Berutti, *Institutiones Iuris Canonici* (6 vols., Vol. III, Taurini-Romae:
Marietti, 1936), III, p. 63, n. 31.

[37] Geser, *The Canon Law Governing Communities of Sisters* (St. Louis,
Mo.: B. Herder Book Co., 1939), p. 82, q. 214.

[38] Schaefer, *De Religiosis*, p. 248, n. 118; Coronata, *Institutiones*, I, p. 657,
n. 538.

riods. Since the duration of a term is computed in years, these years are to be taken as they are found in the calendar.[39] If the term's beginning coincides with the beginning of a day, its end will coincide with that of the beginning of the same date after the completion of the number of years for which the office was assigned. If the beginning of the term of office did not coincide with the beginning of a day, the first day is not counted and the term will end with the last hour of the day having the same date after the lapse of the respective number of years constituting the term.[40]

Asked whether terms of office should be reckoned from the day of appointment or from the date when the Code went into effect, the Pontifical Commission of Interpretation responded that the starting point should be considered the day of appointment.[41] In view of the general law of the Church on ecclesiastical offices,[42] and also in line with the given response, it seems indicated that terms of office are to be considered as beginning from the actual day on which each superioress is designated by the competent authority. However, if a case is found in which confirmation or postulation is involved, the commencement of the term is to be considered as fixed by the date on which confirmation is given or postulation accepted.[43]

Again, since the office of superioress is one that can be exercised without one's actual presence, and there is no law that requires the actual taking of possession, the date on which the designation was made, the confirmation accorded, or the postulation accepted, seems to be the one that must be accepted as determining the moment at which the term of office begins for the superioress.[44] It may be said, however, that this is a subject that the constitutions might well make specific for each institute. If they have made definite regulations, these are, of course, to be followed.

[39] Canon 34, § 3, 1°.

[40] Canon 34, § 3, 2°, 3°.

[41] 25 mart. 1919—*CpR*, II (1921), 65.

[42] Canon 159: "Cuiuslibet officii provisio scripto consignetur."

[43] Maroto, "Annotationes," *CpR*, II (1921), 69; Larraona, "Commentarium Codicis," *CpR*, VII (1926), 379.

[44] Coronata, *Institutiones*, I, p. 656, n. 583; Schaefer, *De Religiosis*, p. 250, n. 120.

Frequently it happens that necessity, such as arises through the death of the incumbent, requires the appointment of a new superioress in the midst of her predecessor's term. In appraising the possible solution of the problem thus presented, it is worthy of note that for the good order of religious institutes it is a common practice to provide either by means of the constitutions or through customary usage that the tenure of all offices shall terminate at the same time, and that all superioresses shall be appointed at the same time. For example, the date of appointments is frequently that of the regular meeting of the chapter or of the general council.

Authors agree that when a situation of this kind arises minor local superioresses substituted for an incompleted term of a predecessor in office cannot be said to have served a regular canonical term. Consequently it is permitted for a superioress who has thus shared a term with a predecessor to be appointed to the same office when her partial term has been completed, and to enjoy the full tenure of office allowed by canon 505, the part term being left entirely unreckoned in the period of her aggregate tenure. Commentators reason that the Code permits, provided that the constitutions are in agreement, two terms of three years each, after which no third term may be granted immediately in the same house. But when a superioress has served only one term of three years plus a partial term, it cannot be said that she has served the two canonical terms allowed by the Code. Thus she may be permitted another term of three years.[45]

This practice is applicable to local superioresses, but some question may arise as to its acceptableness for major superioresses. Augustine (1872-1943) stated that in the case of the latter the matter is disputed.[46] Maroto (1875-1937), on the contrary, felt that an identical application of the rule should be adaptable for major and minor superioresses alike.[47] Canon 505, so he stated, leaves to the

---

[45] Maroto, "Annotationes," *CpR*, II (1921), 66-70; Goyeneche, "Consultationes," *CpR*, V (1924), 29-30; Larraona, "Commentarium Codicis," *CpR*, VII (1926), 379; Schaefer, *De Religiosis*, p. 249, n. 120; Coronata, *Institutiones*, I, p. 656, n. 538.

[46] *Commentary*, III, 121.

[47] "Annotationes," *CpR*, II (1921), 69.

constitutions the determination of the number of terms that major superioresses may have. When the constitutions allow two terms, then, in view of the reasons that have been advanced above, the adding of a partial term to a regular term cannot be said to become the equivalent of two terms, the period of tenure beyond which canon 505 permits no extension.

On the contrary, however, while this benign interpretation seems justified in the matter of estimating the period of tenure of office permitted to minor superioresses it does not seem warranted in the matter of estimating that of major superioresses. First, there does not seem to exist any compelling, or even any solidly expedient, reason for the practice. The number of the major superioresses in a given community is far smaller than that of the minor superioresses, and it is difficult to see how confusion would arise if substitute terms were entirely abandoned. In that event, when death or any other cause required the replacement of an incumbent in office, a regular appointment could be made, and the period of tenure could readily be computed as starting with that point of time.

Secondly, the emphasis of canon 505 in relation to major superioresses is on the temporary characteristic of tenure. It is true that it leaves the determination of the precise time content of a term to the constitutions. But when this time content has been fixed in the constitutions, as for example by the designation of a permissible period consisting of two terms of six years each, or of one term of twelve years, then it must be said that for this particular institute the precise temporary characteristic of tenure is decisively fixed by the limits of the period of twelve years. Any time content beyond these precise limits would in that institute constitute a degree of permanence or of stability contrary to the general law as stated in canon 505.

In view of the fact that the mind of the Holy See disapproves tenures that approximate long terms, it is hard to see how the practice of ignoring partial terms in computing aggregate tenure can be lawfully extended to the tenure of major superioresses. A situation could otherwise occur whereby a superioress general could as a substitute hold office for eleven years, and then be elected for a normal term of twelve years. Such an eventuality does not seem in accord with the mind of the Church on the temporary tenure of office.

A problem may arise inasmuch as the constitutions do not permit appointments to a full term when an office becomes vacant before the term of the incumbent has lapsed. A regulation of this kind is not contrary to the Code, and therefore if it exists as particular law for a religious institute, it must be followed. However, unless the Holy See has approved the practice, as warranted either in the constitutions or through legitimate custom, of not reckoning these partial terms, there does not seem justification for not computing them as part of the aggregate tenure of office.

It seems to the writer that, if a major superioress has in accord with the constitutions of her institute served a partial term, the number of years during which she has held office should always be reckoned, and when together with a full term they would exceed the maximum time content of the tenure of office allowed by the constitutions, she would be ineligible for reappointment. The reason is the one stated above, namely, that any tenure of office beyond the precise limits determined in the constitutions as temporary in character constitutes permanence in office, and therefore is contrary to canon 505.

The reckoning of the date determining the end of a term of office also follows the general laws on the computation of time as enacted in the Code. Related to this problem one finds several pertinent difficulties that demand solution. First, one may ask whether any vestige of authority survives in the superioress after the precise moment at which her incumbency is terminated. Creusen states that no provision in the Code indicates that a local superioress loses all her power at the expiration of her term of office, and that he believes that she continues to exercise her authority validly until her successor is named.[48] Others, holding with him that the term of office ceases, adopt the theory that the superioress may continue her administration as a substitute or delegate.[49] Such prorogation,

[48] *Religious Men and Women in the Code*, p. 50, n. 67.
[49] Larraona, "Commentarium Codicis," *CpR*, VII (1926), 380; Vermeersch-Creusen, *Epitome*, I, p. 446, n. 623; Coronata, *Institutiones*, I, p. 657, n. 538; Schaefer, *De Religiosis*, p. 251, n. 120.

these authors teach, can be accomplished by the constitutions themselves or by the major superioresses.

Canon 505 specifically states that a local superioress may be constituted in office only for three years. Authority therefore seems to be given by the general law for only that period of time. When that period of time has passed, as reckoned by the laws of the Code on the computation of the lapse of time, the office with its power should cease. The view of the authors just cited in opposition to Creusen's, namely, that there must be an explicit act of prorogation by a competent authority, appears more in accord with the Code than his. In regard to the major superioress the same view likewise seems the correct one. Her authority extends simply for the period of time specified by the constitutions of her community. When that period of time has expired, so, too, has the authority granted to her.

Prorogation of authority for the superioress after the expiration of her term of office has been admitted as possible, if there has been an explicit authorization by the constitutions or by an act of a higher superioress. The problem remains regarding the procedure if neither the constitutions nor an act of the higher superioress sanction this prorogation. Larraona notes that when the constitutions are silent and the higher superioress does not take action, the administration of the house should pass to the one who ordinarily substitutes in the absence of the regular superioress.[50] This opinion certainly seems in accord with canon 505. It recognizes the fact that authority ceases with the expiration of office, and offers the natural solution for the problem, namely, that in the absence of a regular superioress the one who ordinarily substitutes is in charge.

A second question calls for consideration at this point. How long must a superioress, if she has held the full tenure of office permitted by canon 505 and the constitutions of her community, wait until she may again have authority as a superioress in precisely the same identical office? The normal time interval would seem to be at least the duration of a full term of office on the part of her successor. However, this conclusion is not necessitated by the wording

---

[50] "Commentarium Codicis," *CpR*, VII (1926), 380-381, nota 292.

of canon 505. As the law stands, provided that a successor has been nominated and has served in office, even though it is only for a short time, the former superioress may be reappointed to the identical office for which, in the absence of that brief interval, she would have been ineligible because of her previous tenure.[51] This procedure, of course, should not be adopted without a sound reason motivating it. There must be no attempt to defraud the law.

As a third and final conclusion cognate to that of the cessation of the term of office, no prohibition of the general law forbids for major or minor superioresses terms of shorter duration than the ordinarily accepted ones. Thus a term might under the constitutions be determined as consisting of two years. In that case these terms could be renewed, if the constitutions so provide, until their total time content consists of that period of time that under canon 505 disqualifies for further appointment, for example, three terms of two years each.[52]

5. *Resignation and Removal*

The powers of the superioress cease by death, by the completion of her term of office, by transfer to other duties, by resignation or removal from office, or by penal suspension.[53] The completion of the terms of office has already been discussed.[54] Cessation of office by death is clear in itself. The other points mentioned above may well be classified under the headings of resignation and removal.

Before one proceeds to discuss these categories, one should state by way of preface that although the superioress does not hold an ecclesiastical office in the strict sense of canon 145, § 1, under the definition of which an office in the strict sense requires participation in the ecclesiastical power of orders or of jurisdiction, still an analogy exists between the latter and the office of the superioress. If, therefore, in a given case affecting the office of superioress there is lack of

---

[51] Fanfani, *De Iure Religiosorum*, p. 62, n. 50; Geser, *The Canon Law Governing Communities of Sisters*, p. 83, q. 218.

[52] Schaefer, *De Religiosis*, p. 250, n. 120; Coronata, *Institutiones*, I, p. 655, n. 538.

[53] Creusen-Garesché-Ellis, *Religious Men and Women in the Code*, p. 71, n. 96; canon 183, § 1.

[54] Cf. *supra*, p. 56.

provision in the general or the particular law, it seems justifiable to apply the canons governing ecclesiastical offices.[55]

The *"Normae of 1901,"* as will be seen, clearly show that it is the intention of the Holy See that the office of superioress should enjoy its legally accredited measure of stability, and that unless just reasons demand otherwise superioresses once instituted should remain in office until their term has been completed.[56] This intent applies to all superioresses, general, provincial and local." [57] In other words, they are not to be placed in office and taken from it at the mere will of a higher superioress.

Again, a superioress who has accepted an office has an obligation to fulfill it. The *"Normae of 1901"* likewise indicate this. Moreover, canon 183, § 1, states that superiors should not accept a resignation without a just cause. Occasions, however, arise when circumstances demand that a superioress resign or be removed. In both of these questions a distinction must be made in regard to the status of the institute in which the office is held. Thus the procedure to be followed will differ depending on whether the institute is of diocesan or of pontifical approval.

In regard to resignation in institutes of pontifical approval, when the superioress general feels that there are good reasons why she should be relieved of the burdens of her office, she should submit them to the Sacred Congregation of Religious, and it is by this Congregation that the decision as to the acceptance of the resignation will be made.[58] The same procedure seems applicable to effect the resignation of a superioress of an independent monastery of nuns. If congregations of diocesan approval are involved, the case of the resignation of the superioress general may become complicated. Certain diocesan institutes have houses only in one diocese; others have spread into several dioceses. In the case of institutes of diocesan

[55] Canon 20.

[56] Art. 269; 270; 310.

[57] Bastien, *Directoire*, p. 333, n. 538; Coronata, *Institutiones*, I, p. 656, n. 538; Balmès, *Les Religieux à Voeux Simples d'après le Code* (Bruxelles: Action Catholique, 1921), p. 61 (hereafter referred to as *Les Religieux*).

[58] *"Normae of 1901,"* p. 46, art. 270; Bastien, *Directoire*, p. 293, n. 466; Mothon, *Institutions Canonique* (3 vols., Paris: Desclée, 1922-1924), I, p. 498, n. 1199; Battandier, *Guide canonique*, p. 371, n. 444.

approval which exist solely in one diocese, the local ordinary is competent to accept the resignation of the superioress general just as the Sacred Congregation of Religious is competent to accept the resignation of the superioress general of institutes which are of pontifical approval.

When these institutes have houses in more than one diocese, the matter is not so clear. Bastien (1866-1940) felt that the resignation should be acted upon by all the ordinaries of the dioceses in which the congregation has houses. The basis for this opinion he saw in canon 495, § 2, which states that, when a diocesan congregation establishes itself in other dioceses, nothing should be changed in its law without the consent of all the ordinaries of these dioceses. Again, he pointed to the Constitution *"Conditae a Christo"* of Leo XIII, which enacted that nothing should be changed in the nature of these institutes without the consent of all the ordinaries.[59] Resignation he regarded as a matter so like those thus reserved as to demand the same procedure.

On the other hand, when asked which ordinary had the right of presiding at an election and of confirming the election of the superioress general of these polydiocesan institutes, the Sacred Congregation of Religious answered that it is the ordinary of the place where the election is held, not necessarily the ordinary of the diocese in which the mother house is situated.[60] In the mind of the Sacred Congregation, then, even in a matter so important as the election of the superioress general, anyone of the ordinaries and not necessarily all of them together is capable of confirming an election, so that his capacity is determined solely by the locality in which the election is held. It seems, then, justifiable to the writer to conclude *a pari* that the ordinary of the place where the superioress general is residing would be able to accept her resignation.

In the question of the resignation of provincials and of local superioresses the general law provides no norm. Canon 187, § 2, provides that resignation should be made to that superior who by ordinary law has the right of confirmation, admission or institution.

---

[59] Bastien, *Directoire,* p. 293, n. 467.

[60] *De celebratione capituli generalis in congregationibus iuris dioecesani,* 2 iul. 1921—*AAS,* XIII (1921), 481.

Under the terms of this canon, the resignation of these superioresses should be made to those who placed them in office, normally the superioress general and her council.

In all cases the one offering the resignation remains in office until notification has been received of the acceptance of it.[61] The resignation, in order to be valid, must be made in writing, or orally before two witnesses.[62] A resignation made through grave fear, deceit, substantial error or simony is null.[63] Once the resignation has been legitimately accepted and notification of this fact has been communicated to the superioress who is resigning, the latter may not change her mind and demand the office back.[64]

As was said above, the office of superioress carries with it a limited but certified measure of stability, and before a transfer or a deprivation can be effected there must exist very grave reasons to justify it. According to the Code the deprivation of office is effected either by law or by the act of a legitimate superior.[65] In the case of superioresses, no automatic deprivations of office are listed in the Code. The determination of the legitimate superiors for the deprivation of office in regard to superioresses depends again on the distinction between pontifical and diocesan congregations. The *"Normae of 1901"* state that, if it seems necessary to deprive a superioress general of her authority, the council should refer the matter to the Sacred Congregation of Religious for a decision. Authors generally accept this as the proper procedure today in the removal from office of a superioress general of an institute of pontifical approval.[66]

The same procedure seems applicable for the deprivation of office of a superioress of an independent monastery of nuns. Since the Holy See is the legitimate superior for the removal from

[61] Canon 190, § 2.

[62] Canon 186.

[63] Canon 185.

[64] Canon 191, § 1.

[65] Canon 192, § 1.

[66] Pejška, *Ius Canonicum Religiosorum* (3. ed., Friburgi Brisgoviae: Herder & Co., 1927), p. 219; Balmès, *Les Religieux*, p. 61; Schaefer, *De Religiosis*, p. 232, n. 109; Battandier, *Guide canonique*, p. 370, n. 443; Bastien, *Directoire*, p. 293, n. 467; Mothon, *Institutions Canonique*, I, 498, n. 1199.

office of a superioress general in pontifical institutes, in similar cases
in diocesan institutes the ordinary of the place seems to be the one
competent to act.[67]   As with resignation, there is no difficulty if the
congregation exists solely in one diocese.   But if it has established
houses in more than one diocese, the question again arises as to which
ordinary is competent to act, or whether the matter is one that demands joint action.   Bastien demanded the latter for the same reasons which he adduced in requiring joint action for the acceptance
of the resignation.[68]   To the writer the case seems one in which the
ordinary of the place where the superioress general resides is competent to act.   The reason for this conclusion is the same as that
presented in the treatment of resignation, namely, that there exists
an analogy between removal from office and the procedure prescribed
in election, the Holy See having in that case made one ordinary
competent.

While it is the common view that a deprivation of office which
involves the superioress general can be effected solely by some authority outside the actual community, some authors feel that the
general chapter would have the power to perform this act.[69]   Lewis
holds the contrary view on the grounds of canon 195, which states
that those who put a cleric in office may not remove him from it.[70]
Over and above this, the *"Normae of 1901"* would seem to deny deposition as a power of the general chapter.[71]

In regard to the removal from office of other major superioresses
and of local superioresses guidance can again be derived from the
"Normae of 1901."   Article 310 states that local superioresses are
not to be removed without grave reasons and a decisive vote by the
council.   While there is silence in the *"Normae of 1901"* as regards

[67] Bastien, *loc. cit.*

[68] *Loc. cit.*

[69] Coronata, *Institutiones*, I, p. 649, n. 535; Augustine, *Commentary*, III,
108.

[70] *Chapters in Religious Institutes*, The Catholic University of America
Canon Law Studies, n. 181 (Washington, D. C.: The Catholic University of
America Press, 1943), pp. 62-65.

[71] Art. 269: "Si necessarium videretur, moderatricem generalem officio et
auctoritate privare, sorores a concilio rem ad S. Congregationem deferant, eiusque
decisioni submittant."

the removal from office of provincials, it seems justifiable in their case also to accept the same procedure as that recommended for the removal of local superioresses. Augustine held that their removal from office was within the competence of the council of religious which serves the province.[72] Bastien taught that it was an act which falls within the competence of the council of the province, but he further required the confirmation of the superioress general and of the general council of the institute.[73]

Whether it be a matter for the general council of the institute or for the council of the province seems to depend on the general competence for grave matters as accorded to these councils in the constitutions of the various institutes. If the ordinary powers of the council of the province are very extensive, then this council seems competent in this instance also; if not, then the matter seems to be one which is reserved to the general council of the institute.

In article 310 of the *"Normae of 1901"* the procedure for the transfer of local superioresses is made identical with that of their removal from office. Consequently, when their transfer to another office occurs, the same grave reasons should exist and the same action should be taken by the proper council as that described in the case of removal from office. The case of the transfer of provincials is a rather rare one, but if it were contemplated, then article 310 again would seem to provide the proper norm.

Thus far no attempt has been made to distinguish specific causes that would justify the removal of a superioress from office. It is not within the scope of this work to treat in detail the many canons of penal law applicable in this matter.[74] Inasmuch as the last four canons of the Code enact penalties for the delicts of superioresses as such, these particular canons will be discussed briefly. Canon 2411 states that religious superioresses who, contrary to the prescription of canon 544, have received to the novitiate an unsuitable candidate, or who, contrary to the prescription of canon 571, § 2, have admitted

---

[72] *Commentary,* III, 108.

[73] *Directoire,* p. 333, n. 538.

[74] Cf. Smith, *The Penal Law for Religious,* The Catholic University of America Canon Law Studies, n. 98 (Washington, D. C.: The Catholic University of America, 1935).

a novice to profession, shall be punished according to the gravity of their fault, even to the extent of being deposed from office. More will be seen of the implications of canons 544 and 571 in other parts of this work, where the subject matter of these canons will be dealt with specifically. Here it may be said that the superior who is competent to impose these penalties is the one who, according to what has been said above is qualified in relation to the removal from office. Thus, as the situation calls for it, these penalties will be imposed by the local ordinary or by the Holy See.[75]

Canon 2412 states that superioresses even of exempt religious shall be punished by the local ordinary according to the gravity of their fault, even to the extent of being deposed from office, if contrary to canon 599 they have presumed to spend dowries, or if contrary to the prescription of canon 522 they have omitted to inform the local ordinary concerning the approaching admission of a subject to the novitiate or to profession. Here the one to punish is explicitly designated as the ordinary of the diocese in which the fault is committed.

Canon 2413, with reference to superioresses who interfere in any way with a canonical visitation, lists the same punishments as those enumerated in canons 2411 and 2412. The penalties, however, are to be imposed by the visitor. When a visitation has been announced, the superioress is forbidden, without the permission of the visitor, to transfer any of the members of the community to be visited. She may not, either directly or indirectly, personally or through others, induce anyone to conceal the truth, and she likewise may not in any way molest anyone for the answers given. Augustine stated that the visitor spoken of in this canon is the local ordinary or the prelate regular. He doubted that sisters who acted in the office of visitor for their community in accord with canon 511 were to be included among those who were competent to inflict the penalties.[76] The Code does not make this distinction. Moreover, canon 511 prescribes the regular visitation by the higher superioresses within the community, just as canon 512 prescribes the visitation by the local ordinary.

---

[75] Vermeersch-Creusen, _Epitome_, I, p. 611, n. 827; Schaefer, _De Religiosis_, p. 485, n. 222.

[76] _Commentary_, VIII, p. 521, note 9.

Thus each of the two is constituted as a canonical visitation, and accordingly, so it seems, either of the visitations receives legal consideration in canon 2413.[77] The law of canon 2413 applies to the superioresses of all religious institutes, not excluding societies living a common life without vows.

The Pontifical Commission of Interpretation, when asked the question whether societies of clerics living in common but without vows were subject to this law of canon 2413 answered in the affirmative.[78] In view of this response, and also in the light of the principle of applied interpretation as stated in canon 490, it may safely be said that societies of women living in common but without vows would likewise be obliged by this law.

Larraona limits the penal power of the visitor to the superioresses who are subject to the visitation. Thus a provincial could not depose a superioress general who had violated canon 2413, for example by the transfer of a member of the community from a house to be visited.[79] A power of this kind would be incongruous. A penalty may be inflicted only on one who is a subject, hardly on one who is a superior of the one who conducts the visitation. This opinion seems the acceptable interpretation of canon 2413, and is the one adopted by Reilly who has made a thorough study of the matter.[80] Moreover, action of this kind by the visitor is not essential, since the ordinary means provided by law for the effecting of deprivation of office are available, if the visitor discovers abuses committed by one beyond his jurisdiction.

Finally, canon 2414 rules that if a superioress, after once having been warned, again offends against the laws enacted in canons 521, § 3, 522 and 523 regarding matters of confession, she shall be removed from office by the local ordinary. In these cases, after inflicting the penalty, the local ordinary must immediately notify the Sacred Congregation of Religious. This law applies to all con-

---

[77] Reilly, *The Visitation of Religious*, The Catholic University of America Canon Law Studies, n. 112 (Washington, D. C.: The Catholic University of America, 1938), p. 170, note 5.

[78] 3 iun. 1918—*AAS*, X (1918), 347.

[79] "Studia Canonica," *CpR*, X (1929), 371-372.

[80] *The Visitation of Religious*, pp. 173-175.

gregations of women religious regardless of whether their status is one of pontifical or of diocesan approval.[81]   The law likewise applies to societies living in common without vows.[82]

ARTICLE 3. THE SUBJECTS OF THE SUPERIORESS

Canon 501, § 1, states that superioresses have governing powers over their subjects in accordance with the constitutions of their congregation and the general law.   Canon 502 states that the superioress general has authority over all the provinces, houses, and members of the institute, to be exercised as prescribed by the constitutions; and that other superioresses have authority within the limits of their charge.   In a later chapter the nature of this power will be discussed, but in view of these two canons the question, who in particular are to be included under the terms "subjects" and "members" as used by the legislator, may well be given its full attention here.

First, it may be definitely said that all those who have been professed, having bound themselves by the vow of obedience, certainly are subjects of their local superioress of the provincial, and of the superioress general.   By their vows they have been constituted members of a particular institute, and as such they come under the authority of its directors.[83]

Secondly, those who are known as postulants and as novices likewise are subjects of the various superioresses, that is, of the house (local), of the province (provincial), and of the institute (general), in view of their affiliation with a specific house, province, and institute.   No vow in their case, it is true, exists, but they have, by means of an explicit or implicit contract which they have made of their own free will, created a relationship between these superioresses and themselves,, and this relationship carries with it an obligation to follow their direction.[84]

---

[81] Ayrinhac-Lydon, *Penal Legislation in the New Code of Canon Law* (New York: Benziger Brothers, 1936), p. 325 (hereafter referred to as *Penal Legislation*); O'Brien, *The Exemption of Religious in Church Law*, p. 75.

[82] P. C. I., 3 iun. 1918—*AAS*, X (1918), 347.

[83] Fanfani, *De Iure Religiosorum*, p. 64, n. 51; Geser, *The Canon Law Governing Communities of Sisters*, p. 30, q. 77.

[84] Wernz-Vidal, *Ius Canonicum*, III, p. 86, n. 93; Vermeersch-Creusen, *Epitome*, I, p. 442, n. 619; Clancy, *The Local Religious Superior*, The Catholic

These two groups of professed and non-professed persons of a religious institute are subjects in all those matters which the general law, the rule, and the constitutions of the institute place within the competence of their superioresses. The submission that they have made is commensurate with the limits as indicated in the general law, the rule, and the constitutions. They are bound to obey any lawfully constituted superioress who has been placcd in charge over them whenever she requires an act of them within the sphere of her office. Moreover, as long as these groups retain their status they are bound by obedience to their superioresses no matter where they or their superioresses happen to be. The power of their superioress is personal as well as local. Thus though she or they are temporarily absent from the house or the province, the same relationship continues, and with it the same obligations obtain.[85]

A second group which falls under the category of subjects comprises those who form a part of the community, not as members of the religious institute or as persons who intend to become such, but as persons who actually dwell in the community as members of the household, for example, for the purpose of education, health or service. They, too, come under the power of the superioress. In their case, however, at least so far as the passive subjects are concerned, the relationship is not measured by the constitutions or the rule. Rather, it arises for them from the nature of the office of the superioress as head of the community and from her consequent concurrent responsibility for its good order, and also in consequence of the obligations created by means of the specific contract entered into by them with the community. As members of the household then, these persons can be said to be subjects of the superioress who is in charge of that household. Her authority is to be respected by them, and the definite relationship of superior to inferior must be recognized. While she cannot impose upon them the rule and the constitutions, she can look upon them, as long as they wish to remain in the community, as a group of persons over whom her power extends, and for whose welfare she has a responsibility.

University of America Canon Law Studies, n. 175 (Washington, D. C.: The Catholic University of America Press, 1943), p. 38.

[85] Cocchi, *Commentarium*, IV, p. 52, n. 23; Beste, *Introductio in Codicem*, p. 330.

CHAPTER V

QUALIFICATIONS FOR OFFICE

Article 1. General Notions

NEEDLESS to say, the one to be chosen for the office of superioress should be outstanding in character and ability. Her qualities should be those of humility, piety, firmness, studiousness in the observance of discipline, patience, charity, knowledge, prudence, affability, justice, and good example.[1] Apart from the possession of these virtues, which certainly are to be hoped for, the one who is to become a superioress is required to be legally eligible. It is required that she has never been deprived of eligibility for election in her community, either by law or by a sentence of an ecclesiastical judge. Examples of persons thus deprived of eligibility for office are those who are infamous in law or in fact,[2] those who have conspired against the Holy Father,[3] those who once apostatized from their religious institute, even though upon repentance they later returned to their community,[4] those who have taken a consenting part in elections in which lay or secular power has dared to interfere with canonical freedom,[5] those who have occupied an office by their own authority, or taken office before they received the necessary letters of institution or of confirmation,[6] those who have knowingly accepted an office that was not vacant,[7] those who have interfered with a canonical visitation,[8] and finally those who are disqualified in consequence of the lack of any of the conditions set in canon 505, as was seen in the previous chapter in the article dealing with tenure of office.[9]

---

[1] Cocchi, *Commentarium*, IV, p. 53, n. 24.

[2] Canon 2294.

[3] Canon 2331.

[4] Canon 2385.

[5] Canon 2390, § 2.

[6] Canon 2394.

[7] Canon 2395.

[8] Canon 2414.

[9] Cf. *supra*, pp. 48, 52.

The two extremes with reference to the qualifications in a prospective candidate for appointment to the position of superioress have now been seen, namely, the desired virtues, and what may loosely be called the precluded vices. These qualifications should be verifiable for all who are being considered for the office of superioress. The Code further specifies in some detail additional qualifications for those eligible for the office of major superioress. Canon 504 states: Without prejudice to the constitutions proper to each institute which requires a maturer age and other important qualities, those are unfit for the office of major superioress who have not spent at least ten years in the same institute to be reckoned from the date of their first profession, those who have not been born of legitimate marriage, and, in the case of the superioress general of an institute or the superioress of a monastery of nuns, those who have not completed their fortieth year; their thirtieth year in the case of other higher superioresses.

Two sets of qualifications are listed then by the general law, and these under pain of nullity of the appointment. They are, first, those which are demanded in canon 504 just cited above, and secondly, those which are under like sanction required by the various constitutions. In the matter of specifically postulated qualifications the Code thus sanctions and places on a par with its own law the particular laws of each institute.[10] It does not, however, demand that in the particular constitutions any disqualifying requisites be added to those proposed in canon 504. Still, on the other hand, it clearly forbids that the constitutions set any qualifications less strict in character than the qualifications which are postulated in the law of the Code itself.[11]

It is impractical in a general treatise to discuss particular points as found in specific constitutions, but the impediments set down in the Code will be treated in detail in the following three articles. Before proceeding to this discussion one should observe that, since these qualifications are a matter of the general law, only the Holy See can dispense from the lack of them, whether they be specified exclusively in canon 504, or also in the particular constitutions as

---

[10] Berutti, *Institutiones Iuris Canonici*, III, p. 56, n. 29.
[11] Augustine, *Commentary*, III, 117.

well, and also whether the institute be one of pontifical, or one of diocesan, approval.[12]

ARTICLE 2. PROFESSION

As its first requirement, demanded under pain of nullity in the person to be appointed to the office of major superioress, canon 504 states that the candidate must have been professed for at least ten years in the same institute. No distinction is made in the canon between temporary and perpetual profession. All commentators, therefore agree that the time is to be reckoned from that profession which is commonly made after the novitiate.[13] The ten years of required profession are to be computed according to the calendar,[14] and in as much as the act of profession does not coincide with the beginning of the opening day of the ten year period of time, that day is not to be counted as a part of the requisite decennium.[15] Moreover, these years are to be understood as ten complete years. Canon 504 does not mention this explicitly, but Fanfani notes that it is the practice of the Roman Curia thus to interpret this canon.[16] The time requirement, then, can be said to have been fulfilled only when the day of the same date on which the profession was made has been completed after ten intervening years have elapsed.[17]

Besides specifying the factor of time to be passed in religious profession, the Code in canon 504 likewise rules that this period is to be passed in the same institute. In canon 504 there is no mention of any restriction that would require that time to have been spent in the same province. Further, for the purpose of the computation of this period, there seems not be entailed any interruption in the months or the years if a religious was transferred from one independent monastery to another of the same congregation, since

---

[12] Schaefer, *De Religiosis*, p. 244, n. 115; Augustine, *Commentary*, III, 119.

[13] Larraona, *"Commentarium Codicis," CpR*, VII (1926), 247; Augustine, *Commentary*, III, 117; Schaefer, *De Religiosis*, p. 242, n. 115; Fanfani, *De Iure Religiosorum*, p. 58, n. 48.

[14] Canon 34, § 3, 1°.

[15] Canon 34, § 3, 3°.

[16] *De Iure Religiosorum*, p. 58, n. 48.

[17] Canon 34, § 3, 3°.

according to canon 633 no new profession is required in these cases.[18]
On the contrary, if a change was made to another institute, the required ten year period of profession is to be computed from profession in the second community. Under any other interpretation the word "same" in canon 504 cannot be said to be given its ordinary meaning.[19]

Further questions of a similar nature arise when indults of exclaustration or of secularization have been received by prospective candidates for the office of major superioress, and when nevertheless such candidates thereupon legitimately returned to the same institute. As regards those for whom the indult granted merely an exclaustration, the years and the months that pass during this period are still available for computation in the matter of determining the candidate's eligibility, since the vows of an exclaustrated religious remain intact and uncancelled.[20] The same cannot be said for candidates who have been secularized or dismissed. Canon 640, § 2, provides that the seniority status of those who, after secularization, have returned to the community with an apostolic indults is to be reckoned from their new profession, and not their first.[21]

ARTICLE 3. LEGITIMACY

The second requirement for the office of major superioress, as mentioned in canon 504, demands that no person is to be raised to this rank who was not born of legitimate wedlock. From this it is naturally expected to follow that those who are to be elected or chosen as major superioresses must be the offspring of parents united by a legitimate marriage. Moreover, it would seem that the parents' legitimate union should exist prior to the birth of the child, that is, that the legal requirements for such a union should be previously

[18] Schaefer, *De Religiosis*, p. 244, n. 115; Berutti, *Institutiones Iuris Canonici*, III, p. 57, n. 29.

[19] Coronata, *Institutiones*, I, p. 653, n. 538; Larraona, "Commentarium Codicis," *CpR*, VII (1926), 247.

[20] Berutti, *Institutiones Iuris Canonici*, III, p. 57, n. 29; Larraona, "Commentarium Codicis," *CpR*, VII (1926), 247.

[21] Coronata, *Institutiones*, I, p. 653, n. 538.

fulfilled by the parents so as to constitute for the child what is known as a natural legitimacy.[22]

There is, however, a second type of legitimacy, namely, a juridic legitimacy.[23] This is a benefit extended by the law or by the lawgiver to one not endowed with natural legitimacy, and restoring some or all the rights proper to a legitimate child.[24] With this definition of juridic legitimacy in mind one may find that even though a natural legitimacy is wanting, at times a juridic legitimacy will be sufficient, and that one so legitimized, other requisite conditions being properly fulfilled, may become a major superioress.

The first type of juridic legitimation to be considered is that arising from a particular rescript or privilege. In accordance with the norms of canons 49 and 67, the effects of legitimation so granted can be measured only from the tenor of the rescript or privilege. It may or may not permit accession to the office of major superioress.[25]

Canon 1117 speaks of a second means of legitimation. "Children legitimated by subsequent marriage," it states, "are, in so far as the canonical effects are concerned, held equivalent in all things to legitimate offspring, unless the canons expressly rule otherwise."[26] There are listed in the Code three exceptions with reference to which a legitimation of this type is not sufficient to qualify one for dignities from which those of illegitimate birth are barred. They are the cardinalate,[27] the episcopate,[28] and abbacies and prelacies

----

[22] McDevitt, *Legitimacy and Legitimation*, p. 65.

[23] Cappello, *Tractatus Canonico-Moralis de Sacramentis* (3 vols. in 6, Vol. III, 4. ed., Romae: Apud Aedes Universitatis Gregorianae, 1939), Vol. III, Pars 2, n. 745 (hereafter referred to as *De Sacramentis*).

[24] Vermeersch-Creusen, *Epitome*, II, p. 290, n. 419.

[25] Larraona, "Commentarium Codicis," *CpR*, VII (1926), 296; Cappello, *De Sacramentis*, Vol. III, Pars 2, n. 751.

[26] Cf. Ayrinhac-Lydon, *Marriage Legislation in the New Code of Canon Law* (New, Revised Ed., New York: Benziger Brothers, Inc., 1943), p. 298 (hereafter referred to as *Marriage Legislation*). Legitimation by subsequent marriage according to canon 1116 always presumes that the parents were able to contract marriage at the time of the conception, of the pregnancy, or of the birth.

[27] Canon 232, § 2, 1°.

[28] Canon 331, § 1, 1°.

nullius.[29]   No such restriction is made with reference to the office of major superioresses.   Therefore a child legitimated by the subsequent marriage of her parents attains a status juridically identical with that of a child born from legitimate wedlock and is consequently eligible for the office of major superioress.[30]

Another question for consideration is that of canon 1051.   There it is stated that the offspring becomes legitimated by means of a dispensation from a diriment impediment granted in virtue of ordinary power or delegated faculties possessed by general indult, provided that the offspring is not the fruit of adultery or of sacrilege.   The case contemplated by the concession of canon 1051 is one in which a dispensation is given, for example, from disparity of cult, with a view to the convalidation of a marriage.   Legitimation occurs when the dispensation is given.   If the parents through no fault of their own later do not actually proceed with the marriage, the legitimation is not deprived of its effect.   If through their own fault the marriage did not take place, the matter is disputed.[31]

McDevitt in his treatment of the subject concludes that the effects deriving from a use of the concession of canon 1051 are not determined sufficiently to indicate whether a person so legitimated is eligible for an office of major superioress.   This is a matter, he says, to be decided by the legislator.[32]   Other authors place canon 1116 and canon 1051 side by side as equal in their effects in favor of the eligibility of a candidate for the office of major superioress.[33]

---

[29] Canon 320, § 2.

[30] Larraona, "Commentarium Codicis," *CpR*, VII (1926), 296; McDevitt, *Legitimacy and Legitimation*, p. 169; Schaefer, *De Religiosis*, p. 242, n. 115.

[31] Ayrinhac-Lydon, *Marriage Legislation*, p. 84, n. 84.   A comparison between canons 1051 and 1116 reveals what seems to be a greater leniency on the part of the legislator in cases where impediments exist.   Under canon 1051 legitimation of offspring is granted without demanding a subsequent marriage; canon 1116 which contemplates only those cases where no impediment is present makes the subsequent marriage a necessary requisite for the effect of legitimation.   Nevertheless, the wording of canon 1051 is clear.   The legitimation is effected under this canon by the concession of the dispensation and not by a subsequent marriage.

[32] *Legitimacy and Legitimation*, pp. 169-170.

[33] Larraona, "Commentarium Codicis," *CpR*, VII (1926), 296; Schaefer, *De Religiosis*, p. 243, n. 115.

While it is true that, unlike canons 1116-1117, canon 1051 does not specifically state that its effects render one so legitimated equal in all things to one born of legitimate wedlock unless exceptions are noted in law, still the legislator's purpose in both cases was to remove the hinderances brought on by illegitimacy. Disqualification for office of major superioresses is nowhere indicated in the law as exemplifying the exceptive clause which is written into canon 1117. Therefore this exception should not be introduced in canon 1051 when the legislator himself did not introduce it.

Two more cases affecting legitimacy as a requisite qualification for the office of major superioress remain to be discussed. The first is that of the legitimizing effect produced on the children by the radical sanation of marriages; the second is that of the legitimizing effect produced on the person who is admitted to solemn profession. From canon 1138 it is clear that the children of a sanated marriage are to be considered as though born of a true marriage. They are in the eyes of the Church born of lawful wedlock. Thus they are certainly, at least in this regard, eligible for the office of major superioress. Harrigan, who devotes much space in his work to the effects of canon 1138, § 2, passes over the effect of eligibility for the office of major superioress, seemingly taking it for granted, and concerns himself with the application of the canon to the exceptions produced by illegitimacy in relation to promotion to the cardinalate, the episcopate, and to abbacies and prelacies *nullius*.[34] Vermeersch-Creusen merely remark that the sanated marriage is to be considered as having its effects from the time to which the sanation is retroactive.[35]

Regarding the legitimizing effect of solemn profession, it may be said briefly that while according to canon 984, § 1, this act removes the irregularity of illegitimacy, this effect cannot be called legitimation. Solemn profession does not produce legitimation as

---

[34] *The Radical Sanation of Invalid Marriages* (The Catholic University of America Canon Law Studies, n. 116, Washington, D. C.: The Catholic University of America, 1938), pp. 65-72.

[35] *Epitome*, I, p. 445, n. 622.

such.[36] Consequently it does not remove the ineligibility for the office of major superioress incurred by illegitimate birth.[37]

ARTICLE 4. AGE

Canon 504 is specific in its age requirement for major superioresses. Those are ineligible for the office of superioress general who have not completed their fortieth year. Therefore no one may become a superioress general until she has passed her fortieth birthday. The fortieth year must be completed, not merely begun. The first day of eligibility is the day that follows the fortieth birthday.[38] The legislator likewise extends this identical age limitation to superioresses of independent monasteries of nuns. This limitation is of obligation whether the members of the institute actually profess solemn vows or by way of exception and by apostolic precept make only simple profession.[39]

In the case of other major superioresses the law demands that they must have completed their thirtieth year. This is the age minimum that is required by law for all provincials. No distinction is made in canon 504, however, between the supreme moderator of an institute and the president of a monastic congregation.[40] Rather, the canon specifically refers only to the supreme moderator. Therefore, if among institutes of women religious a structure of organization would exist like that which is found in certain institutes of men religious, by which a monastic congregation elects a president, the person elected to the latter office would be included under the law requiring the age of thirty years in the incumbent. This application of canon 504 is based on the words, "among other higher superiors." [41]

[36] Larraona, "Commentarium Codicis," *CpR*, VII (1926), 296, nota 249.

[37] Larraona, *loc. cit.;* Schaefer, *De Religiosis*, p. 243, n. 115; Berutti, *Institutiones Iuris Canonici*, III, p. 57, n. 29; Fanfani, *De Iure Religiosorum*, p. 58, n. 48.

[38] Canon 34, § 3, 3°; Fanfani, *loc. cit.*; Larraona, "Commentarium Codicis," *CpR*, VII (1926), 297.

[39] Berutti, *Institutiones Iuris Canonici*, III, p. 57, n. 29; canon 488, 7°.

[40] Canons 488, 8°; 510; 516.

[41] Oesterle, *Praelectiones Iuris Canonici* (Romae: In Collegio S. Anselmi, 1931), p. 253; Schaefer, *De Religiosis*, p. 253, n. 115.

CHAPTER VI

THE POWER OF THE SUPERIORESS

ARTICLE 1. NATURE OF THE POWER

ONE after another the early rules written for women religious insist on the right of the superioress to obedience.[1] Part of the very essence of religious life was subjection to the latter's will. With the growth of religious communities there was a corresponding growth in the sphere of power acknowledged to the superioress. It became her prerogative to administer and to rule the monastery in temporal matters, to appoint officers, to remove them, and as a mother over a family to correct and to punish her subjects. She was limited only by the inherent nature of her power, by the rule of her community, and by the obligation of consultation with other members of the community under certain circumstances.

The existence of a very definite power has been recognized as a right of the superioress from the earliest foundations of religious communities. It has not been radically challenged down through the centuries, but rather accepted and assumed. In providing legislation for religious, the Church has always had in mind the sphere of authority in the superioress. The scope of the latter was adequate to cope with situations, and the superioress possessing it was able to meet the ordinary problems of her community, and to solve them without the aid of specific legislation.

Various names have been offered to describe the power of the superioress, sometimes as a description of it in its entirety, sometimes of only a part of it. Thus it is often called domestic power.[2] Again, it is termed economic power.[3] A third title for it is social

---

[1] St. Jerome, *Regula Monachorum*, c. 7—*MPL*, XXX, 400; St. Augustine, *Epistola CCXI*, n. 15—*CSEL*, LVII, 369; St. Aurelian, *Regula ad Virgines*, n. 19—*MPL*, LXVIII, 400.

[2] Augustine, *Commentary*, III, 103.

[3] Ferreres, *Institutiones Canonicae* (2. ed., 2 vols., Barcinonae: Subirana, 1920), I, p. 366, n. 808.

power.[4] The common term and the one that the Code uses to describe it as a whole is *dominative* power.[5] This term takes its origin from that used to describe the relationship between a master and a servant brought on by a free agreement. Later it was extended to describe the power in any imperfect society.[6] In the discussion in this article of the nature of the power of the superioress, since ultimately the various terms designate the same power, it shall be referred to as dominative power.[7]

Canon 501, § 1, states that all superioresses have dominative power, but adds nothing as to its nature or origin. As an approach to this problem it seems logical to start with the definition of a society. Ottaviani, citing Cavagnis (1841-1906), defines society as a union of a number of men using common means to attain the same end.[8] The note that is of particular interest in this definition is that of the common means. Without this adjunct no society can exist, because without common means a society cannot even attempt to attain its end. One of these means on which every society rests as a necessary condition for its existence is authority.[9] The source of dominative power has its very root, then, in the very nature of a society itself. It is ultimately the product of the natural law for the reason that the essential elements of a society stem from the natural law. They must derive from the inherent nature of man as a social being destined to social contacts with his fellow man.

A second aspect of the problem of the authority of the superioress has reference to the source of membership in a society or the means by which one becomes subject to this authority. Subjection to this authority can arise in various ways. First, it can be the result of a necessary membership in a society, as for example, in the subjection of the child in a family to its parents. From this natural re-

---

[4] Schaefer, *De Religiosis*, p. 222, n. 105.

[5] Canons 501, § 1; 1312, § 1.

[6] Lewis, *Chapters in Religious Institutes*, p. 51.

[7] Wernz-Vidal, *Ius Canonicum*, III, p. 85, n. 93; Ferreres, *Institutiones Canonicae*, I, p. 366, n. 808.

[8] "Plurimum hominum unio ad eundem finem communibus mediis consequendum."—*Compendium Iuris Publici Ecclesiastici Ad Usum Auditorum S. Theologiae* (Typis Polyglottis Vaticanis, 1936), p. 11.

[9] *Ibidem*, p. 14.

lationship the parent has authority over the child, and the child is obliged to obey him. Again, the society can be one in which a person is free either to become a member or to forego membership. The consequence of the choice is subjection or non-subjection. While the person remains a member, the obligation of submission exists. To be noted, too, is that fact that certain types of submission in their inception voluntarily become irrevocable as, for example, the one assumed under vow.

Every religious institute forms a society, and, in accord with its constitutions and the common law which specify its end and purpose, is endowed with dominative power. Its members are subject to their legitimate superiors in whom the society has vested this power. Authors, but more in passing than in detail, point out the fact of the necessity of dominative power in a religious institute and the foundation of this power in natural law.[10]

The greater interest of canonists, however, concerns the manner of and the title by which the subjection of others to this power is affected. All agree that there is a clear and voluntary submission resulting in a consequent right granted to the authorities of the institute in the act of profession through the vow of obedience.[11] Profession is clearly an act of the will freely made placing oneself under the authority of superioresses. Moreover, there is a formal acceptance of the person who makes profession on the part of the community or society. The vow of obedience makes the obligation irrevocable and binding under the virtue of religion.

While it is clear that dominative power extends over those who have made profession and taken vows, as was pointed out above the act of profession is not necessary that one be embraced by this power.[12] This is the case with postulants and novices. The power

[10] Augustine, *Commentary, III,* 104; *Ferreres, Institutiones Canonicae,* I, p. 366, n. 808; Schaefer, *De Religiosis,* p. 221, n. 105; Lewis, *Chapters in Religious Institutes,* pp. 52-53.

[11] Wernz-Vidal, *Ius Canonicum,* III, p. 86, n. 93; Fanfani, *De Iure Religiosorum,* p. 64, n. 51; Berutti, *Institutiones Iuris Canonici,* III, p. 48, n. 23; Vermeersch-Creusen, *Epitome,* I, p. 442, n. 619; Cocchi, *Commentarium,* IV, p. 50, n. 23; Geser, *The Canon Law Governing Communities of Sisters,* p. 30, q. 77.

[12] Cf. *supra,* pp. 66-67.

of the superioresses by virtue of a pact or implicit contract extends to them.[13] They have handed themselves over to the community. They are not bound to render their submission under the virtue of religion, and they are free to leave the community at will, but as long as they remain in it they are bound to submit to the authority of their superioresses under the virtue of obedience. If they leave the community, they are no longer subject to this power.

A third group of persons subject to the dominative power of superioresses are those who are members of the individual household of a religious community, but who, unlike the professed, the novices and the postulants, have no direct connection with the religious institute as such. They are subject to the dominative power of the head of the house because this power is necessary for its good order, and because they have submitted themselves to it in establishing their residence in the house. The extent of their subordination is limited to those matters which are intimately connected with the good order of the house, qualified further by the conditions of their relation to the house as expressed in their contract. Authors frequently use the term domestic power, rather than dominative power, to describe this species of the authority of the superioress.[14]

Thus far in the study of the nature of dominative power it has been seen that there is a twofold aspect, the power itself, and those whom it embraces as its subjects. The use of the power remains to be discussed, but a definition of the power itself may now be ventured as a preliminary to that discussion. *Dominative power is that private authority existing in at least every imperfect society arising from the very nature of the society, limited by its end and purpose, and embracing all who by a necessary relation or by an act of free will have become subject to it.*

The degree of dominative power which is inherent in any society and which consequently governs its use, as has just been noted, depends on the purpose and the end of the society. Measured by the

---

[13] Wernz-Vidal, *Ius Canonicum*, III, p. 86, n. 93; Coronata, *Institutiones*, I, p. 646, n. 534; O'Brien, *The Exemption of Religious in Church Law*, p. 25.

[14] Schaefer, *De Religiosis*, p. 22, n. 105; Vermeersch-Creusen, *Epitome*, I, p. 442, n. 619; Geser, *The Canon Law Governing Communities of Sisters*, p. 31, q. 78.

end and the purpose of the society, its extent will be greater or lesser.
A purely literary society would not enjoy the same degree of governing authority as a religious society. Canon 501, § 1, points out that
dominative power in a religious institute is limited by the constitutions and the general law. These sources of law are those in which
one precisely finds stated the end and the purpose of the institute.

In religious societies, then, stemming from dominative power as
their source, certain general rights inhere. First, from a negative
aspect, unlike jurisdiction, dominative power is a private power dealing with a private group of persons. Therefore it cannot be either
executive, or judicial, or legislative; it is simply preceptive.[15] In
virtue of dominative power the superioress may command her subjects
and direct them, urging the fulfillment of the constitutions and the
rule.[16] These precepts may be given by her to a whole or a part
of the community. They may be given, if expressly so stated, by all
superioresses in virtue of the vow of obedience, although cases of
invoking the vow may be limited by the constitutions. Certainly prudence forbids frequent recourse to this sanction.[17]

The *"Normae of 1901"* remark in article 136 that superioresses
should impose these precepts only rarely and for grave reasons, issuing them either in writing or before two witnesses, and in article 137,
that the local superioress would do well never to impose them. The
superioress in no case may make her precept binding under grave sin
when the nature of its object is not serious enough of itself to constitute a grave matter.[18]

Precepts issued by superioresses are personal and bind every-
where, unless the contrary is evident from the nature of the precept or the manner in which it is given. They are, however, temporary, and therefore cease with the loss of office by the superioress

---

[15] Farrell, *The Rights and Duties of the Local Ordinary Regarding Congregations of Women Religious of Pontifical Approval*, The Catholic University of
America Canon Law Studies, n. 128 (Washington, D. C.: The Catholic University of America Press, 1941), p. 2.

[16] Ferreres, *Institutiones Canonicae*, I, p. 366, n. 808; Geser, *The Canon Law
Governing Communities of Sisters*, p. 71, q. 177.

[17] Creusen-Garesché-Ellis, *Religious Men and Women in the Code*, p. 42, n.
58; Berutti, *Institutiones Iuris Canonici*, III, p. 50, n. 25.

[18] Schaefer, *De Religiosis*, p. 229, n. 107.

who imposed them.[19]   The superioress may correct and punish her subjects.   Because of the lack of jurisdiction in the superioress, these punishments are not ecclesiastical penalties, and no formal process is required to impose them.[20]   They are rather penances to be imposed in a maternal or administrative way, and only for external faults.   They are to be marked by a proportion to the number and the seriousness of the external faults committed.   They should be salutary and appropriate to provide for the amendment of the wrong-doer.[21]   Such penalties might well include fasts, vocal prayers, manual labor and acts of mortification.[22]

Canon 595, § 3, specifically states that if a religious since her last sacramental confession has given grave scandal or committed a grave external fault, the superioress may forbid her to receive Holy Communion until she has approached the Sacrament of Penance. These conditions must obtain if such respective action is to be permissible, and no superioress may deny the reception of Holy Communion as a public penance.[23]   Finally, a religious who has taken recourse against a penance imposed by her superioress is not exempt from the observance of it until a contrary decision has been given by the higher superior.[24]   Since it is a penance and not an ecclesiastical penalty that is invoked in such a recourse, the rules for the latter type of punishment are not applicable.[25]

Just as the infliction of ecclesiastical penalties is beyond the competence of the superioress, so, too, is dispensation from ecclesiasti-

---

[19] Van Hove, *Commentarium Lovaniense in Codicem Iuris Canonici* (Vol. I, Tom. II, *De Legibus Ecclesiasticis*, Mechliniae-Romae: Dessain, 1930), I, pp. 364-365, nn. 358-359; Vermeersch-Creusen, *Epitome*, I, p. 128, n. 136.

[20] Creusen-Garesché-Ellis, *Religious Men and Women in the Code*, p. 42, n. 58; Schaefer, *De Religiosis*, p. 229, n. 107.

[21] Creusen-Garesché-Ellis, *Religious Men and Women in the Code*, p. 42, n. 58.

[22] Goyeneche, "Consultationes," *CpR*, III (1922), 142; Berutti, *Institutiones Iuris Canonici*, III, p. 51, n. 25; Schaefer, *De Religiosis*, p. 229, n. 107.

[23] Creusen-Garesché-Ellis, *op. cit.*, p. 43, n. 58.

[24] Cf. canon 345, which speaks of recourse from precepts at the time of visitation.   These precepts are likewise of a maternal nature; Schaefer, *De Religiosis*, p. 229, n. 107.

[25] Canon 2287: "Ab inflictis poenis vindicativis datur appellatio seu recursus in suspensivo, nisi aliud expresse in iure caveatur."

cal laws.[26] Thus the superioress may not dispense either herself or her subjects from the general law of the Code or even the particular law of her community, except in those cases in which this power is specifically granted to her by the Code or by the constitutions.[27] Even in these cases there exists a strong doubt whether the relaxation of the law is a dispensation in the strict sense. The power of relaxing the law as granted by the constitutions can be known only from the text of the constitutions itself.

In the Code itself, canon 589, § 2, gives the supreme moderator and in particular cases other superioresses the right to exempt teachers and students from some community exercises and from choir, especially from the office recited during the night, whenever they prudently see a need for this exemption. The question whether this is a dispensation in the strict sense is a difficult one to answer. Jurisdiction is required to dispense, and canon 118 limits the exercise of jurisdiction to clerics. However, as was seen in the historical synopsis of this work, it seems to the writer that at one time certain superioresses by privilege did possess ecclesiastical jurisdiction.[28]

It is further the opinion of the writer that women religious are not incapable of possessing this power in view of any intrinsic incapacity or of any prohibition of the divine law. Consequently, today by special law, privilege, or apostolic indult there seems no reason why superioresses could not be granted this power. Canon 589, § 2, is certainly not a clear case of the power of dispensation being granted to superioresses. Rather, it seems to give them a right to decide whether in their institute teachers and students are no longer obliged to observe certain precepts of the law, inasmuch as if they were observed the effects would be detrimental to them. Whether superioresses actually do have the power to dispense, and whether canon 589, § 2, is an example of this power, can be determined only by the legislator himself.

For particular cases, dominative power itself warrants a superioress to declare authoritatively that in view of an existing cause subjects are excused from the observance of the rule or the con-

---

[26] Augustine, *Commentary*, III, 106.

[27] Berutti, *Institutiones Iuris Canonici*, III, p. 51, n. 25.

[28] Cf. *supra*, p. 31.

stitutions.[29] These are not dispensations in the strict sense, but merely declarative decisions in regard to a fact that already exists, namely, that the law does not bind in this particular case.

In virtue of dominative power another right accorded to every superioress is that of annulling non-reserved private vows of her subjects. Canon 1312, § 1, states that those who have dominative power over the will of those who make a vow may validly, and if a just cause is present, also licitly, render the vow null. The obligation of the vow in no case revives once this has been done. The subjects referred to in canon 1312, § 1, are all those who are professed religious.[30] The vows subject to nullification by the superioress are all those which have not been officially accepted by the Church with the exception of the two reserved private vows, namely, that of perfect and perpetual chastity, and that of entering a religious institute of solemn vows, both made absolutely and after the completion of the eighteenth year.[31]

Paragraph two of canon 1312 states that those who have power not over the will of the one making the vow, but over the matter, that is, over the substance of the vow itself, may suspend the obligation of the vow as long as it offers an obstacle to the fulfillment of duty. Thus, the superioress may suspend the non-reserved private vows of novices and postulants.[32] The superioress has the same power of granting a suspension for the private vows of all who are members of the household to the extent that the vows interfere with their duties to the house.[33]

Canon 1320 states that all who are able to nullify or suspend vows are, in regard to the subjects whom they can affect in this manner, likewise competent to nullify or suspend promissory oaths, provided that the nullification or suspension will not be harmful to

[29] Schaefer, *De Religiosis,* p. 240, n. 113; Berutti, *Institutiones Iuris Canonici,* III, p. 51, n. 25; Geser, *The Canon Law Governing Communities of Sisters,* p. 77, q. 197.

[30] Creusen-Garesché-Ellis, *Religious Men and Women in the Code,* p. 45, n. 62.

[31] Canon 1309.

[32] Berutti, *Institutiones Iuris Canonici,* III, p. 51, n. 25; Creusen-Garesché-Ellis, *Religious Men and Women in the Code,* p. 45, n. 62.

[33] Schaefer, *De Religiosis,* p. 239, n. 112.

others who refuse to relinquish their rights under the obligation. The basis for the use of this right is again dominative power. It may be pointed out that this power of nullification or suspension may be exercised in regard to both oaths and vows, even if the superioress had approved them at the time they were made.[34]

Other rights of the superioress arising from dominative power are, according to the norms of law, the erection of new houses, the administration of temporal goods, and the admission and dismissal of religious.[35]   These rights will be treated more fully in later chapters.

ARTICLE 2. LIMITATIONS OF POWER

As has been seen, the superioress enjoys a very definite power over her subjects.   There are, however, certain sources from which spring limitations to this authority.   These fall into three categories. In the first group are found both the common law and the particular law of each institute as expressed in the constitutions; in the second, the chapters and councils; and in the third, all other offices involving such a restriction.

1. *From Law*

All religious, as baptized Catholics, are members of the Church and subject to its laws.[36]   Entrance into a religious society in no way exempts a Catholic from the general law of the Church. Superioresses are no exception, and they are therefore first and foremost bound by the Code of Canon Law.   This obligation includes the law as prescribed for the faithful in general and for religious in particular.[37]

A second determinant of the power of the superioress is the rule and the constitutions of her community.   The rule comprises a body of principles regarding the religious life.   It offers norms directing all acts toward the end of religious profession, and it serves to promote the observance of the evangelical counsels.[38]   These rules were

---

[34] Creusen-Garesché-Ellis, *op. cit.*, p. 545, n. 62.

[35] Vermeersch-Creusen, *Epitome*, I, p. 443, n. 620; Wernz-Vidal, *Ius Canonicum*, III, pp. 86-87, n. 93.

[36] Canon 12.

[37] Fanfani, *De Iure Religiosorum*, p. 36, n. 29.

[38] Creusen-Garesché-Ellis, *Religious Men and Women in the Code*, p. 204,

proposed to their disciples by the first organizers of the religious life, for example, by St. Basil, St. Augustine, and St. Benedict. They have been adopted, and are still followed by certain religious institutes. Not all religious institutes have rules. For those communities which have been approved with an obligation to follow them, they have a binding force.[39] Superioresses must govern in accord with the rule, and cannot dispense from it without authorization, except in the cases explained above.[40]

Over and above the rule, every religious institute is required to have a set of constitutions. These are statutes or particular laws which give individual institutes their specific character. They determine and declare the specific ends of the institute and the means to attain these ends.[41] Constitutions contain exhortations to practice certain virtues with great care; they define the obligations of vows as effective in the particular community; they list the disciplinary prescriptions of the general law; they outline with some detail the routine of life in the society.[42]

The Code itself specifically points out that the power which the superioress possesses is to be exercised according to the general law and the constitutions.[43] Thus, these constitutions are elevated to the status of collections of ecclesiastical law. They must be revered as such, and alterations and dispensations are to be governed by the regular procedure which controls the relaxation or the modification of law.

n. 271; Schaefer, *De Religiosis*, p. 104, n. 54; Geser, *The Canon Law Governing Communities of Sisters*, p. 35, q. 84.

[39] Canon 593: "Omnes et singuli religiosi, Superiores aeque ac subditi, debent, non solum quae nuncuparunt vota fideliter integreque servare, sed etiam secundum regulas et constitutiones propriae religionis vitam componere atque ita ad perfectionem sui status contendere."

[40] Cf. *supra*, p. 82.

[41] Berutti, *Institutiones Iuris Canonici*, III, p. 18, n. 9.

[42] Creusen-Garesché-Ellis, *Religious Men and Women in the Code*, p. 204, n. 27.

[43] Canon 501, § 1. "Superiores et Capitula, ad normam constitutionum et iuris communis, potestatem habent dominativan in subditos; in religione autem clericali exempta, habent iurisdictionem ecclesiasticam tam pro foro interno, quam pro externo."

2. From Assemblies

A third source of limitation on the power of the superioress is the chapter. Lewis defines the chapter as: "A collegiate moral person composed of those members of the religious institute who, according to the prescriptions of the constitution and the common law, possess the right of active suffrage, and constituted as an independent subject of authority in the internal government of the institute."[44] These chapters may be general, provincial, or local. They may be convened for the consideration of general business or for elections, or for both. They, too, have dominative power.[45] And, although the extent of this power can be determined only from an examination of the constitutions, the chapter's authority is above that of the superioress, and she is subject to it.

Chapters may be convoked by the terms of the law itself or by the superioress acting under authorization of the law.[46] An example of convocation by the very terms of the law would be revealed in constitutions or in established custom if either of these set the time and the place for the meeting, requiring no further action on the part of any person in authority.[47] If there are no regulations available from these sources, canon 162, § 1, names the *collegii praeses* as the one in possession of this right. This is the superioress of the moral person represented by the chapter, and not the official who presides at the chapter.[48]

The Sacred Congregation of Religious when asked whether the right to determine the place for the meeting of the general chapter was proper to the local ordinary of the mother house of a polydiocesan community or to the superioress general, responded that it was proper to the superioress.[49] From this it may be deduced that the competent superioress is the local superioress for the local chap-

---

[44] *Chapters in Religious Institutes,* p. 3.

[45] Canon 501, § 1.

[46] Canon 162, § 1.

[47] Coronata, *Institutiones,* I, p. 268, n. 229.

[48] Lewis, *Chapters in Religious Institutes,* p. 73.

[49] *De celebratione capitula generalis in congregationibus iuris dioecesani,* 2 iul. 1921—*AAS,* XIII (1921), 481.

ter, the provincial for the provincial chapter, and the superioress general for the general chapter. Lewis adds that unless constitutions prohibit it the superioress general would be competent to convoke all types of chapters, and the provincial superioress not only the provincial but also the local chapter.[50]

Ordinarily the person enjoying the right to convoke the chapter has the right also to preside over it. But in a chapter for the election of the superioress of an independent monastery or of the superioress general of a congregation, the general law has set down exceptional norms appointing the presiding officer. When the case is that of the election of a superioress of a monastery subject to the local ordinary, he or his delegate presides; if the nuns are subject to a regular superior, the right belongs to this superior, unless the local ordinary chooses to preside personally or by delegate. In both cases the local ordinary is to be informed in due time of the approaching convocation of the chapter.[51] In congregations the local ordinary or his delegate presides; if the congregation is diocesan, he also has the right of granting confirmation.[52]

During the course of the chapter, business is to be conducted in accord with the norms governing the acts of any moral person, namely, through balloting.[53] The conclusion of the chapter is reached by a reading of the acts and the signing of them by the secretary, the president and the tellers.[54]

A second type of advisory assembly provided by law as a limitation upon the exercise of power by the superioress is the council.

---

[50] *Chapters in Religious Institutes,* p. 74, note 25.

[51] Canon 506, § 2: "In monasteriis monialium, comitiis eligendae Antistitae praesit, quin tamen clausuram ingrediatur, Ordinarius loci aut eius delegatus cum duobus sacerdotibus scrutatoribus, si moniales eidem subiectae sint; secus, Superior regularis; sed etiam hoc in casu Ordinarius tempestive moneri debet de die et hora electionis, cui potest una cum Superiore regulari per se ipse vel per alium assistere et, si assistat, praeesse."

[52] Canon 506, § 4: "In mulierum Congregationibus electioni Antistitae generalis praesideat per se vel per alium Ordinarius loci, in quo electio peragitur; cui, si agatur de Congregationibus iuris dioecesani, peractam electionem confirmare vel rescindere integrum est pro conscientiae officio."

[53] Canon 101.

[54] Canon 171, § 5.

The Code prescribes that every superioress, at least of a formal house, must have a council whose consent or advice she must invite according to the norms of the canons and the constitutions.[55] This council must be stable,[56] and its members must reside in the same house with the superioress.[57] The members of the council are not superioresses and have no authority to govern. Their duty is to approve or reject measures which the law requires the superioress to submit to them before she takes action.[58] The initiative in the manner and order of discussion of affairs submitted by her to her council is left to the individual superioress.[59]

The superioress is obliged to convoke the council whenever such a convocation is prescribed by the Code or by the constitutions. In accord with the norms of the common law governing this assembly, recourse to individual members of the council is not a sufficient compliance with this required formality. The members must be called together for the consultation; their action must be a collegiate one.[60] If the convocation was legitimately made but no one appeared in answer to the summons, the superioress still may not act without the requisite consultation; [61] if, however, only one member appears she may proceed, unless some specific law states otherwise.[62] Should the superioress neglect to invite at least two-thirds of the ordinary members of the council, all acts pursued by it during that meeting would be invalid; if only the two-thirds are called, the acts are valid, but they would be subject to nullification at the insistence of any one of the absent members.[63] The superioress in accordance with her

[55] Canon 516, § 1.

[56] Coronata, *Institutiones,* I, p. 671, n. 541.

[57] Creusen-Garesché-Ellis, *Religious Men and Women in the Code,* p. 73, n. 97.

[58] *Loc. cit.*

[59] Vermeersch, "De consiliariis superiorum," *Periodica,* XV (1926-1927), (63).

[60] Canon 105, 2°; Goyeneche, "Consultationes," *CpR,* III (1922), 216.

[61] Schaefer, *De Religiosis,* p. 328, n. 155.

[62] Cf. canon 655, § 1, which demands at least four members to be present for the dismissal of a religious.

[63] Canon 162, § 3, 4°.

power to impose punishment seems authorized to compel the council to appear in answer to her invitation by imposing penances if necessary.[64]

The Code is specific as to certain matters in the execution of which the council must give consent, and as to others in which mere consultation is sufficient. Constitutions may provide in a similar way for affairs not mentioned by the Code. If consent is required by the Code or by the constitutions, the superioress who acts against the decision of the council acts invalidly.[65] In matters in which consultation of the council suffices under the terminology of the Code, the latter does not require that the superioress follow the recommendations given her. There is an implication, however, that she should.[66]

Authors dispute whether the superioress would act invalidly if she did not in this latter case even hear the views of the council. This is a long standing dispute based on the meaning of the words of canon 105, 1°, *"satis est ad valide agendum."* Renowned authors are found in support of either side of the question.[67] To argue this point that canonists for so long have been unable to settle seems without merit. The opinion which interprets the words of the text *"it is sufficient for a valid action"* to mean that consultation is necessary for a valid action seems the more probably correct doctrine. In practice, since it certainly would be a violation of law if the superioress did not hear the council when consultation is prescribed, there is no choice left her. *Post factum,* the probable opinion which favors the validity of the act despite the omission of the required consultation will serve, in view of the argued doubtful import of the law, to remove anxiety in the individual case.

[64] Cf. *supra,* p. 81.

[65] Canon 105, 1°.

[66] Canon 105, 1°.

[67] Among those who hold that consultation is required for valid action are: Oesterle, *Praelectiones Iuris Canonici,* p. 297; Coronata, *Institutiones,* I, p. 187, n. 153, nota 8. Among those who deny this are: Vermeersch-Creusen, *Epitome,* I, pp. 198-199, n. 229; Schaefer, *De Religiosis,* p. 326, n. 155.

3. *From Persons*

The nature of a religious society makes it such as to have within it persons who are endowed with authority. In no sense, however, are these societies autonomus, that is, independent of the universal Church. Consequently they are affected by an external as
well as an internal ruling authority. Representing the former are
the superiors who hold this right from their place in the hierarchy
of the Church.[68]

First and foremost, all religious are subject to the Roman Pon-
tiff, and this by virtue of their vow of obedience. He is the Supreme
Superior of every religious institute.[69] In most cases the Holy Father
does not act directly, but through the Sacred Congregations. As
his representatives they too have a right to exact and receive obedience. To the Sacred Congregation of Religious this obedience is
owed, as to the Holy Father, in virtue of the vow itself.[70] It is from
the Sacred Congregation of Religious that all dispensations from the
common law are to be sought, and to which cases are to be submitted
for solution by religious. For all pontifically approved institutes
dispensations from their particular law must likewise be obtained
from this Sacred Congregation. For diocesan institutes the same
procedure must be followed for those things which are reserved by
the Congregation to itself.[71]

The authority of the other Sacred Congregations in matters pertaining to religious appears, for example, in the so-called reserved
major causes. These are the specific cases listed in the Code in
which all superioresses are forbidden to interfere. They pertain to
the Holy Office.[72] In nature they are all cases which pertain to doc-

---

[68] Cocchi, *Commentarium*, IV, p. 46, n. 18; Beste, *Introduction in Codicem*,
p. 325; Wernz-Vidal, *Ius Canonicum*, III, p. 77, n. 83.

[69] Canon 499, § 1.

[70] Schaefer, *De Religiosis*, p. 179, n. 91.

[71] Examples of the things that must be referred to the Sacred Congregation
are changes in the title of an institute, in the style of the habit, and in the scope
of the work.—Const. *"Dei Providentis,"* 16 iul. 1906—*ASS*, XXXIX (1906),
344-346.

[72] Canon 501, § 2.

trines of faith and morals, including all delicts of heresy and schism.[73]
In a decree issued by the Holy Office on May 15, 1901, it is stated
that superiors cannot and should not under any guise or pretext make
inquiry, receive accusation, question witnesses, inflict punishment,
or otherwise concern themselves in any way in these matters.[74]

It is true that the concern of the law in these canons is the juridical process for which the superioress is never competent, but it seems
important also to point out that in the subject matter reserved as
major causes the superioress may not act even in her usual capacity
of disciplinarian. The ordinary of the place is the inquisitor in all
matters pertaining to heresy and schism.[75] Consequently, all questions in this matter must be referred to him. Nothing, however,
seems to militate against action on her part for the sake of prevent-
ing or removing scandal arising from such delinquency on the part
of her subjects, for instance, by a transfer of the delinquent to another house.[76]

Immediately beneath the Holy Father and the Roman Curia, the
next in rank authorized to exercise a limitation on the power of the
superioress is the local ordinary or residential bishop.[77] As to his
competence in this respect a distinction is to be made between exempt
and non-exempt communities. In the latter category one must
further distinguish between pontifical and diocesan communities.
Exempt women religious are subject to the bishop only in such
matters as are assigned to his jurisdiction by the Holy See. Their
immediate superior is the one in the coordinate institute of men religious designated by their constitutions.[78]

In the United States, all nuns have been placed under the jurisdiction of their local ordinaries.[79] This does not mean that the

---

[73] Canon 247, § 1.

[74] *Fontes*, n. 1254.

[75] Schaefer, *De Religiosis*, p. 223, n. 106.

[76] Larraona, "Commentarium Codicis," *CpR*, VII (1926), 96, nota 191.

[77] Canon 500, § 1.

[78] Clancy, *The Local Religious Superior*, pp. 38-39.

[79] S. C. Ep. et Reg., *Americana Votorum*, 2 sept. 1864—*Coll. S. C. Ep. et Reg.*, p. 723; *Archiepiscopo Baltimorensi*, 30 sept. 1864—*ibidem*, p. 735; O'Brien, *The Exemption of Religious in Church Law*, p. 68; Creusen-Garesché-Ellis, *Religious Men and Women in the Code*, p. 39, n. 53.

communities of these nuns have thereby acquired a diocesan status.[80] They do not enjoy the privilege of exemption, but they do retain the status of institutes that have received pontifical approval. By papal indult an individual institute could receive the privilege of exemption, and some communities of nuns in the United States have recently received this privilege.

Congregations of women religious of pontifical approval are partially withdrawn from the local ordinary's jurisdiction, inasmuch as canon 618 states that the local ordinary may not interfere with their internal government and discipline, except in the cases designated in the law. Internal government includes the reception of candidates, the admission to vows, dismissal, appointments, and the administration of temporal goods.[81]

The ordinary, however, must according to canon 618 inquire concerning the maintenance of discipline, the status of doctrine and morals, the law of the enclosure, and the frequency with which the sacraments are received. If a superioress, after being warned, does not remedy an abuse detected by him in the course of his supervisory investigation, he has a right to provide for its correction himself. He must, however, refer matters of greater importance to the Sacred Congregation of Religious; but even as to these, if their nature demands prompt action, the bishop may act at once and report his procedure to the Holy See. Orders of women religious in the United States are subject in these matters to the local ordinary in the same manner as congregations of women religious.[82]

[80] In a decree in reference to the status of monastic nuns in France and Belgium, who like the nuns in the United States had been made dependent on the ordinaries of places, the Sacred Congregation of Religious pointed out that these nuns were subject to the jurisdiction of ordinaries of places in those matters in which the Code gives bishops jurisdiction over monastic nuns. These nuns, the decree states, are true monastic nuns of pontifical law in the sense of canon 488, 7°.—23 iun. 1923—*AAS*, XV (1923), 357.

[81] Geser, *The Canon Law Governing Communities of Sisters*, p. 331, q. 1001.

[82] It is beyond the scope of this work to develop in detail the subject of the relation between external and internal superiors of women religious, since this dissertation concerns mainly the office of the internal superioress. For a detailed study of the question cf. Farrell, *"The Rights and Duties of the Local Ordinary Regarding Congregations of Women Religious of Pontifical Approval."*

The degree of intervention permitted to the local ordinary in the case of diocesan institutes of women religious is somewhat more extensive than that just described as granted to him in the case of communities of women religious of pontifical approval. Here the religious depend more directly on him. This dependence is always of course to be in conformity with the general law and the constitutions. Each bishop exercises jurisdiction over the houses of the community in his own diocese, and it is to him that these institutes must recur for the permissions required by the Code or by the constitutions.

The diocesan institute, however, is not so completely dependent on the local ordinary as not to remain a moral person under the direction of its own superioresses. The ordinary may not interfere in the internal government of the institute except in the matters prescribed by the law. The bishop is not a governing religious superior. This power belongs solely to the superioresses of the institute in accordance with the limitations imposed by the law in favor of the local ordinary or of the Holy See.[83] Thus the bishop may not admit candidates for the postulancy or the novitiate, or dismiss the professed or the non-professed; he may not assign duties to them, and he may not appoint to or remove from office the various superioresses of the institute.

More closely connected with the subject of this work is the relationship between the superioress and the persons who do not pertain to the hierarchy of the Church, but who by their office are obliged to minister to the community or to assist the superioress in the government of its institute. Of these, the first to be considered is the office of the chaplain. He is the priest who performs the divine services for the community. He may be the parish priest or a special priest placed in charge of this work by the local ordinary.[84]

The free appointment of the chaplain to a community of women religious is a right possessed by the local ordinary, unless the institute enjoys the privilege of exemption. In this latter case the appointment is to be made by the regular superior of the correlative order

[83] Gallik, *The Rights and Duties of Bishops Regarding Diocesan Sisterhoods* (St. Paul, Minnesota: Wanderer Printing Co., 1939), p. 32.

[84] Canon 464, §§ 1, 2.

of men religious. However, it remains the devolved right of the local ordinary to make the appointment if it were neglected by the regular superior.[85] Moreover, even in the case of women religious in monasteries directly subject to the Holy See, the local ordinary likewise appoints the chaplain.[86]

The rights of the chaplain and his obligations are known from the Code, from particular law, and from his letter of appointment. His essential functions consist in the celebration of Mass, the distribution of Holy Communion, and the performance of other divine services held in the oratory of the community. Regarding the administration of Extreme Unction and of Holy Viaticum, if the convent is a monastery of nuns, the confessor is authorized to exercise this right; in other institutes of women religious it is the right of the chaplain.[87]

The right of the chaplain in the latter case is, of course, predicated on the assumption that the community has been withdrawn from the jurisdiction of the parish priest.[88] On the same assumption the right of the chaplain extends to the conducting of the funeral rites. If the religious are not under the care of the pastor, the chaplain performs these in the convent oratory; otherwise the pastor conducts them in the parish church.[89]

Chaplains are in no way to interfere with the internal government of the community. The obligation to see that the religious make a retreat once a year, are present for daily Mass, make their daily meditation, perform their spiritual exercises, and approach the Sacrament of Penance once a week, rests on the superioress.[90] Again, it is the duty of the superioress to encourage her subjects to

---

[85] Canon 529.

[86] Creusen-Garesché-Ellis, *Religious Men and Women in the Code,* p. 100, n. 133.

[87] Canon 514, §§ 2, 3: The right of the confessor to administer Extreme Unction and Holy Viaticum in a monastery of nuns extends both to monasteries where the nuns have pronounced solemn vows and also to monasteries where by papal precept the nuns have pronounced only simple vows. Cf. Schaefer, *De Religiosis,* p. 317, n. 149.

[88] Canon 464, § 2.

[89] Canon 1230, § 5.

[90] Canon 595, § 1.

receive Communion frequently and even daily.[91] Should a religious now and again abstain from receiving daily Communion, the superioress may not manifest displeasure.[92]

It is also the right of the superioress to grant or to refuse admittance to the convent chapel to the faithful who come to hear Sunday Mass. The local ordinary is to judge whether their admittance interferes with the instruction that they should receive in the parish church. On his judgment in this matter he may forbid them to attend Mass at the convent.[93]

According to an Instruction of the Sacred Congregation of the Sacraments, the custody of the tabernacle key is the responsibility of the chaplain.[94] The same Instruction orders that in monasteries of nuns the key should be kept in a safe in the sacristy, the safe being securely sealed by means of two different locks. The superioress is required to keep the key to one of these locks, and the sacristan the key to the other lock. The Instruction does not distinguish between nuns who have pronounced solemn vows and those who by papal precept have pronounced only simple vows. It is clear in the Instruction, though, that in no monastery of women religious is the tabernacle key to be kept within the walls of the monastery. Therefore the regulations of this Instruction extend to the monasteries of all nuns. If a community of sisters of simple profession has no chaplain, Creusen believes that the foregoing directive may well be followed in their case also.[95]

Authors differ in their interpretation of the law with regard to what authorization is required before one may preach to non-exempt women religious. Canon 529 states that it is the right of the local ordinary to approve and to appoint preachers who are to speak to non-exempt religious. Canon 1338, § 3, however, prescribes that the preacher cannot use this faculty without the consent of the re-

[91] Canon 595, § 2.

[92] Geser, *The Canon Law Governing Communities of Sisters*, p. 117, q. 350.

[93] Creusen-Garesché-Ellis, *Religious Men and Women in the Code*, p. 103, n. 137.

[94] *De Sanctissima Eucharistia sedulo custodienda*, 26 maii 1938—*AAS*, XXX (1938), 198.

[95] Creusen-Garesché-Ellis, *Religious Men and Women in the Code*, p. 108, n. 144.

ligious superior. Augustine held that the rule of canon 1338, § 3, does not apply to women religious at all.[96] This negative position is not evident in the text. Fanfani believes that its meaning is that the superioress is authorized to choose any preacher from those already approved.[97]

While it is true that the law warrants this practice, there remains the difficulty that the law on the one hand seems to suggest that the local ordinary has the right to make a specific appointment, while on the other it speaks of assent on the part of the superioress. Vermeersch-Creusen state that ordinaries generally permit superioresses to choose freely from those preachers who have already received approval. These same authors add, however, that it would be within the right of the ordinary to designate a specific priest for a retreat. They note further, though, that the Holy See would hardly consider such action on the part of the bishop as opportune.[98]

This leaves the problem suggested by the writer still unanswered. Under the text of canon 1338, § 3, the action of the superioress is certainly included as a requirement in the authorization of the preacher, and the legislator gives every evidence of intending that there be a twofold action in an amicable agreement between the ordinary and the superioress.[99] To the writer it seems, then, that in the matter of the authorization of preachers to non-exempt women religious two rights must be respected, namely, that of the ordinary to approve and to appoint preachers, and that of the superioress to express her satisfaction or dissatisfaction with the appointees. Should the superioress express dissatisfaction, the ordinary should make a new appointment.

All superioresses are strictly forbidden to induce any of their subjects to make a manifestation of conscience to them.[100] This refers not only to every superioress, but also to those who act as substitutes or delegates for them. It rules out every possible means of inducement, of command, of threat, of counsel, and even all in-

---

[96] *Commentary*, VI, 354.
[97] *De Iure Religiosorum*, p. 440, n. 430.
[98] *Epitome*, I, 468, n. 649.
[99] Cf. Beste, *Introductio in Codicem*, p. 654.
[100] Canon 531, § 1.

direct methods of praise or flattery.[101]   The subjects referred to as protected against these inducements are all such persons as come under the authority of the superioress: the professed religious, the novices, the postulants, and the members of the household.[102]

Manifestation of conscience as forbidden in canon 531, § 1, means the revealing of one's virtues or faults, one's temptations, and one's likes and dislikes, or one's inclinations and propensities as touching the moral sphere of life.   More, it includes all those things which, when revealed at all, are usually told only in confidence and under secrecy.[103]   Once these matters become noticeable to others or occasion a problem of discipline, they no longer form a part of the realm of conscience, and the superioress may have a duty to make inquiries.   This duty on the part of the superioress may also arise from the general obligation of charity when there are external evidences betrayed by a religious of internal unhappiness or anxiety. In this latter case the superioress must exercise extreme caution in order that she will not trespass on the internal forum.   Should any doubt regarding this matter exist in the mind of the superioress, a better course of action for her would be to recommend to the religious that she consult her confessor and make a manifestation of conscience to him.[104]

Further, it may be said that the law applies as a prohibition which affects the superioress, and not her subjects.   The latter are permitted to speak freely and to open their minds to her.[105]   Permission may also be given by the subjects to the superioress in order that the latter may propose to them even such questions as touch on these reserved matters.   However, this permission must be spontaneous, and it may freely be withdrawn at any time.[106]

[101] Schaefer, *De Religiosis,* p. 402. n 183.

[102] Cf. *supra,* pp. 66-67.

[103] Creusen-Garesché-Ellis, *Religious Men and Women in the Code,* pp. 94-95, n. 128.

[104] Chelodi, *Ius de Personis iuxta Codicem Iuris Canonici* (ed. altera a Sac. Ernesto Bertagnolli recognita et aucta, Tridenti: Libr. Edit. Tridentum, 1927), p. 431, n. 258.

[105] Canon 530, § 2.

[106] Creusen-Garesché-Ellis, *Religious Men and Women in the Code,* p. 99, n. 132.

Every superioress has the obligation to see to it that her subjects approach the Sacrament of Penance at least once a week.[107] There is no precept in the common law regarding the day or the time for this confession. It would be within the right of the superioress to demand that permission be asked if confession is to be made by a religious at a time when the order of community exercises does not allow it. Thus, even if the superioress does not explicitly require it, permission should be obtained if for the purpose of making her confession a religious wished to leave a class or a common work. The obtaining of such permission would not be necessary on the part of a religious to absent herself at a time when common exercises are being held in the chapel.[108]

The one designated to hear the confessions of women religious may or may not be the chaplain. Generally he will not be their chaplain, but if he were, then needless to say, he must meet all the qualifications demanded of him in the canons. The Code lists six possible types of confessors for the hearing of the confessions of women religious. The first is the ordinary confessor. He is the priest chosen by the local ordinary and given the special jurisdiction required for this office.[109] It is his task regularly to afford the means of confession to all the religious of the convent to which he is appointed. Any religious, however, is free, should she feel the need, to ask the bishop for a special ordinary confessor.[110] The decision as to her need is to be made by the religious, with the approval of the local ordinary, and not of the superioress.

The third type of confessor contemplated by the Code is the extraordinary confessor. He is appointed for a specific convent by the ordinary, and is obliged to offer the opportunity for confession to the religious residing there at least four times a year.[111] The superioress must see to it that on these occasions all the religious,

---

[107] Canon 595, § 1, 3°.

[108] Creusen-Garesché-Ellis, *Religious Men and Women in the Code*, p. 88, n. 121.

[109] Canons 876; 520, § 1; 525.

[110] Canon 520, § 2.

[111] Canon 521, § 1.

herself included, present themselves to him at least to receive his blessing.[112]

Besides looking to the appointment of ordinary and extraordinary confessors the bishop is obliged to provide also for the appointment to each convent of supplementary ·confessors, to whom the community is authorized to confess in particular cases without obtaining any further permission.[113] The number of these supplementary confessors depends on the judgment of the ordinary. The reason for a plurality is to give an opportunity of choice to the individual religious, but not to the superioress except for her own confession.[114] The superioress should acquaint herself with the names of those appointed to this office, and then inform her subjects of this right communicating also the names of the priests so authorized. At the petition of any of her subjects she is obliged without question or sign of displeasure to summon the priest designated.[115] The same rule applies if the religious names one of the extraordinary confessors.[116]

The superioress would offend directly against the rule of canon 521, § 3, if she asked the penitent for her reasons in making the request; she would offend indirectly if she sought these reasons from other sources.[117] As has been intimated in the foregoing, the ordinary approach to these confessors is through the superioress, but this need not always be the case. If a religious uses other legitimate means, the superioress may not object.[118] Finally, it may be said that the superioress herself may in special cases ask one or the other of the supplementary confessors to hear the confessions of the whole community. This request would be justified, for example, if the ordinary confessor were unable to come.[119]

[112] Wernz-Vidal, *Ius Canonicum*, III, p. 147, n. 179.

[113] Canon 521, § 2.

[114] S. C. Ep. et Reg., 14 aug. 1891—*Fontes*, n. 1053.

[115] Canon 521, § 3.

[116] Paragraph 3 of canon 521 uses the words *"ex iis"* and includes the extraordinary as well as the supplementary confessors.

[117] Coronata, *Institutiones*, I, p. 681, n. 550.

[118] Larraona, "Commentarium Codicis," *CpR*, XI (1930), 30; Schaefer, *De Religiosis*, p. 373, n. 175.

[119] Cf. Creusen-Garesché-Ellis, *Religious Men and Women in the Code*, p. 84, n. 175.

As though not satisfied with the foregoing provisions to insure freedom in matters of confession for women religious, the Code offers another means to this end. It permits any religious to approach in a church or even a semi-public oratory any confessor approved in the respective territory to hear the confessions of women. Moreover, the superioress may not prohibit the use of this privilege, nor are the religious obliged to tell her that they have availed themselves of it.[120]

The question immediately arises as to how a religious may avail herself of the privilege of consulting a confessor in this manner. The Sacred Congregation of Religious, on being asked this question, did not deem it expedient to answer directly, but one of the consultors in a private response noted that in his opinion canon 522 in no way obliged the superioress when seeking to afford such an opportunity to make any change in the discipline of the cloister or in the constitutions. The religious should, therefore, await an occasion when such a confessor may be approached without any violation with reference to the observance of the cloister.[121]

Thus it may be said that, if a religious is legitimately outside her convent, all other conditions being duly fulfilled, she is free without informing anyone to approach the confessor described in canon 522. She is also free to approach him, if he is hearing confessions or if on some other occasion he is present in the convent. In this latter case, of course, the proper place for hearing confessions must be used. As to permission to leave the convent solely for the sake of approaching a confessor in a church or in a public or a semi-public oratory, the superioress may grant it or refuse it according to her best judgment. However, unless she had adequate grounds for her refusal, it would not be in accord with the mind of the Church that she should deny this permission when it was asked.[122] Finally, the superioress, with the one exception to be noted below, is not obliged

---

[120] Canon 522.

[121] Bouscaren, *The Canon Law Digest* (2 vols., Milwaukee: The Bruce Publishing Company, 1934-1943), I, 296-297.

[122] Fanfani, *De Iure Religiosorum*, p. 141, n. 127; Schaefer, *De Religiosis*, p. 379, n. 176.

to call a priest to the convent for the confession of a religious, unless he is an ordinary, extraordinary, or supplementary confessor.[123]

The Code makes special provision for the confession of a sister who is seriously ill. To her is given the right to call any priest who is approved for the hearing of the confessions of women. The superioress may not prohibit this.[124] Briefly, it may be stated that, unlike the case of a sister who is not ill, in this instance the superioress is obliged to carry out the request whenever it is made.

It is most clear that the Church wishes to preserve freedom as much as it can reasonably be done in matters of the confession of women religious. The superioress is never free to infringe on the rights granted to religious. Should she do so, the bishop is warranted, after administering a warning at the first offense, in removing her from her office when the offense is repeated. He is, however, to notify the Sacred Congregation of Religious of his action.[125] If a superioress believes that abuses have arisen in her convent in matters of confession, whether they derive from the confessor or from the penitents, her sole remedy is to notify the local ordinary and to accept his decision.

Another limitation is placed on the power of the superioress by reason of the rights of other officers within the community. First, every superioress must exercise her power with due respect to the authority, not only of her higher superioresses, but also, if there be any, of lower superioresses. Every duly authorized superioress has within the scope of her charge an independence which cannot be encroached upon. Lower superioresses are not mere representatives of higher superioresses, but they have, as has been seen in the early part of this chapter, a dominative power of their own.[126]

The Code and the constitutions frequently note the extent of the power of the individual superioress. These specifications must be followed. When a particular power is not inherently or by prescription of the Code the right of one superioress only, nothing for-

---

[123] Wernz-Vidal, *Ius Canonicum*, III, p. 161, n. 199; Creusen-Garesché-Ellis, *Religious Men and Women in the Code*, p. 87, n. 120.

[124] Canon 523.

[125] Canon 2414; cf. *supra*, p. 65.

[126] Cf. *supra*, p. 77.

bids that it be reserved by the constitutions to a higher superioress, but certainly not in a way that all power is retained by the highest superioress, with a complete denial of power to lower superioresses.[127]

Again, from within the community, an office which limits the superioress in the use of her authority is that of the bursar or econome. The institute as a whole, each province, and each house, must have besides the superioress a bursar.[128] This office, so canon 516, § 2, states, is to be administered under the direction of the superioress. Thus it is clear that it is not the council but the superioress who is to guide and to advise the bursar. The council does, however, in particular cases according to law have to be informed.[129] Again, because of the clear statement in the Code, no custom or contrary rules of constitutions may exempt the bursar from informing the superioress of all the transactions in which she has participated.[130]

The superioress general and the provincial may not hold the office of bursar respectively of the institute or of the province. In the local superioress the offices may be united, but this should not be done unless it is necessary.[131] If a superioress general or a provincial also served at the same time as local superioress, it would be permitted for her to hold the office of local bursar.[132] It may also be said that the law does not prohibit a superioress general from being also a provincial bursar, or the superioress of a province from being the general bursar.[133]

Finally, the method of choosing the bursar is left by the common law to the constitutions. If these are silent in the matter, the bursar is to be designated by the higher superioress with the consent of her council, that is, the general bursar by the superioress general; the provincial bursar and the local bursars by the provincial.[134]

---

[127] Larraona, "Commentarium Codicis," *CpR*, II (1921), p. 135, nota 203.

[128] Canon 516, § 2.

[129] Cocchi, *Commentarium*, IV, p. 66, n. 31; Larraona, "Commentarium Codicis," *CpR*, X (1929), 33-38.

[130] Creusen-Garesché-Ellis, *Religious Men and Women in the Code*, p. 74, n. 99.

[131] Canon 516, § 3.

[132] Vermeersch, "Annotationes," *Periodica*, X (1922-1923), 35.

[133] Oesterle, *Praelectiones Iuris Canonici*, p. 259.

[134] Canon 516, § 4.

CHAPTER VII

THE OBLIGATIONS OF THE SUPERIORESS

ARTICLE 1. RESIDENCE

ALL superioresses are obliged by the law of residence. They must reside in the house entrusted to their office, and leave it only in accord with the norms of the constitutions of their institute.[1] Thus the superioress general must live at the mother house, the provincials at the respective provincial houses, and the local superioresses at the convents entrusted to their charge. The place of residence of the local superioress offers no difficulty. That of major superioresses should be fixed and stable in a place convenient for their respective administration.

Moreover, the residence of the superioress general may not be changed without consultation of the Holy See. This is not prescribed by law, but it is the customary practice of the Sacred Congregation of Religious to demand a statement to this effect in constitutions submitted for approval.[2] If thus forbidden in the constitutions, a change in the residence of the superioress general would be a change in the constitutions, and for this act the competent superior, i. e., the Sacred Congregation of Religious, must be consulted.[3] Bastien pointed out, however, that this permission is needed only when the change is to be permanent and not merely temporary.[4]

As was noted above, the law of residence binds all superioresses, but most rigorously the local superioress. The latter is chosen for her personal qualities to exert authority and influence over a particular community, and for the accomplishing of this aim her presence is needed.[5] Moreover, her duties are naturally confined to a special place, and reasons are normally wanting for any frequent or lengthy absence.[6] On the other hand, there are many duties that normally

---

[1] Canon 508.

[2] Fanfani, *De Iure Religiosorum*, p. 138, n. 125.

[3] Bastien, *Directoire*, p. 278, n. 442.

[4] *Directoire*, p. 278, n. 442.

[5] Augustine, *Commentary*, III, 129.

[6] Geser, *The Canon Law Governing Communities of Sisters*, p. 115, q. 344.

call higher superioresses away from their habitual residence. Visitations, attendance at chapters, the erection of new houses—these are but a few of the considerations that may necessitate an absence from the place of habitual residence.[7]

The Code makes the law of residence binding on all superioresses in accord with the norms set by the constitutions. Thus, whether an absence is legitimate or illegitimate, is not simply determined by the duration of the absence, but also by the existence or non-existence of a justifying cause, and by the fulfillment or non-fulfillment of the conditions defined in the constitutions.[8]

When superioresses are unlawfully absent, they may be punished.[9] What the penalty will be in a specific case must be determined in relation to the seriousness of the violation of the law. Certainly, if a superioress has gravely neglected her duties by her absence, she could be deprived of her office.[10] The penalties, however, are not to be identified with those which receive mention in canon 2381, for that canon concerns only ecclesiastics who hold an office which requires residence.[11]

The competent superior to inflict punishments for the violation of the law of residence will, then, be the superior normally competent as designated in the constitutions for the punishment of other offenses. If the penalty to be inflicted on the culpable superioress is deprivation of office, the procedure to be followed will be the one regularly required for the removal of a superioress.[12]

Article 2. The Enclosure

Closely allied with the duty of residence is the obligation of the superioress to safeguard the observance of the enclosure or cloister. The cloister consists of that section of the convent which is to be

---

[7] Balmès, *Les Religieux*, p. 65.

[8] Fanfani, *De Iure Religiosorum*, p. 138, n. 125; Vermeersch-Creusen, *Epitome*, I, p. 450, n. 627.

[9] Berutti, *Institutiones Iuris Canonici*, III, p. 65, n. 32.

[10] Cf. Schaefer, *De Religiosis*, p. 293, n. 143.

[11] Ayrinhac-Lydon, *Penal Legislation*, p. 292, n. 351; Wernz-Vidal, *Ius Canonicum*, III, p. 121, n. 143.

[12] Cf. *supra*, pp. 61-63.

kept exclusively for the habitation and the use of the religious. The law concerning the observance of the cloister not only forbids the religious to leave this section, but also prohibits outsiders from entering it.[13]

As to the papal cloister, the superioress must see to it that without the permission of the Holy See no one enters it, with the exception of those who have the right of entering it by concession of the common law. In this latter group are those who perform a local canonical visitation, the confessor or his substitute for the purpose of administering the duties of his office, the highest official of the state with his wife and retinue, and cardinals.[14] Besides these persons the superioress may also, with due precautions, admit doctors and others whose service is needed for the maintenance of the house. For the admission of these persons she must have at least the habitual approval of the ordinary.[15] The practice of submitting to the bishop at the beginning of each year the names of persons whose work will be needed has been approved by the Sacred Congregation of Religious as satisfactory.[16]

In urgent cases in which no time interval is available in order to ask the ordinary's approval, this permission may be presumed. In admitting these persons the superioress must ascertain that they are of good reputation and character, and must see to it that they are accompanied by two elderly nuns in going to the place where they are to render service. Further, she should take care that no nun speaks to them except in regard to their work.[17] She must see to it that the discipline is not relaxed through repeated visits of externs, and that the religious spirit is not weakened by useless conversation.[18]

In accordance with her obligation to guard the observance of the papal cloister, it is the duty of the superioress to keep the keys of the cloister night and day, and to give them only to designated nuns

---

[13] Geser, *The Canon Law Governing Communities of Sisters*, p. 298, q. 952.

[14] Canon 600, 1°, 2°, 3°.

[15] Canon 600, 4°.

[16] "Instructio de Clausura Monialium Votorum Solemnium," 6 febr. 1924, III, 2, n, o)—*AAS*, XVI (1924), 99-100 (hereafter referred to as "Instructio de Clausura").

[17] *Ibidem*, p. 100.

[18] Canon 605.

when there is need for them.[19] If without the required permission she allows anyone entry to the cloister, she is guilty of grave sin and automatically incurs an excommunication the absolution of which is reserved in a simple manner to the Holy See.[20]

The church and the sacristy are not considered a part of the enclosure, but if the services of the nuns are required to keep these places clean and ornamented, the superioress may obtain permission from the Holy See to allow as many nuns as are necessary to enter them at stated occasions to take care of this work, always, however, at times when no one else is present in these places.[21]

Apostolic legates and local ordinaries frequently have extensive powers to permit admission to the cloister. Hence superioresses may apply to them when permissions are needed for the admitting of others to the cloister.[22] Finally, the superioress may not allow a religious to leave the cloister without the permission of the Holy See except in imminent danger of death or in other grave peril. If time permits, the local ordinary should attest in writing to the existence of these facts.[23]

The enclosure prescribed for congregations of simple vows, although modeled after that specified for orders of solemn vows, is not so severe in its implications. Persons of the other sex are generally not admitted even within this type of cloister, with the exception of those privileged by law as mentioned above. The superior, however, for a just and reasonable cause may admit others.[24] To do this she needs no authorization from the local ordinary unless the constitutions provide otherwise.[25] This permission may be granted by both the higher and the lower superioresses, but it would

---

[19] "Instructio de Clausura," IV—*AAS*, XVI (1924), 100.

[20] *Loc. cit.*; cf. canon 2342, 1°.

[21] "Instructio de Clausura," III, 1, d)—*AAS*, XVI (1924), 98.

[22] Creusen-Garesché-Ellis, *Religious Men and Women in the Code*, p. 218, n. 289.

[23] Canon 601, §§ 1, 2.

[24] Canon 604, § 1.

[25] Schaefer, *De Religiosis*, p. 733, n. 363; Creusen-Garesché-Ellis, *op. cit.*, p. 221, n. 291.

not at all be contrary to the common law if the matter were reserved to the higher superioresses alone.[26]

As regards religious leaving the cloister of congregations, and visitors coming to the convent to see religious, the superioress must take care that all regulations of the constitutions are faithfully observed.[27] The judgment of the superioress is the deciding factor for the religious under her charge in the matter of their going out from the convent. She may not allow them to remain outside the convent except for a brief-time, and for a just and grave cause. No religious may be permitted to be absent from her convent for more than six months, except for study, without the permission of the Holy See.[28] This permission is needed even when the cause is one of health.[29]

The superioress has the further duty of seeing that no religious goes out alone.[30] Constitutions approved by the Sacred Congregation at times permit the religious to go out alone, for example, in the case of communities whose members do visiting nursing. Although particular law may require it, the common law does not demand that the companion to be another religious. Any respectable woman would serve as a suitable companion. No automatic penalty is attached to any violation of the episcopal cloister, but the bishop has a right to safeguard its observance by means of penal sanctions, and in special circumstances even with censures.[31]

As a further means of protecting religious discipline and spiritual advancement the constitutions of almost every religious institute grant the superioress the right to demand that her permission be asked for the sending and receiving of letters. The superioress also may have the further right of inspecting these. It is hardly necessary to say that from the very nature of this question the superioress is obliged to keep these matters secret. No superioress,

---

[26] Schaefer, *De Religiosis*, p. 734, n. 363.

[27] Canon 606, § 1.

[28] Canon 606, § 2.

[29] Schaefer, *De Religiosis*, p. 735, n. 364; Geser, *The Canon Law Governing Communities of Sisters*, p. 301, q. 962.

[30] Canon 607.

[31] Canon 604, § 3.

however, may inspect letters sent to or received from the Holy See, its legates or delegates, the cardinal protector of the institute, the local ordinary, the higher superioresses, or a local superioress absent from her convent.[32] Permission is needed for the sending of letters to a confessor or a spiritual director, or also of letters which are marked as dealing with matters of conscience, but they may not be inspected, neither may the reply to them be inspected, even though a previous permission to write has been given.[33] At times charity may advise that a superioress omit reading purely family secrets, particularly when the envelope containing them is marked "personal." This would not be the case if there were grounds for suspecting the existence of an abuse.[34]

ARTICLE 3. VISITATION

The canonical visitation is the examination by a competent religious superioress of the religious discipline of each house and of the spiritual life of those residing there.[35] Canon 511 makes the canonical visitation an obligation. It leaves to the constitutions of particular institutes the designation of the particular major superioresses so obliged, and the times when the visitations are to be made. It further permits these superioresses, when legitimately impeded, to delegate another to perform the visitation. The obligation to make the canonical visitation is a grave one.[36]

The visitor may be the superioress general, the provincial, or another member of the institute who has as her ordinary office that of carrying out visitations. The latter, in such a case, are major superioresses.[37] At times independent monasteries enter into a form of union. In these instances one of the abbesses is designated by the

[32] Canon 611.

[33] Creusen-Garesché-Ellis, *Religious Men and Women in the Code*, p. 224, n. 294.

[34] *Ibidem*, n. 295.

[35] Fanfani, *De Iure Religiosorum*, p. 80, n. 69; Geser, *The Canon Law Governing Communities of Sisters*, p. 120, q. 361.

[36] Schaefer, *De Religiosis*, p. 308, n. 148; Cocchi, *Commentarium*, IV, p. 62, n. 27; Fanfani, *op. cit.*, p. 81, n. 70.

[37] Larraona, "Commentarium Codicis," *CpR*, IV (1923), 46.

constitutions of the federation to make the visitation.[38] The visitation of the superioress general generally takes place every three or six years, and that of the provincial every year, but the Code does not specify the periods at which either is to comply with this obligation. The constitutions furnish the determining law in this matter. No authorization is needed from the local ordinary, even in communities of diocesan approval, to proceed with these visitations.[39]

The superioress obliged by the common law to make the visitation has the right to delegate a substitute, but this only when she herself cannot carry out her office. She may be morally or physically impeded.[40] Impediments justifying an act of delegation on her part would be extreme distance, sickness, or old age. At times constitutions approved by the Sacred Congregation permit the superioress to delegate freely even without cause. In these instances the constitutions name two possible visitors, namely the superioress or her appointee.[41]

It is the customary practice of the Sacred Congregation of Religious to permit the superioress general to designate as her substitute for visitation, even apart from a special reason, one of the members of her council, but to require that she must have the consent of this council if she wishes to name a religious who is not a member of this body.[42] The delegate must follow the instruction given by the superioress who named her. If the superioress should die before the visitation has begun, the delegation ceases unless it was given by the constitutions.[43] The substitute is considered to have begun her office on the day that her letter of delegation has been read to or even presented to those subject to the visitation.[44]

In so far as they are subject to the superioress, all houses should be visited by her or her delegate, the latter enjoying competence under the terms described above. All persons attached to these houses

---

[38] Larraona, "Studia Canonica," *CpR*, VIII (1927), p. 365, nota 462.

[39] Reilly, *The Visitation of Religious*, p. 77.

[40] Schaefer, *De Religiosis*, p. 309, n. 148.

[41] Reilly, *The Visitation of Religious*, p. 78.

[42] Vermeersch-Creusen, *Epitome*, I, p. 453, n. 631.

[43] Augustine, *Commentary*, III, 135.

[44] Coronata, *Institutiones*, I, p. 667, n. 540.

are liable to questioning. Every visitation should thus be both local and personal. The constitutions frequently set down the norms that must be followed in the procedure of the visitation. They may exempt certain houses; on the other hand, they may require that in the houses visited all the members be called for an interview.

Under the common law the visitor is obliged to interview only those who according to her judgment should be summoned.[45] These may include the professed religious—superioresses being in no way excepted by the constitutions—the novices, and the postulants, for all of these are members of the community.[46] She should give all who desire it an opportunity to be heard.[47] If any member of the community is legitimately absent, the visitor has a right to question her by means of a letter, and these letters are not subject to the inspection of the local superioress.[48] The religious are obliged to answer questions truthfully, and no superioress may in any way prevent them from fulfilling their duties in this regard.[49]

The subject matter of the personal visitation concerns the general religious discipline of the house, the observance of the vows, of the rules, and of the constitutions, the relations of the superioresses with their subjects, the performance of their duties by the officials, the respect shown by superioresses for the laws on the manifestation of conscience and the reading of the prescribed decrees, the administration of temporal goods, the carrying out of the spiritual exercises, the observance of the various fasts and abstinences, and the cultivation of fraternal charity. There should also take place in every visitation an inspection of the buildings, and questions should be asked concerning their repair and arrangement.[50]

The visitor may not, however, propose questions on matters of conscience, nor may she demand that the occult faults of the supe-

---

[45] Canon 513, § 1.

[46] Larraona, "Commentarium Codicis," *CpR*, IX (1928), p. 25, nota 516; Schaefer, *De Religiosis*, p. 312, n. 148.

[47] Reilly, *The Visitation of Religious*, p. 149.

[48] Berutti, *Institutiones Iuris Canonici*, III, p. 71, n. 32.

[49] Canon 513, § 1; canon 2413, § 1.

[50] Augustine, *Commentary*, III, 138; Wernz-Vidal, *Ius Canonicum*, III, p. 125, n. 148; Geser, *The Canon Law Governing Communities of Sisters*, pp. 121-122, q. 365.

rioresses or of other members of the house be revealed to her unless a crime is involved that will eventually lead to the public detriment of the institute.[51]   In some institutes the religious renounce their right to the observance of secrecy concerning their occult faults on the part of their fellow religious, and the visitatrix could inquire even concerning such failings.[52]   The visitatrix should proceed in a kindly and benevolent manner.[53]   Her purpose is to correct by secret admonitions and salutary directives.[54]   Her interviews should be personal and private, and throughout the whole procedure secrecy should be preserved.[55]

The visitatrix, however, is a true superioress, and not merely an inspector or a reporter.[56]   She has a right to give formal precepts, and these, when her discretion suggests it, may be imposed in virtue of holy obedience. After the completion of her investigations she may draw up precepts which are to be carried out as she directs. Under the common law these precepts, to be obligatory, need not be put in writing, but for future examination a written record is recommended.[57]

Recourse from these decrees is available under the law, but their binding force is retained until a contrary decision by the higher authorities is given.[58]   Thus no pretext may be seized upon to justify a delay in putting them into effect. They must be obeyed first, and then recourse may be made. The same must be said of a command involving the performance of a penance.[59]

ARTICLE 4. THE QUINQUENNIAL REPORT

According to canon 510 every superioress general of communities of pontifical approval must send a report to the Holy See on the

---

[51] Fanfani, *De Iure Religiosorum*, p. 84, n. 72; Augustine, *op. cit.*, III, 139-140.

[52] Geser, *op. cit.*, p. 125, q. 377.

[53] Canon 345.

[54] Cocchi, *Commentarium*, IV, p. 64, n. 27.

[55] Augustine, *Commentary*, III, 141.

[56] Larraona, "Commentarium Codicis," *CpR*, IX (1928), 23-31.

[57] Reilly, *The Visitation of Religious*, p. 163.

[58] Canon 513, § 2.

[59] Cf. the article on removal from office, *supra*, pp. 64-65.

state of the institute. The person always responsible for these reports is the supreme moderator of the society. If the institute has but one house the obligation is not relaxed, since the superioress is nonetheless a superioress general of a congregation and is embraced by canon 510.[60]

The prescription binds also pontifical societies living in common although without vows. This is evident not only from canon 675, which states that these societies are subject to the laws of canons 490-530 regarding religious institutes with vows, but also from the decree of the Sacred Congregation of Religious which assigns particular years for these societies to make their reports.[61] On the contrary, the superioress of an independent monastery of nuns is not obliged. It is true she is a major superioress, but she cannot be said to be a superioress general.[62] The case would be different if the monasteries were united with a hierarchy established among those in authority under an abbess president. In that instance the latter would be a counterpart of the abbot president of a congregation of monasteries of men religious. Canon 510 specifically obliges the abbot president to make the report.

The report must be in writing,[63] and according to the law must be submitted every five years. This five year interval is the maximum time interval allowed. Constitutions may require that the report be submitted more often, and then these of course must be followed.[64] For such institutes there would be no obligation of submitting the report at the normally assigned five year periods.[65]

According to the decree *"Sancitum est,"* institutes of women religious are to make their reports as of January 1, 1923, and every

---

[60] Schaefer, *De Religiosis*, p. 299, n. 145; Creusen-Garesché-Ellis, *Religious Men and Women in the Code*, p. 65, n. 88.

[61] Decr., *"Sancitum est,"* 8 mart. 1922—*AAS*, XIV (1922), 161.

[62] Vermeersch-Creusen, *Epitome*, I, p. 453, n. 630; Coronata, *Institutiones*, I, p. 665, n. 540, nota 10; Fanfani, *De Iure Religiosorum*, p. 49, n. 37.

[63] Canon 510 requires a document, and thus an oral report would not be sufficient.

[64] Vermeersch-Creusen, *op. cit.*, I, p. 452, n. 630; Geser, *The Canon Law Governing Communities of Sisters*, p. 118, q. 354.

[65] Berutti, *Institutiones Iuris Canonici*, III, p. 69, n. 32; Creusen-Garesché-Ellis, *Religious Men and Women in the Code*, p. 65, n. 88.

fifth year thereafter, as follows: first year: Italy, Spain and Portugal; second year: France, Belgium, England, Ireland, and Holland; third year: all other countries in Europe; fourth year: North and South America (reports from the United States are thus due on the first and sixth years of each decade, i. e., in 1946, in 1951); fifth year: societies living in common without vows (from the United States in 1947, in 1952).

All reports are to be signed by the superioress general, the members of her council, and by the ordinary of the place where they reside.[66] The part of the ordinary is merely to testify to the authenticity of the document.[67] The report is to be sent to the Sacred Congregation of Religious, unless the institute is subject to the jurisdiction of the Sacred Congregation for the Propagation of the Faith, which then is exclusively competent for the receiving and the reviewing of the report.[68]

The form of the report is determined by a list of questions as published by the Sacred Congregation of Religious. The use of this form is obligatory for certain institutes. The arrangement of the questionnaire treats persons, property, and discipline.[69] If the report is being submitted for the first time, it should contain a history of the foundation of the institute, a statement on the facts of its approval by the Holy See, and it should be accompanied with a copy of the constitutions by which it is governed. Further, it should describe the internal government of the institute, the nature of the vows pronounced, and any changes in administration or in the constitutions that have taken place since the institute's foundation as well as any relaxations in the observance of the rule. It should be noted by what authority these modifications or relaxations were effected.[70]

[66] Canon 510.

[67] Larraona, "Commentarium Codicis," *CpR*, VIII (1927), 282.

[68] Schaefer, *De Religiosis*, p. 306, n. 147.

[69] *De quinquennali relatione a religionibus facienda*, 25 mart. 1922—*AAS*, XIV (1922), 161; an English version was published in *AAS*, XV (1923), 459. Other copies of the English text may be found in Bouscaren, *The Canon Law Digest*, I, 284, and in Creusen-Garesché-Ellis, *Religious Men and Women in the Code*, Appendix III, p. 299.

[70] S. C. de Rel., decr., "*Sancitum est*," 8 mart. 1922—*AAS*, XIV (1922), 161.

Institutes which were obliged to send a report to the Holy See before the promulgation of the Code are required to follow the form given by the Sacred Congregation of Religious. Other institutes, until they are given some further specific direction, are obliged to draw up their reports in a complete and truthful manner in a form that is best suited to their institute. Their reports are to be sufficiently complete, so that the Holy See can acquire a full knowledge of the material and also of the moral and disciplinary condition of the society.[71] Therefore it seems best that in preparing their reports all superioresses have before them the questions as drawn up by the Sacred Congregation.[72]

ARTICLE 5. DUTIES OF THE LOCAL SUPERIORESS

The specific duties of a local superioress are for the most part defined in the constitutions of her institute. Common law, however, over and above what these may state, places certain obligations upon her. First, she must take care to have the constitutions of the institute read publicly at least once a year on fixed days.[73] This may be done in the refectory or in some other place at a time when the community is gathered together. The obligation would be fulfilled even though one or other of the members were absent.[74] The custom of reading the customarily accepted summary of the constitutions may be considered sufficient.[75]

Secondly, also under canon 509, the superioress has an obligation to read publicly and to enforce any decrees which the Holy See will prescribe. This is not a promulgation of the decrees, but rather an imparting of the knowledge of what they contain, in order that they may be known and obeyed.[76] In reality all superioresses, no

---

[71] *Loc. cit.*

[72] Coronata, *Institutiones*, I, p. 666, n. 540.

[73] Canon 509, § 2, 1°.

[74] Berutti, *Institutiones Iuris Canonici*, III, p. 66, n. 32.

[75] Vermeersch-Creusen, *Epitome*, I, p. 451, n. 628; Creusen-Garesché-Ellis, *Religious Men and Women in the Code*, p. 62, n. 86.

[76] Schaefer, *De Religiosis*, p. 293, n. 144.

matter what their rank, have this obligation, but its fulfillment naturally falls to the local superioress.[77]

To be obliged to proceed to the reading of these decrees the local superioress need not have received any special communication from any higher authority within or outside the institute.[78] Once the local superioress is in possession of the official text, she must follow its directions. The reading should be from an authorized translation in the language spoken by the members of the community.[79] At times the execution of these decrees may require the action of several superioresses. The local superioress must then await the possibility of this coordinated activity before she proceeds to the public reading of them in her own house.[80]

Prior to the promulgation of the Code certain decrees of this kind existed. Their provisions, with some modifications, are now embodied in the common law. No obligation exists to continue reading them. Canon 509, § 2, 1°, refers to decrees which will be prescribed in the future. To date no such decree binds superioresses of women religious.[81] It is opportune to note at this point that superioresses, although not specifically in virtue of canon 509, have nevertheless an obligation to acquaint themselves and their subjects with a knowledge of the Code of Canon Law in those aspects which concern religious.[82] It is of absolute necessity that religious know the law if they are to keep it.

---

[77] Fanfani, *De Iure Religiosorum*, p. 138, n. 126; Geser, *The Canon Law Governing Communities of Sisters*, p. 116, q. 348.

[78] Wernz-Vidal, *Ius Canonicum*, III, p. 121, n. 143.

[79] Wernz-Vidal, *loc. cit.*; Creusen-Garesché-Ellis, *Religious Men and Women in the Code*, p. 62, n. 86.

[80] Vermeersch-Creusen, *Epitome*, I, p. 451, n. 628.

[81] Berutti (*Institutiones Iuris Canonici*, II, p. 66, n. 32), states that the decree of the Sacred Congregation of Religious regarding the life of externs of a monastery of nuns must be read at least four times a year. While it is true that these sisters must be informed of their obligations as given in this decree, and must conform to them, there does not seem to be any directive in the decree itself obliging that it be read publicly. For the text of the decree cf. *Jus Pontificium*, XIII (1933), 196. Bouscaren (*Canon Law Digest*, II, 170) gives a translation of the general preceptive clauses of the decree, but includes only a summary of its statutes.

[82] Coronata, *Institutiones*, I, p. 664, n. 540.

Besides bringing a knowledge of the constitutions and of the decrees of the Holy See to their subjects, local superioresses have an obligation to provide for the giving of catechetical instruction at least twice a month both to the lay sisters, i. e., as contrasted with choir sisters, and also the domestics living in the house, and over and above this that pious exhortations be given to all the sisters at the same intervals.[83] The instruction and the exhortations should not merely consist of spiritual reading, unless circumstances make this to be the only feasible arrangement.[84]

The superioress is not obliged to conduct these exercises herself. They may be given by the parish clergy or by the chaplain at her invitation or at least with her consent. If the domestics attend the parochial Mass, her obligation with regard to them seems adequately fulfilled.[85] If there are no lay sisters in the community, the precept of instruction would not bind.[86] It may be noted that, if the one who conducts these exercises can aptly join the instruction and the exhortations, it would not be contrary to the common law to effect such a conjoint presentation.[87]

Beyond the provisions regarding religious instruction and exhortations as found in the law of the Code, the Sacred Congregation of Religious has issued an Instruction to superioresses on the knowledge of Christian doctrine that must, under their diligent care, be made available to their subjects.[88]

In this Instruction the following points are stressed: (1) During the postulancy and the noviceship Christian doctrine shall be re-

---

[83] Canon 509, § 2, 2°.

[84] Coronata, *Institutiones*, I, p. 665, n. 540; Schaefer, *De Religiosis*, p. 295, n. 144 bis.

[85] Creusen-Garesché-Ellis, *Religious Men and Women in the Code*, p. 64, n. 87.

[86] Schaefer (*op. cit.*, p. 296, n. 144 bis), points out that canon 509, § 2, 2°, uses the technical term *"conversis,"* and that although all the members of an institute may be lay religious as contrasted with clerical religious, this canon embraces only those members who are lay religious as contrasted with choir religious.

[87] Vermeersch-Creusen, *Epitome*, I, p. 452, n. 629.

[88] *Ad supremos moderatores et moderatrices Religiosarum laicarum familiarium de obligatione subditos in doctrina Christiana rite imbuendi*, 25 nov. 1929— *AAS*, XXII (1930), 28-29.

viewed and learned thoroughly, and an examination shall be suc-
cessfully taken in proof of this before the profession; (2) after the
novitiate all who are to teach catechism must be so trained in this
subject and in the methods of teaching it that they shall be able to
pass an examination before the ordinary or his delegate; (3) the
program of preparation for this examination may follow that used
by the Vicariate of Rome; [89] and (4) if the teaching of Christian
doctrine is to be done by the religious in a parish and not in the
schools, then the members of the institute shall procure a testimonial
of fitness from the diocesan Curia.

Goyeneche remarks that the examination prescribed in number
(1) is determined in its matter by the superioress; that the prescript
of number (2) pertains only to those who are going to teach in
schools; and finally, that all books to be used and the methods of
administration to be employed are matters which rest entirely under
the authority of the bishop.[90]

[89] This program may be found in the *Periodica*, XIX (1929), 201-206.
[90] "Consultationes," *CpRM*, XVI (1935), 122.

CHAPTER VIII

ADMINISTRATION OF TEMPORAL GOODS

ARTICLE 1. ADMINISTRATION IN GENERAL

WITH specific reference to religious communities temporal administration may be defined as "the control or care of temporal goods of a religious institute that they may serve the purposes for which they were acquired." [1]

Temporal administration is divided into two general types: ordinary and extraordinary. Ordinary administration itself may be viewed from two aspects. First, it embraces all acts that are regularly necessary for the care of temporal goods.[2] This category includes all those acts which the accustomed manner of living demands, be it revenue or be it expenditure that is involved.[3] Secondly, it refers to all those acts which the regular administrators of any institute may perform validly in virtue of the power invested in them by virtue of their office.[4]

Extraordinary administration refers to all those acts of administration for which a special faculty must be received by the administrator from a higher authority in order that she may act validly. They are generally acts which have as their object the disposition of capital or the contraction of large debts, and which thus endanger the financial stability of an institute.[5] Extraordinary expenditures for building and repairs, even though the money was on hand and not funded as stable capital, would also constitute extraordinary administration.

[1] McManus, *The Administration of Temporal Goods in Religious Institutes*, The Catholic University of America Canon Law Studies, n. 109 (Washington, D. C.: The Catholic University of America, 1937), p. 79.

[2] Larraona, "Commentarium Codicis," *CpR*, XII (1931), 356.

[3] Vermeersch-Creusen, *Epitome*, I, p. 471, n. 605.

[4] McManus, *ibidem*, p. 80.

[5] McManus, *The Administration of Temporal Goods in Religious Institutes*, p. 82.

The Code points out to everyone who is called on to perform
acts of administration that it is her duty: (1) to see that the goods
placed in her care do not perish or suffer any damage; (2) to observe the norms of canon and civil law as well as the rules imposed
by a donor or by legitimate authority; (3) to collect all revenue due,
protect it, and spend it according to the mind of the founder and
the norms of law; (4) to invest with the consent of the proper authority all moneys remaining after expenses have been paid; (5) to
keep accounts in good order; and (6) to preserve in a safe place
the documents which serve as proof for the established rights and
acquired claims.[6]

In regard to the actual methods to be used, or the way of going
about the various acts of administration, the Code explicitly states
that these considerations are matters for regulations by the constitutions of each religious institute, and that once inscribed there they are
the law for that institute.[7] Thus the common law of the Church
concerning the norms of administration becomes identified with the
particular law of each institute. Constitutions are thus entrusted
with the determination of the details necessary both for the valid
and the licit acts of administration, with the exception of certain
explicit requirements contained in the Code itself.[8] The latter must
be obeyed,[9] but for the most part they appear only in cases in
which a higher authority external to the institute must be approached.[10]

Since a moral person cannot act for itself, administration pertains to that person who by office is commissioned to govern it. Thus
the administration of its very nature pertains to the religious superioress, whether she be the superioress general, the provincial, or the
local superioress, for all have the right of administration over either
the institute as a whole, or the province, or the individual house.[11]

---

[6] Canon 1523.

[7] Canon 532, § 1.

[8] Schaefer, *De Religiosis,* pp. 417-418, n. 195.

[9] Canon 1495, § 2.

[10] Larraona, "Commentarium Codicis," *CpR,* XII (1931), 355-356.

[11] Wernz-Vidal, *Ius Canonicum,* III, p. 172, n. 221; Schaefer, *De Religiosis,*
p. 415, n. 192.

For this natural right residing in the moral person and its accredited representation, the Code provides additional confirmation by explicitly stating that every superioress is competent to perform acts of administration.[12] However, it also decrees that the superioress should not as a general rule perform these acts personally. For this work there should be a specially appointed official or econome for each institute, for each province and for each house, namely, an official who has as her distinct office the duties pertaining to the administration of temporalities.[13] This is obviously a reasonable regulation, because the main concern of the superioress, and her first obligation, must always be the spiritual welfare of her subjects. Time does not permit her to give herself to the details of any other task.

While the superioress is then in virtue of her office competent to act in the sphere of administration, her main sphere of action in this regard assumes the form of supervision. It is her duty to see that the temporal needs of the community under her charge are effectively supplied and cared for, but she is to do this by her vigilance and direction of the official who is appointed to discharge this task directly and in detail. She must, of course, require regular reports of accounts and study them carefully. For more important acts she may demand that individual permission be obtained by the econome before an act is placed.[14] Her power, too, includes that of correction and punishment when officials appointed to the task of administration neglect their duty.[15] If in a given case the superioress should prefer to carry out a transaction personally or to perform a particular function pertaining to the administration of temporalities, as long as the act is one of ordinary administration for which no further faculty is required by the Code or particular law, she would act validly.[16]

Other limitations placed on the superioress, besides that which

---

[12] Canon 532, § 2.

[13] Canon 516, § 3; cf. *supra*, p. 102.

[14] McManus, *The Administration of Temporal Goods in Religious Institutes*, p. 89.

[15] Berutti, *Institutiones Iuris Canonici*, III, p. 116, n. 57.

[16] Canon 532, § 2.

restricts her in the regular personal performance of acts of administration, are found in the obligation placed upon her to confer with
others, and even to receive their consent, before authorizing certain
more important acts. Directions in this regard are noted in the
Code and in particular constitutions when it is prescribed that the
.superioress must consult her council or obtain their consent by
deliberative vote.[17] In other matters she is required .to receive the
consent of the local ordinary.[18] There are also certain acts for which
she requires the consent of the Holy See.[19] Finally, since the Code
canonizes civil law in matters of contracts, in many instances this,
law too must be followed by the superioress if she is to place an act
valid even in canon law.[20]

As a further point it may be mentioned that superioresses may
not appear in court in the name of their community except according to the norm of the constitutions.[21] Noval (1861-1938) remarked on this canon that if the constitutions merely forbid this,
the acts of the superioress would still be valid, since such acts are
part of the ordinary administration and therefore, according to canon
532, § 2, are within the competence of the superioress. If the constitutions are silent, he stated that the acts would be not only valid
but also licit.[22]

In the matter of contracting debts, the superioress must be most
assiduous in seeing that no debts are contracted, unless it is fore-
seen that they can be paid off without the lapse of a long duration of
time.[23] However, when a superioress acting in accordance with the
duties of her office gives permission for an act of administration, any
obligations that arise from this act bind the moral person which
she represents, and not herself.[24] On the contrary, if the supe-

[17] Creusen-Garesché-Ellis, *Religious Men and Women in the Code*, p. 119,
n. 160.

[18] Canon 523.

[19] Canon 534, § 1.

[20] Canon 1529.

[21] Canon 1653, § 6.

[22] *Commentarium Codicis Iuris Canonici*, lib. IV, *De Processibus* (2 vols.,
Romae: Marietti, 1920-1932), Pars I, *De Iudiciis*, p. 164, n. 261.

[23] Canon 536, § 5.

[24] Canon 536, § 1.

rioress authorizes or executes an act beyond the competence of her office, she herself is held responsible, and not her community, for the ensuing obligations.[25]

ARTICLE 2. INVESTMENTS

Every religious institute, its provinces, and individual houses are capable of acquiring temporal goods unless the constitutions impede or surrender this right.[26] It is left to the constitutions to determine the norms that each institute is to follow in the internal distribution of authority to acquire and to hold property,[27] but because of the risks involved and the danger of imprudent transactions, the Code sets down special regulations in the matter of acquisition by means of investment and alienation. The latter will be discussed in the next article; the former may be opportunely considered at this point. Investment is the allocating of the wealth or resources of an institute to the production of new wealth whereby the capital remains undiminished while yielding income.[28]

The process is clear in the purchase of stocks or bonds, but authors disagree whether bank deposits are also to be considered investments, and therefore governed by the laws controlling the latter. Augustine dismissed the question with the statement that to consider bank balances an investment would lead to absurdities.[29] Cocchi [30] and Coronata [31] hold that an investment exists only when permanence is apparent in the allocation of wealth, and that this is not found in a deposit in a bank that may be withdrawn at will. Vermeersch-Creusen are of the same opinion, for as they say, a bank deposit is a means of protecting money rather than an investment.[32]

---

[25] Coronata, *Institutiones*, I, p. 701, n. 552; Fanfani, *De Iure Religiosorum*, p. 175, n. 157.

[26] Canon 531.

[27] Canon 532, § 1.

[28] Larraona, "Commentarium Codicis," *CpR*, XII (1931), 436; Schaefer, *De Religiosis*, p. 419, n. 196; McManus, *The Administration of Temporal Goods in Religious Institutes*, p. 91.

[29] *Commentary*, III, 181.

[30] *Commentarium*, IV, p. 102, n. 54.

[31] *Institutiones*, I, p. 693, n. 559.

[32] *Epitome*, I, p. 470, n. 652.

Other authors favor the opposite opinion on the ground that, since interest accrues from the capital, bank deposits have the nature of an investment.[33]   McManus distinguishes between the two conflicting opinions, saying that if the deposit is made merely for the purpose of convenience or of security, it is not to be considered an investment; but that if, on the other hand, its purpose is to make the money which is banked productive, it must be considered as an investment, and the regulations of the Code controlling the latter must be followed.[34]   To the writer it seems that the small rate of interest paid by the banks today can hardly be considered in the light of income. This conclusion, not to mention their present security, would seem to exclude bank deposits from the regulations of the common law on investments.

Canon 533 decrees that, in certain cases, before investments can be made, the superioress must receive the consent of the local ordinary. These cases will be seen in detail, but first it may be said that this consent may be oral or in writing,[35] and it may be received by the competent superioress personally or through a delegate.[36] Moreover, these regulations bind whether the investment to be made is an initial venture or whether it is a change from an old to a new one.[37]

First on the list of those superioresses whom canon 533 obliges to obtain this permission are the superioresses of all monasteries of nuns and the superioresses of diocesan institutes. They must approach the local ordinary before each investment. If the monastery is subject to a regular superior, his consent is also necessary.[38]   The nuns referred to include those who are professed with solemn vows and also those who, under papal indult, are professed with simple vows.[39]

The question arises whether not only the local superioress of

---

[33] Schaefer, *De Religiosis*, p. 419, n. 196; Fanfani, *De Iure Religiosorum*, p. 172, n. 155; Geser, *The Canon Law Governing Communities of Sisters*, p. 174, n. 540.

[34] *The Administration of Temporal Goods in Religious Institutes*, pp. 94-95.

[35] Schaefer, *De Religiosis*, p. 421, n. 197.

[36] McManus, *op. cit.*, p. 96.

[37] Canon 533, § 2.

[38] Canon 533, § 1, 1°.

[39] Berutti, *Institutiones Iuris Canonici*, III, p. 117, n. 58.

diocesan institutes must obtain this consent, but also the provincial and the superioress general. The majority of the authors does not discuss the point, evidently seeing no difficulty in the canon in this respect, but Larraona takes the stand that only the local superioress of diocesan institutes is obliged in the matter. He bases his opinion on the wording of canon 535, § 3, 1°, which, in speaking of the local ordinary's right to review the financial status of diocesan communities, refers to the religious house rather than to the province or institute as a whole.[40] It is difficult to see the justification of this view, for first of all canon 533, § 1, 1°, speaks specifically of the superioress of a diocesan institute without any qualification of her rank.[41] Moreover, McManus sums up well the reasons why the provincial and the superioress general are likewise included.[42] Diocesan institutes, which are usually far more inexperienced and less developed than pontifical institutes, would thus in the absence of any dependence on the local ordinary be subject to fewer restrictions than the latter in regard to investments. All pontifical institutes are bound by the quinquennial report to indicate in detail to the Sacred Congregation the extent and character of their investments. Institutes of diocesan approval do not make this report.[43] Further, the local ordinary bears to the diocesan institute a position analogous to that held by the Holy See in relation to pontifical institutes, and under this aspect his jurisdiction extends to the province and to the institute as a whole as well as to individual houses. Finally, since investments are ordinarily made in all institutes by the superioress of the province and by the superioress general rather than by the local superioress, the law would hardly omit the former from its regulation, which aims at protecting the property of the institute. It is difficult to see how any other view is tenable.

While the law demands the permission of the local ordinary for every investment or change of investment in an institute of diocesan approval, it does not seem contrary to the law if for small amounts a general permission would be granted. Thus the local ordinary may

---

[40] "Commentarium Codicis," *CpR*, XII (1931), 440-441.
[41] Cf. Schaefer, *De Religiosis*, p. 420, n. 197.
[42] *The Administration of Temporal Goods in Religious Institutes*, p. 96.
[43] Canon 510.

establish a set sum and specific types of investments for which a blanket authorization exists.[44]

As to investments made by institutes of pontifical approval, the legislator in the Code, aware of their usually more financially acute internal hierarchy, is far less demanding. The consent of the local ordinary is demanded, in their case, only for the investment of dowries.[45] The dowry is the money or property brought to a religious institute by a postulant for her support.[46] The superioress must, after the religious has made her first profession, place this money in a safe and fruitful investment.[47] Before doing this, she must take the matter up with her council, and receive the consent of the local ordinary as to the particular means of investment.[48] The consent of the council is not specifically required by the Code; thus consultation suffices.[49] At no time may the superioress use the capital of the dowry before the death of the religious, unless the consent of the Holy See has been received.[50]

The particular superioress obligated by this law is the provincial or the superioress general. Canon 550, § 1, indicates this in noting that the administration of dowries is to take place at the residence of either the provincial or the superioress general. In monasteries of nuns the obligation of course is imposed upon the superioress of the house.

While in the general matter of investments as discussed above the superioresses of nuns of diocesan institutes must receive the consent of the local ordinary for all investments, and the superioresses of pontifically approved communities for the investment of dowries,

---

[44] Berutti, *Institutiones Iuris Canonici*, III, p. 117, n. 58; Creusen-Garesché-Ellis, *Religious Men and Women in the Code*, pp. 119-120, n. 161.

[45] Canon 533, § 1, 2°.

[46] Canon 547, § 1.

[47] Canon 549.

[48] Canon 549: Superioresses of nuns and of diocesan institutes must receive permission for the investment of dowries just as for any other investment, and, in the case of the former, the permission must be obtained not only from the local ordinary but also from the regular superior of the order of men religious to whom they may perchance be subject.

[49] Vromant, *De Bonis Ecclesiae Temporalibus* (Louvain: Desbarax, 1927), n. 255.

[50] Canon 549.

special regulations are made in canon 533, § 1, 3°, for all local superioresses of religious congregations in regard to the investment of funds that have been received for the furtherance of divine worship or the promotion of a local charity. Under its provisions, whenever property, money, or other things convertible into property or money, are donated with the intention that the income from them is to be used for divine worship or charity in the neighborhood, the superioress of the house to which the donation has been given must obtain the consent of the bishop before investing it. In reference to works of charity these include the spiritual and corporal works of mercy to be performed in the locality of the religious house.

Some authors interpret this reference to locality as including the whole diocese where the religious house is established.[51] Others accept the word as designating a more limited area, as for example the city or the town in which the house is situated.[52] The broader interpretation seems more in line with the normal exercise of the bishop's jurisdiction which extends to the whole diocese.[53]

Much clearer is the fact that only funds donated to an individual house are in question. Consequently, if the donation is made to a province or to the institute as a whole, the superioress of a province or the superioress general of a pontifical institute may administer it without further permission.[54]

Lastly, in canon 533, § 1, 4°, the Code requires that every religious, and therefore every superioress, must receive the consent of the local ordinary to invest any money given to a parish or a mission or for their benefit. The law embraces in this restriction all types of religious, exempt and non-exempt, while in section 3 of this canon the law extends only to religious congregations. Again, the donor must have made a specific designation in the making of the gift to a specific mission. The case would not be the same

---

[51] Vermeersch-Creusen, *Epitome*, I, p. 472, n. 656; Schaefer, *De Religiosis*, p. 424, n. 197.

[52] Larraona, "Commentarium Codicis," *CpR*, XIII (1932), 34; Coronata, *Institutiones*, I, p. 694, n. 559, nota 7.

[53] Cf. McManus, *The Administration of Temporal Goods in Religious Institutes*, pp. 108-109.

[54] Fanfani, *De Iure Religiosorum*, p. 173, n. 155; Coronata, *op. cit.*, I, p. 694, n. 559, nota 4; Schaefer, *op. cit.*, p. 422, n. 197.

if the donor's intention as expressed was for the missions in general.[55]
The local ordinary authorized to give permission in the case of canon
533, § 1, 4°, is the bishop under whose jurisdiction the beneficiary
mission exists.[56]

ARTICLE 3. ALIENATION

Alienation in the canonical sense is any act by which there is a
transfer of ownership of ecclesiastical property to another proprietor,
or any contract made by an ecclesiastical moral person from which
the ecclesiastical property of that person can become less secure.[57]
Thus acts of alienation would be constituted by sale, exchange, gift,
lease, mortgage, assumption of debt, and similar contracts.

Certain preliminary requisites are prescribed in the Code as
necessary to be fulfilled before a superioress may proceed with the
formalities necessary for an act of alienation. First, she must ascertain that a just cause exists for alienation; this means urgent
necessity, the evident utility of the Church, or the performance of
a work of piety.[58] Secondly, there must be an appraisal made in
writing by skilled men of unimpeachable reputation and integrity.[59]
The choice of these men seems to be within the province of the
superioress, who in virtue of her office is competent to authorize the
procedure preliminary to the actual petition to alienate. Thirdly,
permission must be obtained from the superior whom the law makes
competent for the specific case.[60] This superior may be, as will be
seen shortly, the Holy See, the local ordinary, or one of the internal
superioresses of the community as designated by the constitutions.

In all acts of alienation the Code requires that the price accepted
must not be less than the estimated value set by the experts.[61] It

---

[55] Vermeersch-Creusen, *Epitome,* I, pp. 472-473, n. 656; Schaefer, *De Religiosis,* p. 426, n. 197; Fanfani, *De Iure Religiosorum,* p. 173, n. 155.

[56] Wernz-Vidal, *Ius Canonicum,* III, p. 177, n. 266; Berutti, *Institutiones
Iuris Canonici,* III, p. 118, n. 58; Augustine, *Commentary,* III, 182.

[57] Cf. Schaefer, *op. cit.,* pp. 427-428, n. 199; Augustine, *ibid.,* pp. 183-184;
Creusen-Garesché-Ellis, *Religious Men and Women in the Code,* p. 121, n. 162.

[58] Canon 1530, § 1, 2°.

[59] Canon 1530, § 1, 1°.

[60] Canon 1530, § 1, 3°.

[61] Canon 1531, § 1.

is not forbidden, of course, provided that no injustice be involved, to accept a higher price than that of the estimate. This is evident in the prescription that the transfer of property is to be made by public auction and awarded to the highest bidder, or that at least advance notice of sale be given, unless circumstances demand another method as more advisable.[62] After the act of alienation has been completed, the Code requires that the sum received be placed in a secure and useful investment.[63] As to the making of this investment the requirements reviewed in the preceding article must be observed.

It is the practice of the Holy See at the time it authorizes the act of alienation to note the obligation of the safe investment of the proceeds, or to grant the permission necessary to use the money otherwise. Larraona asserts that when, with the particular case warranting such action, the act of authorization does not come from the Holy See but from an internal superioress, the latter also gives permission if the money is to be used for a purpose other than that of its investment, provided that this is necessary.[64] No formula, he states, exists in the files of the Sacred Congregation of Religious for this permission, and superioresses have always acted without it unchecked by further instruction from the Holy See.

As was noted above, when permission from a higher superior is required for the execution of an act of alienation, this must be obtained if the validity of the act is to be properly assured. Moreover, when the petition is presented to the higher superior, then also for the sake of insuring the validity of the transaction, information must be included regarding all existing debts and obligations that currently burden the moral person.[65] If the alienation concerns real property, then the superioress asking the permission must state, to render the subsequent act of alienation valid, whether any parts of it have previously been alienated.[66]

In a letter addressed by the Apostolic Delegate at Washington,

---

[62] Canon 1531, § 2.
[63] Canon 1531, § 3.
[64] "Commentarium Codicis," *CpR*, XIII (1932), 360-361.
[65] Canon 534, § 2.
[66] Canon 1532, § 4.

D. C., to all religious superiors in the United States, dated November 13, 1936, the following instructions were given with reference to the contents of petitions for permission to execute contracts of alienation.[67]

> The petition which must be presented to the Holy See, according to the provisions of canon 534, for permission and authorization to incur such obligations, must obtain *definite and clear statements of the following facts*:
> 1. The *reason* for contracting the debt or assuming the obligation.
> 2. The *nature* of the debt or obligation. A mere general statement does not comply with the requirements for an explicit declaration of intention. For example, a mere statement that permission for a loan is required does not satisfy the requirements, if an intention exists to issue bonds or debentures.
> 3. The *name* of the person, firm, or corporation with whom the debt or obligation is to be contracted.
> *Moreover, the Sacred Congregation requires the following additional information*:
> 4. The proposed terms of meeting the debt or obligation. This requires a detailed and truthful statement of the arrangements for extinguishing such obligations both as to interest requirements and the principal debt. This requirement demands a statement of the time contemplated for complete payment. In this regard, attention is to be called to canon 536, § 5, which warns Superiors not to allow the contracting of debts unless it is certain that the *interest* on them may be met from *current revenue* and that *within a reasonable time* the *capital* may be paid off by means of a lawful amortization fund. For example:
> (a) Loans—the plan of amortization must be presented.
> (b) Annuities—the amounts, the plan of investing the funds and interest arrangement, and plans for meeting annual payment, etc., must be stated in detail.
> 5. The *economic condition* of the petitioner, which must be illustrated by the following exhibits:
> (a) A balance sheet of current assets and liabilities. The value of each asset ought to be stated at the current price, not at the purchase or nominal price; e.g., bonds should be listed at the current quotation on the exchange; real estate should be listed according to the tax assessment, depreciation, income, etc.
> (b) A statement of receipts and expenditures over a sufficient period of time to give an accurate estimate of normal receipts and expenditures.

[67] Bouscaren, *The Canon Law Digest*, II, 164, n. IV.

(c) A separate list of the obligations which do not appear under (a); e.g., obligations as guarantor, surety, trustee, bondsman, etc. This information is required in order to estimate all the certain or contingent obligations of the petitioner, particularly with reference to the rule regarding coalescence, supra, n. III.

If the petitioner fails to declare in the petition the debts and obligations which actually encumber the institute, Province, or religious house for which the indult or permission is sought, *canon 534, § 2, of the Code of Canon Law declares the apostolic indult or the permission of the Superior null and void.*

Canon 534, § 1, decrees that in order to alienate precious objects, to alienate property whose estimated value is in excess of $6,000, or to contract debts or obligations beyond the same sum, an apostolic indult is required under pain of nullity. Canon 1497, § 2, defines precious objects as those things which have a notable value because of artistic or historical reasons, or because of the material of which they are constructed. The words, "notable value," seem justly interpreted today as synonymous with a sum in excess of $200.[68]

Closely allied with precious objects, and likewise subject to alienation only by papal indult, are important relics and precious images.[69] These relics consist of the body, head, arm, forearm, heart, tongue, hand, leg, or that part of the body of a martyr which was subject to suffering, provided that it is entire and notable.[70] Precious images are those in churches or public oratories, noteworthy because of their antiquity, their artistic value, or the veneration in which people hold them.[71] No relic may be sold, but for a transfer of the relics and precious images described above to another church, permission, under penalty of an invalid act, if the permission is not sought, must be received from the Holy See.

The regulations of canon 534, § 1, regarding the alienation of goods other than precious objects state that when the value involved is above $6,000, then for a valid transaction the administrator must

---

[68] Creusen-Garesché-Ellis, *Religious Men and Women in the Code*, p. 122, n. 163; Schaefer, *De Religiosis*, p. 431, n. 204; Fanfani, *De Iure Religiosorum*, p. 177, n. 158.

[69] Canon 1281, § 1.

[70] Canon 1281, § 2.

[71] Canon 1280.

receive the consent of the Holy See. Included under the scope of this law are all ecclesiastical properties, all contracts of debts, and all obligations. If the value of an individual piece of property or of a contract in itself is not in excess of the specified $6,000, then, in the event that other alienations are contemplated that cumulatively would exceed that total value, the sum of the component items would be regulated by the requirements for alienations of property whose value exceeds $6,000.[72] Further, both the issuing of bonds or debentures, and also the acceptance of annuities, are governed by canon 534, and this holds true whether the issue or acceptance involves $6,000 under one transaction, or under a series of transactions through a coalescence of separate negotiations.[73]

Special regulations are found in the legislation of the Code for the contracts of renting and leasing. For these cases the law decrees that, when the period for which the contract is made extends beyond nine years, and the yearly sum received totals more than $6,000, permission must be obtained from the Holy See for the valid execution of the contract.[74]

While the superioress of religious institutes of pontifical approval is under no obligation in the cases just noted, to approach any other external authority than the Holy See, unless her constitutions prescribe otherwise, on the other hand, if the institute is one of nuns or one of merely diocesan approval, then, besides the consent of the Holy See, the superioress must also obtain in writing that of the local ordinary and of the regular superior.[75]

For acts of alienation in which the intervention of the Holy See is not involved, that is, acts of alienation which do not affect precious objects or stable capital in excess of $6,000, the law prescribes that the necessary permission is that which is given in writing by the superioress designated by the constitutions, provided that she has the consent of her council manifested in a secret vote.[76] Superioresses

---

[72] P. C. I., 20 iul. 1929—*AAS*, XXI (1929), 574; Letter of the Apostolic Delegate, Nov. 13, 1936—Bouscaren, *The Canon Law Digest*, II, 163, n. III.

[73] Letter of the Apostolic Delegate, Nov. 13, 1936—Bouscaren, *op. cit.*, II, 162-163, n. I.

[74] Canon 1541, § 2, 1°.

[75] Canon 534, § 1.

[76] Canon 534, § 1.

of nuns and of diocesan communities, however, must also have the consent of the local ordinary and of the regular superior of the order of men religious to which the nuns (not the sisters of congregations of diocesan approval) may perchance be subject.[77]

The same prescriptions, as to the permissions required and the superioress from whom they must be obtained, holds for contracts of rental and lease, if the time period is not above nine years, or, in the event that it is beyond nine years, if the yearly rental does not exceed $6,000.[78]   These permissions of the superioress and, in the case of diocesan communities, of the local ordinary, again are required for the validity of the transactions.   The same is to be said of the permissions of the local ordinary in the case of monasteries of nuns, and of the permissions of the superior of the order of men religious to whom they may by chance be subject.[79]   If, however, the alienation involves only a small sum, the constitutions may well determine the freedom of local superioresses to act without further formalities.[80]

At the beginning of this article it was noted that gifts are also included among the various acts to be considered as alienation. Canon 537 specifically states that all religious are forbidden to give away anything belonging to a religious house, province, or institute, except as alms or in the interests of some other just cause.   Even in the instance of the two exceptions mentioned, the norms of the constitutions must be followed, and permission must be received from the superioress.   This law binds the superioress herself, though at times she may decide that her duty requires her to make certain donations out of charity or gratitude.[81]

A penalty of excommunication, though not reserved, is incurred by any administrator who, knowing the law and its penalty, presumes without first having obtained the consent of the Holy See to dispose of any precious object or to make a transaction of alienation in which

---

[77] Canon 534, § 1.

[78] Canon 1541, § 2, 1°.

[79] Canon 1530, § 1, 3°.

[80] Coronata, *Institutiones*, I, p. 698, n. 560.

[81] Creusen-Garesché-Ellis, *Religious Men and Women in the Code*, p. 125, n. 168.

the value involved exceeds $6,000.[82]   When the conditions noted above, as postulated for the incurring of the penalty, are fulfilled, the penalty falls on all who perform such an act or wrongfully authorize its performance.   Thus the penalty could embrace the administrator, the higher superioress, and the members of her council.

If the unlawful alienation involves a sum over $200 but under $6,000, any superioress who culpably ignores the requisite formalities of the law must be deprived of her office and in other ways amply punished by the competent higher superioress.[83]

If the sum illegitimately alienated is under $200, the proper superior should choose fitting penalties.[84]   The Code does not specify which superior is competent to impose these penalties.   Authors generally fail to treat the question.   In view of the lack of any norm, it seems that the superior competent to authorize the act of alienation would likewise be competent to impose penalties on the person who neglected to obtain the necessary authorization.

ARTICLE 4. THE ACCOUNT OF ADMINISTRATION

Superioresses in their capacity as administrators of the temporal goods of their communities are in no sense proprietors or owners of them.   It is to be expected, then, that they are required not only to discharge the duties of their office faithfully, but also to give an account of their acts to higher authority.[85]   Reports required within the community itself, are left, as to method and frequency, to the determination of the individual constitutions.   In the common law there are also certain prescriptions in this regard.

Canon 1499, § 2, states that the ownership of all ecclesiastical goods rests under the authority of the Holy See, which has, in consequence, a right to a knowledge of the administration of all ecclesiastical goods.   At times it exercises this right directly; at other times through the local ordinary.   Exercising this right directly, it requires the supreme moderator of every pontifically approved re-

---

[82] Canon 2347, 3°.

[83] Canon 2347, 2°.

[84] Canon 2347, 1°.

[85] Cf. Coronata, *Institutiones*, I, p. 699, n. 561; Wernz-Vidal, *Ius Canonicum*, III, pp. 183-184, n. 234.

ligious institute to submit a report on its economic condition at least every five years.[86] In the formula of questions prescribed by the Sacred Congregation of Religious for the execution of the quinquennial report, a detailed account of the financial condition is required.[87]

Canon 535 enacts the prescriptions regulating the return of financial accounts to the local ordinary. If the community is a monastery of nuns, the superioress must at least once a year, and more often if the constitutions call for it, give an account to the local ordinary of her entire administration of the temporal goods of her monastery. If a regular superior enjoys jurisdiction over the community, he must also, under the provisions of this canon, receive a report.[88] In the latter case, then, two financial reports must be returned, one to each ordinary.[89]

In all other communities of women religious the superioress must give an account to the bishop, not of her entire economic administration, but of certain funds, among which are enumerated the funds connected with dowries. As to these, the report is made at the time of his visitation, or also more often if he should require it.[90] The superioress responsible for this report is either the provincial superioress, or the superioress general, according as the obligation of administering these funds falls on the one or the other.[91]

A second type of funds regarding which the making of a report of their economic administration is called for includes all funds donated for the furtherance of divine worship, for the promotion of a local charity, or for the alleviation of the needs of a specific mission. The local ordinary may require an accounting as to the administration of them, and when this is demanded the local superioress must comply with the terms.[92] Concerning other matters of economic administration, the superioress of pontifically approved institutes are not obliged to render an account to anyone other than the Holy See.

---

[86] Canon 510; cf. *supra*, pp. 111-114.

[87] Cf. *supra*, p. 113.

[88] Canon 535, § 1, 1°.

[89] P. C. I., 24 nov. 1920—*AAS*, XII (1920), 575.

[90] Canon 535, § 2.

[91] Canon 550, § 1; cf. *supra*, p. 125.

[92] Canon 535, § 3, 2°; cf. *supra*, p. 126.

As has been seen throughout the treatment of the administration of temporal goods, it is the general tendency of the common law to place more detailed obligations on superioresses of communities of diocesan approval in relation to external authority than on superioresses of religious institutes of pontifical approval. In the matter of rendering accounts, the law, in accord with this tendency, states that the local ordinary has a right to be fully aware at all times of the financial status of all institutes of diocesan approval.[93]

Since canon 535, § 3, 1°, in speaking of the right of the local ordinary to investigate the financial conditions of diocesan communities, refers only to the religious house, the question arises in respect of his relations in this matter with the institute as a whole. Authors seem to agree that even the accounts of the general administration of the institute must be submitted to his inspection, though there is no explicit precept to this effect in the general law of the Code. The reasons given by the authors are the almost unqualified subjection of diocesan institutes to the jurisdiction of the bishop together with his concomitant duty of vigilance,[94] and the analogy which they find in regard to this obligation between the religious house and the institute as a whole.[95]

While it is admitted among the authors that an account of the general administration must be submitted by superioresses of institutes of diocesan approval if such a report is requested by the local ordinary, disagreement is found among them regarding the particular bishop to whom the superioress general is to make the report when the institute is polydiocesan. Schaefer holds that all the bishops of all the dioceses in which the diocesan community has become established have cumulatively the duty of vigilance over the general administration of the institute.[96] McManus merely states that the bishops may appoint one of their number to act

---

[93] Canon 535, § 3, 1°.

[94] Vermeersch-Creusen, *Epitome*, I, p. 476, n. 660; Schaefer, *De Religiosis*, p. 441, n. 209; Gallik, *The Rights and Duties of Bishops Regarding Diocesan Sisterhoods*, p. 78.

[95] Coronata, *Institutiones*, I, p. 700, n. 561, nota 4; Wernz-Vidal, *Ius Canonicum*, III, p. 184, n. 235, nota 27.

[96] *Loc. cit.*

as a delegate.[97]   Gallik looks upon the matter as pertaining to the whole institute, and therefore as constituting under canon 495, § 2, the joint concern and right of all the bishops into whose dioceses the institute has spread.[98]   Coronata,[99] Vermeersch-Creusen [100] and Wernz-Vidal, on the other hand,[101] state without further amplification that the right is that of the ordinary of the diocese in which the mother house exists.

To the writer the second view seems the more tenable one.   The common law is indeed not specific in this matter, and consequently leaves a doubt as to the person of the local ordinary authorized to act. Canon 495, § 2, in a general provision, states that the bishops of all the dioceses into which an institute of diocesan approval has spread are to act in unison when a modification of the constitutions is contemplated.   It cannot be said, however, that the inspection of the financial accounts in any way approaches so fundamental a factor.   Therefore canon 495, § 2, does not seem necessarily to be applicable in this situation.   On the contrary, when in 1921 the Sacred Congregation of Religious was asked who should preside at the election of the superioress general of polydiocesan institutes of diocesan approval, it gave a response that seems to favor the opposite view.[102]

The act concerning which the question was asked is certainly one that involves the institute as a whole, since it carries with it for those entrusted with its execution the power of confirming or of rejecting the particular religious candidate elected to office.   The Sacred Congregation, in solving the doubt proposed, replied that the bishop authorized to preside is the local ordinary of the diocese in which the election is held.   This response surely does not show any absolute policy in the Sacred Congregation in support of cumulative action in all matters affecting institutes of diocesan approval when they have become polydiocesan in character.   Rather it is a fair

[97] *The Administration of Temporal Goods in Religious Institutes*, p. 163.

[98] *Op. cit.*, p. 82.

[99] *Institutiones*, I, p. 700, n. 561, nota 7.

[100] *Epitome*, I, p. 476, n. 660.

[101] *Ius Canonicum*, III, p. 184, n. 235, nota 27.

[102] *De celebratione capituli generalis in congregationibus iuris diocesani*, 2 iul. 1921—*AAS*, XIII (1921), 481.

indication that there are matters in which the authorization to act rests solely with the bishop of the diocese in which the mother house is located.

In view of this response, and in the absence of any specific direction in the common law as to the person of the local ordinary entrusted with vigilance concerning the economic administration of polydiocesan institutes of diocesan approval, it seems that a norm could be taken from the procedure approved by the Sacred Congregation in the matter of election. Thus the local ordinary of the diocese in which the mother house exists seems to be the one entrusted with the right to investigate the financial condition of the institute as a whole whenever his discretion suggests it.

Accordingly the superioress would be obliged to supply to the latter ordinary the necessary information. This would further guarantee the protection for the institute which the lawgiver constantly seeks in matters of temporal administration. If one or the other of the remaining bishops in whose dioceses houses of the institute have been established, would sense the need of information on the financial status of the community, he would not thereby be prevented, in cases in which it would be of advantage to him to have access to it, from obtaining the desired information from the superioress general, or, perhaps even preferably, from the ordinary in whose diocese the mother house is located.

ARTICLE 5. ERECTION AND SUPPRESSION OF HOUSES

The erection and suppression of religious houses is not considered in the Code of Canon Law as a part of the temporal administration of goods, but it is closely allied with it. These acts impose many duties of an economic nature on the superioress, and consequently may appropriately be considered in connection with acts of temporal administration.

Religious institutes constantly increase in membership and in the number of their houses.[103] The greater part of the acts incident

---

[103] The erection and suppression of an institute, as also of a province, is so peculiarly the prerogative of the Holy See or of the local ordinary, that these acts will not be treated in this work. The only action of the superioress in this matter appropriate for consideration in this work is the petition addressed by her to the competent authority for the necessary permission.

to any negotiation for the erection or the suppression of religious houses pertains to authorities outside the community such as the Holy See and the local ordinary. Much, therefore, relating to those acts will be passed over at this point as not pertinent to this work.[104] Reference will be made, then, solely to the duties and the obligations of the superioress in the procedure of the foundation or of the suppression of religious houses.

Before distinguishing between diocesan, pontifical, and exempt communities, one may indicate in general that, while all congregations once legitimately established are capable of erecting new houses, before this is to be attempted there must be evidence that the new house will provide suitable living quarters and that sufficient means will be available for its continued maintenance.[105] The Code is not specific as to who should make the decision regarding the fulfillment of these conditions. Fanfani holds that the right to make it belongs to the local ordinary.[106] Other canonists feel rather that the matter deserves joint action on the part of both the institute and the local ordinary.[107] Joint action seems to provide the better method to carry out the mind of the legislator, since the local ordinary is in the better position to pass a judgment which is based on the needs of the diocese, while the superioress can add much with regard to the needs of the community.

On the contrary, actual permission to erect a new religious house must come entirely from outside the community. The Code does not determine who is to draw up the petition which requests the

---

[104] Cf. Flanagan, *The Canonical Erection of Religious Houses*, The Catholic University of America Canon Law Studies, n. 179 (Washington, D. C.: The Catholic University of America Press, 1943); Farrell, *The Rights and Duties of the Local Ordinary Regarding Congregations of Women Religious of Pontifical Approval*, pp. 58-75; Gallik, *The Rights and Duties of Bishops Regarding Diocesan Sisterhoods*, pp. 45-56.

[105] Canon 496.

[106] *De Iure Religiosorum*, p. 30, n. 21.

[107] Coronata, *Institutiones*, I, 633, n. 523; Larraona, "Commentarium Codicis," *CpR*, V (1924), 332; Farrell, *The Rights and Duties of the Local Ordinary Regarding Congregations of Women Religious of Pontifical Approval*, p. 58; Flanagan, *op. cit.*, p. 43.

needed permission for the new foundation. The constitutions of the individual institutes must be consulted to ascertain the person so authorized. Normally it is the superioress general. The procedure to be followed by her varies with the type of the institute in question. If it is an exempt community, consent must be received in writing from both the Holy See and the local ordinary.[108] If it is a congregation of pontifical approval, consent in writing from the local ordinary is sufficient. The same holds for diocesan congregations.[109]

Canon 497, § 1, states implicitly that the erection of a monastery of nuns always requires the approbation of the Holy See. From this law it would seem that no exception could be permitted in regard to the erection of such a monastery. However, the fact that in some countries communities of nuns are permitted to pronounce only simple vows gives rise to a divergence of opinion among canonists as to the procedure that the superioresses of nuns of simple vows must follow.

Some canonists hold that no distinction is to be made, in this respect, between them and nuns who are professed with solemn vows, and that the approval of the Holy See must be sought by the former as well as by the latter.[110] Other canonists feel that the local ordinary is competent to grant permission for the erection of a monastery when the community of nuns by papal prescription pronounces only simple vows.[111]

Those who hold that the consent of the Holy See is required in all cases base their view on a decree of the Sacred Congregation of Religious which declared that the nuns of Belgium and France are true monastic nuns despite their simple vows authorized by way of exception by the Holy See.[112] Those who hold the contrary opinion claim that this decree did not alter the relationship of their dependence on local ordinaries by which these nuns are bound.

---

[108] Canon 497, § 1.

[109] Canon 497, § 1.

[110] Schaefer, *De Religiosis*, p. 158, n. 81; Berutti, *Institutiones Iuris Canonici*, III, p. 33, n. 14; Vermeersch-Creusen, *Epitome*, I, p. 437, n. 607.

[111] Larraona, "Commentarium Codicis,"—*CpR*, V (1924), 421; Maroto, "Annotationes,"—*CpR*, II (1921), 168.

[112] Decr., *Circa moniales in Gallia et in Belgio*, 23 iun. 1923—*AAS*, XV (1923), 357.

While the matter remains controverted it is to be observed that the text of canon 497, § 1, speaks of nuns without any qualifications, and the decree of the Sacred Congregation of Religious noted above includes the nuns professed with simple vows under this title. Therefore, according to the first norm of interpretation, namely, the clear text of the law, it seems that for the erection of a new monastery all nuns need the approval of the Holy See, and that it is the duty of the superioress to obtain it.[113]

In the case of diocesan communities a multiple permission is frequently necessary, and this gives rise to the need of clarity as to the person from whom the superioress is to seek the permission to erect a new house. This situation confronts the superioress when a community seeks to open a house in a diocese in which the community has not yet become established. In this case two permissions are required, namely, that of the local ordinary of the diocese in which the mother house is situated, and that of the local ordinary of the diocese in which the new house is to be erected. Thus it may be said that whenever a diocesan institute plans to open a new house, if that house is to be the first of the institute in the diocese, these two permissions must always be obtained by the superioress.[114] The erection of additional houses in the same diocese require only the permission of the local ordinary of the diocese in which the house is to be erected.[115]

When the superioress has received the necessary permission or permissions to erect a new house, she obtains with this consent the right for the community to conduct all the works proper to it. This is so, however, only if the local ordinary has not placed restrictions upon that right at the time his consent was given, and has not restrictively determined a specific work as the one to be carried out in the newly erected house.[116] For example, if the community is devoted to both teaching and nursing, the local ordinary could

---

[113] Cf. canon 18.

[114] Canon 495, § 1.

[115] Larraona, "Commentarium Codicis,"—*CpR*, V (1924), 326-327; Gallik, *The Rights and Duties of Bishops Regarding Diocesan Sisterhoods*, p. 51; Flanagan, *The Canonical Erection of Religious Houses*, p. 63.

[116] Canon 497, § 2.

stipulate, at the time when he gives his permission, that the newly erected house is to be used for teaching only. To avoid future difficulties the superioress should see to it that these matters are, from the very beginning, clearly provided for and understood by both parties in an identical sense.

Every religious house established in accord with the rules that have just been noted forms a moral person. The superioress must see to it, therefore, that all the requirements for canonical incorporation are fulfilled. Canon 100, § 1, decrees that subordinate moral persons receive their juridic personality from the law itself, or in consequence of a formal decree of a competent ecclesiastical superior. The superioress cannot in the strict sense of the term be called an ecclesiastical superior. She does not enjoy jurisdiction, and consequently is not capable of an act that postulates the possession of this power. No decree that she would issue could confer juridic personality on any group.[117] Nevertheless some authors, while they agree that the superioress has no jurisdiction, feel that the superioress must issue a formal decree in the erection of a religious house.[118]

Nowhere in the Code, however, is a formal decree of erection required of the superioress. The juridic personality proceeds entirely from the law itself. Any decree issued by the superioress would be merely an act of recognition of the operation of the law. It is unnecessary as a fulfillment of any requirement of law, but is certainly invaluable as a matter of record, and should, therefore, not be neglected.[119] The superioress should, moreover, provide that the canonically erected house is composed of at least three permanent members. This number is required by law as requisite for the establishment of a moral person.[120]

Several other questions remain which are pertinent to the permission needed by the superioress in the erection of religious houses. These concern the procedure to be followed in the erection of separate

---

[117] Canon 118.

[118] Coronata, *Institutiones*, I, p. 632, n. 522; Vromant, *De Bonis Ecclesiae Temporalibus*, n. 19.

[119] Larraona, *ibid.*, 418; Flanagan, *op. cit.*, p. 35.

[120] Canon 100, § 2.

buildings, in making alterations, and in the transfer of the house to another location. Canon 497, § 3, states that for the erection of buildings which are separate from the religious house, a permission in writing from the local ordinary is sufficient. This, of course, refers to a new building which is not a new foundation of a religious house, for in the latter event the regular formalities, as just outlined, would be required. Again the new building involved must connote more than an expansion which simply serves the necessities of the internal life of the community, inasmuch as apart from specifically made limitations this right is contained in the original permission.[121]

Finally, if the new building is to be on the same property, and no stipulations were made by the local ordinary at the time when he gave his consent for the erection of the house, it can be considered a part of the original house, since nowhere in the law is a religious house limited to one building.[122] Consequently, by way of eliminating the contingencies just ruled out of the context of canon 497, § 3, it may be said that a special permission is needed from the local ordinary and from him alone, when any institute wishes to erect a new filial edifice, but only when it is to be erected outside its original property, and when it will have an external influence on the clergy or the laity.[123]

With regard to alterations which are simply the equivalent of repairs no permission is required from any authority outside the community, unless to carry out the work it is necessary to alienate property or to contract debts.[124] In this latter case the general laws with regard to alienation must be obeyed. On the other hand, any formal change increasing the extent of the work of the house

---

[121] Canon 497, § 2: Canon 554, § 1, makes an exception for congregations of pontifical approval with regard to the erection of a novitiate. Permission is always necessary from the Holy See, even though the novitiate be established in a house already erected.

[122] Farrell, *The Rights and Duties of the Local Ordinary Regarding Congregations of Women Religious of Pontifical Approval*, p. 70.

[123] Flanagan, *The Canonical Erection of Religious Houses*, p. 106; Farrell, *op. cit.*, p. 71.

[124] Schaefer, *De Religiosis*, p. 168, n. 87; Coronata, *Institutiones*, I, p. 637, n. 525.

or prejudicing the laws of the foundation, presupposes the need of all the formalities attendant upon the erection of a new house, if its influence extends beyond the community itself.[125] Indeed, a change in the extent of the work of the institute would even amount to a change in the constitutions, and would therefore require the consent which is necessary for so radical a move. Thus an institute of pontifical approval would need permission from the Holy See; a diocesan institute would need permission from the local ordinary if it existed only in one diocese, and from all the local ordinaries of all the dioceses in which it had houses.[126]

Finally, permission for the erection of a new house is needed if the house is to be transferred to another diocese, or if, even within the same diocese, it is to be transferred to a new cite outside the confines of the old property. This is so because one of the purposes of the permission for the erection of any religious house is to ascertain that the work of the institute is needed in a given locality.[127]

From time to time, because of circumstances beyond the control of anyone, a need will arise for the suppression of a religious house. If the house to be suppressed is the last one owned by the institute, no matter what status the institute has, the action of the Holy See is required.[128] If the institute possesses more than one house, the procedure for the suppression of a house will differ with the varying type of the institute. A house of an exempt community can be suppressed only by the Holy See; the suppression of a house of a congregation of pontifical approval falls within the competence of the supreme moderator, provided that she has the consent of the local ordinary; the suppression of a house of a diocesan institute, on the contrary, falls within the competence of the local ordinary, but he is obliged to consult the supreme moderator.[129]

It is to be noted, if the congregation is of pontifical approval, that the supreme moderator cannot act unless she has the consent of the local ordinary, while with the diocesan community the matter

---

[125] Canon 497, § 4.

[126] Canon 618, § 2; canon 495, § 2.

[127] Flanagan, *The Canonical Erection of Religious Houses*, p. 116.

[128] Canon 493.

[129] Canon 498.

is one of consultation. Therefore, even though after consultation
the superioress of a diocesan congregation is of a different opinion than
the local ordinary, he is free to act. In all cases the religious community has the right to take recourse to the Holy See, and once
this recourse is lodged the decree of suppression becomes inopera-
tive until the Holy See has decided the merits of the case.[130]

[130] Canon 498.

CHAPTER IX

ADMISSION AND DISMISSAL OF RELIGIOUS

Canon 538 states that any Catholic capable of undertaking the burdens of the religious life, provided that he is imbued with the right intention and disqualified by no legitimate impediment, may be admitted into a religious institute. This canon, however, is but a preliminary to many laws which set down in detail the steps that one must take to become a religious in the true sense of the word. The Church requires periods of testing. These are called postulancy, novitiate, and temporary profession. In most cases only after all these periods have elapsed is one permitted to take the final step which deprives one permanently of the right to leave an institute of one's own free will. In this chapter consideration will be given in four articles to the part played by the superioress in regard to postulancy, novitiate, profession, and dismissal.

Article 1. Postulancy

As just noted, the postulancy is a time of probation. Its purpose, on the one hand, is to give the candidate an opportunity to experience personally the nature of the life of a religious, and, on the other, to give the superioress an opportunity to judge the validity of the religious vocation of the candidate.[1]

The common law prescribes that every aspirant to membership in an institute of women religious who take perpetual vows must pass through this period of probation; it leaves to constitutions to determine its necessity in other institutes of women religious.[2] The postulancy, as required in the present law, is not a condition on which the validity of the novitiate or of the profession demands.[3] How-

---

[1] Cf. Creusen-Garesché-Ellis, *Religious Men and Women in the Code*, p. 129, n. 171; Geser, *The Canon Law Governing Communities of Sisters*, p. 191, q. 589.

[2] Canon 539, § 1.

[3] Coronata, *Institutiones*, I, p. 705, n. 567; Vermeersch-Creusen, *Epitome*, I, p. 478, n. 665; Wernz-Vidal, *Ius Canonicum*, III, p. 194, n. 244.

ever, no superioress has a right to dispense from it any more than she has authority to dispense from any other law of the Code.[4]

It is within the province of the constitutions or of approved custom to determine the one who has the right to admit postulants. Generally it is the major superioress who is authorized to act in this matter. If the constitutions are silent, and if the community has but one house, the superioress of that house enjoys this authority; if the community has many houses, and is not yet divided into provinces, the superioress general is the competent superioress for granting admission to the postulancy.[5] So far as the common law is concerned, no vote or even consultation of any chapter or council is needed on the part of the superioress in admitting postulants.[6]

While it is clear that a superioress may not admit a candidate to the novitiate without having obtained all the testimonials specified in canon 544, the same cannot be said to be required in the admission of a candidate to the postulancy. Certainly, to forestall the possibility of future difficulties and the danger of delays when these documents are needed, it is expedient that the superioress should demand them from the beginning. The requirements of canon 538 demand for the admission into religion only that the candidate be baptized, confirmed, loyal to the Faith, free from impediments, capable of assuming the burdens of the religious life, and possessed of a right intention. The superioress should ascertain through adequate investigation that the candidate possesses these requisite qualifications. For instance, she should insist on the presentation of certificates of baptism and confirmation.[7]

It is true that canon 544, § 1, § 2, 6°, when it demands testimonials for prospective novices, uses the term aspirants, which is frequently applied in general usage to postulants. However, the general heading of the chapter in the Code under which this canon is placed refers not to the postulancy but to the novitiate. Therefore

---

[4] Schaefer, *De Religiosis*, p. 454, n. 214.

[5] Cf. Schaefer, *De Religiosis*, p. 455, n. 215; Fanfani, *De Iure Religiosorum*, p. 213, n. 190.

[6] Coronata, *Institutiones*, I, p. 706, n. 567.

[7] Larraona, "Consultationes," *CpR*, I (1920), 179; Vermeersch, "De variis litteris exigendis ante ingressum," *Periodica*, IX (1920), (5).

the presumption should be that the application of this law is restricted to those who are about to be admitted to the novitiate, and not extended to those who are preparing for admission to the postulancy.[8] Moreover, the proposed argument is not nullified by any specific sense applied by the Code to the term "aspirant," for this term is applied indiscriminately by the Code to novices and to postulants alike.[9] It seems, then, safe to say that the superioress is not obliged to be in possession of these testimonials at the time of admitting the candidate to the postulancy.[10]

Unless the constitutions offer more definite regulations, the postulancy commences at the moment the candidate takes up residence in the religious house with the permission of the superioress.[11] No special act or formality to mark the starting point is required by law.[12] Canon 539, § 1, prescribes, however, that in all institutes of women religious who take perpetual vows the postulancy must continue for at least six months, while in other institutes of women religious, if the constitutions require a postulancy, they are the source of the law determining its duration.

It is important to note that in those institutes in which a postulancy is required by the common law, the minimum period is stated, but not the maximum. The former is six months, but the constitutions may within the terms of the common law require a longer period. The major superioress must see to it that the law, whether of the Code or of the constitutions, as it applies to her institute, is properly observed. By special permission of the Code major superioresses may lengthen the time of the postulancy, but not beyond six months.[13] This of course should be done only for a just cause.

An example of such a cause is either the desire of the postulant to consider further the state of her will, or that of the superioress

---

[8] Schaefer, *De Religiosis,* p. 456, n. 215.

[9] Cf. canons 570, § 2; 2411.

[10] Cf. Vermeersch-Creusen, *Epitome,* I, p. 480, n. 667; Wernz-Vidal, *Ius Canonicum,* III, p. 195, n. 244; Goyeneche, "Consultationes," *CpR,* VIII (1927), 33.

[11] Fanfani, *De Iure Religiosorum,* p. 213, n. 190; Geser, *The Canon Law Governing Communities of Sisters,* p. 192, q. 597.

[12] Coronata, *Institutiones,* I, p. 706, n. 567.

[13] Canon 539, § 2.

to resolve doubts about the candidate's fitness. Since the Code itself gives the major superioress the right to lengthen the term of the postulancy by an additional term of six months, it would not be within the right of the superioress general, unless particular law established this power of limitation as within the latter's competence, to limit or exclude the provincial superioress from the function of making this decision.[14] For this prorogation, moreover, no vote or consultation of the council is required by the common law.[15]

Some confusion has arisen as to the exact meaning of the words which restrict the extent to which the major superioress may prolong the period of postulancy, i. e., "not beyond six months." The questions disputed are the following: Do these words mean that the superioress may always with a just cause add any period within a maximum of six months to the period already prescribed by both the common and the particular law? Or may she simply add six months to the period of postulancy as specified in the Code, so that the total period of the postulancy, prorogation included, would never exceed a year?

Authors admit that the wording of the law makes it difficult to ascertain the correct interpretation. The common opinion today is this: Whether the prolongation extends the minimum six month period of the Code, or the longer period as designated by the constitutions, the superioress may, whenever she feels the need to do so, demand a longer period of probation. Never, however, may she extend this added period beyond six months.[16] On the other hand, it would not seem indefensible, if for a just cause, the superioress shortened the period of postulancy by a few days.[17] For example, this could be done to avoid a long delay in the beginning of the postulant's novitiate.

[14] Schaefer, *De Religiosis*, p. 458, n. 216.

[15] Schaefer, *loc. cit.*

[16] Vermeersch-Creusen, *Epitome*, I, p. 497, n. 666; Schaefer, *De Religiosis*, p. 458, n. 216; Fanfani, *De Iure Religiosorum*, pp. 211-212, n. 189; Bastien, *Directoire*, p. 52, n. 79; Battandier, *Guide Canonique*, p. 96, n. 123; Berutti, *Institutiones Iuris Canonici*, III, p. 134, n. 65.

[17] Creusen-Garesché-Ellis, *Religious Men and Women in the Code*, p. 130, n. 172; Schaefer, *op. cit.*, p. 457, n. 216; Vermeersch-Creusen, *Epitome*, I, p. 479, n. 666.

While a postulant remains in the religious community she is subject to the local superioress, to the provincial superioress, and to the superioress general; she must obey them not under vow, but under the virtue of obedience.[18]   She has no obligation to remain in the institute, and accordingly may leave whenever she so wills. The ultimate decision whether she may stay, however, rests with the major superioress.[19]   There is no formality prescribed for the dismissal of postulants, and unless the constitutions direct otherwise, the superioress may act without any consultation with her council.[20]

ARTICLE 2. NOVITIATE

After the period of postulancy has been completed or, if this is not required, immediately on entrance to a community, the candidate seeking to become a religious commences the period of probation known as the novitiate. It is a time in which the aspirant studies and practices the life of one in religion and demonstrates to those in charge her possession of the qualities necessary to live this life.[21] All candidates must make the novitiate, and this for the validity of their future profession.[22]   The place in which this period of study and probation must be spent is a house canonically erected for that purpose,[23] and, unless constitutions require a second year, the duration of the novitiate must be a full and continuous year.[24]

Canon 543 decrees that the right to admit candidates to the novitiate belongs to all major superioresses, who however, to exercise this right, must obtain the vote of their council or of the chapter according to the norms of the constitutions. The admitting authority is the major superioress specifically determined by the constitutions, which may provide, for instance, that the right is to be

---

[18] Cf. *supra*, p. 66.

[19] Berutti, *Institutiones Iuris Canonici*, III, p. 136, n. 67.

[20] Schaefer, *De Religiosis*, p. 460, n. 218.

[21] Cf. Cocchi, *Commentarium*, IV, p. 134, n. 63; Fanfani, *De Iure Religiosorum*, p. 214, n. 191.

[22] Canon 555, § 1.

[23] Canon 555, § 1, 3°.

[24] Canon 555, § 1, 2°; § 2.

exercised cumulatively by the provincial and the superioress general, or by either one acting alone.[25]

It is clear that the right to admit candidates to the novitiate is proper to the major superioress, and not to the ordinary of the place.[26] The major superioress, however, who enjoys this right, no matter what the status of her institute is, must notify the local ordinary of the admission of new candidates at least two months prior to the time designated for it.[27]   Should she fail to do this, she is to be punished by him according to the gravity of her fault, and, if it be warranted, even with deprivation of office.[28]

Under the Code the part allotted to the chapter or to the council in the admission of candidates to the novitiate is less clear than the part allotted to the major superioress. Is it required that in approaching the council or the chapter in this matter the superioress receive a decisive vote, or only a consultative vote, if the constitutions permit it? Creusen holds that the vote must be decisive in character.[29]

He bases his opinion on the fact that canon 543 speaks of the right of granting admission to the novitiate and to profession at the same time and in the same way, and then adverts to the fact that according to canon 575, § 2, the part of the council in granting admission to profession is clearly of a decisive character. Other authors, admitting a lack of clarity in canon 543 in the placement of the words, "according to the constitutions" hold that the superioress is bound to act by a decisive vote of her council only when the constitutions specifically require this.[30]

Until further instruction is given in this matter, it seems safe to conclude that the major superioress must, in admitting novices,

[25] Wernz-Vidal, *Ius Canonicum*, III, pp. 215-216, n. 261.

[26] Coronata, *Institutiones*, I, 717, n. 572; Vermeersch-Creusen, *Epitome*, I, p. 493, n. 690.

[27] Canon 552, § 1.

[28] Canon 2412.

[29] Creusen-Garesché-Ellis, *Religious Men and Women in the Code*, p. 139, n. 181.

[30] Fanfani, *De Iure Religiosorum*, p. 218, n. 194; Coronata, *Institutiones*, I, pp. 716-717, n. 572; Schaefer, *De Religiosis*, p. 486, n. 223; Vermeersch-Creusen, *Epitome*, I, p. 493, n. 690.

obtain only the consultative vote of her council unless the constitutions require a decisive vote. Coronata, in adding a note to this question, states that if the major superioress should be unwilling to admit a candidate, she is not obliged to consult the council at all, and that even though the council should desire the admission of the candidate, it may not act on it unless the major superioress presents her name for their vote.[31]

Before the admission of a candidate to the novitiate may take place, there must be fulfilled, besides the requisites noted above in the article on the postulancy, a detailed list of other requirements specifically prescribed in the Code.[32]

1°. The following may not be validly admitted to the novitiate: (1) anyone who has adhered to a non-catholic sect; (2) anyone who has not reached the age of fifteen years complete; (3) anyone who is acting under compulsion resulting from grave force or threats, or anyone who is being admitted by a superioress constrained in the same way; (4) anyone actually bound by the bond of matrimony; (5) anyone professed in another religious institute; (6) anyone liable to penalty because of a past grave crime, whether she has already been accused or whether with great probability such accusation will follow.

2°. The following may not be licitly admitted to the novitiate, though the admission would be valid: (1) anyone who is burdened with debts that are beyond her ability to pay; (2) anyone implicated in secular affairs from which there is danger of lawsuits or of other secular annoyances; (3) anyone whose grandparents or parents are in grave need of her help; (4) anyone who is a member of an Oriental rite in reference to admission to the novitiate of the Latin rite, unless written permission has been obtained from the Sacred Congregation for the Oriental Church.

A detailed study of each of these requisites is far beyond the scope of this work. Suffice it to say that the superioress charged with the admission of candidates to the novitiate should be familiar with them, and should consult authors who have dwelt in detail on

---

[31] *Op. cit.*, I, p. 717, n. 572.

[32] Canon 542.

their precise implications.[33]   She should remember that in matters prescribed by the Code as necessary for the validity of the admission, if the requisites are not fulfilled, regardless of her ignorance of them, the admission is invalid.[34]

Besides the obligation to examine candidates in order to establish the fulfillment of the above listed requisites, there rests on the major superioress the duty of obtaining certain testimonials.   To fail in this regard is to draw upon herself penalties in accord with the gravity of her fault, not excluding deprivation of office.[35]   Of primary importance among these testimonials are two which in all probability were demanded at the time of admission to the postulancy, namely, the certificates of baptism and confirmation.[36]

If the candidate has attended a college for aspirants to the religious life, or has previously been accepted as a postulant or as a novice in another religious institute, letters of testimony are required from the major superioresses of these institutes.[37]   It may be noted that the text of the law clearly provides that the local superioress or the mistress of novices may not issue these letters.

Authors generally agree that the interpretation of the word "college" in paragraph three of canon 544 is not that which ordinarily comes to mind with the use of this term, namely, an institution of higher learning in which students prepare for all walks of life. They say that it refers rather to an institution destined solely for the training of candidates for the religious life.[38]   They base this interpretation not only on the source of the law which contained the word "college" with this meaning,[39] but also from the position of

---

[33] Bakalarczyk, *De Novitiatu*, The Catholic University of America Canon Law Studies, n. 36 (Washington, D. C.: The Catholic University of America, 1927); Geser, *The Canon Law Governing Communities of Sisters*, pp. 195 ff.

[34] Canon 16.

[35] Canon 2411; cf. *supra*, p. 63.

[36] Canon 544, § 1.

[37] Canon 544, § 3.

[38] Vermeersch-Creusen, *Epitome*, I, pp. 495-496, n. 694; Fanfani, *De Iure Religiosorum*, p. 206, n. 182; Coronata, *Institutiones*, I, p. 720, n. 574; Schaefer, *De Religiosis*, p. 491, n. 225; Berutti, *Institutiones Iuris Canonici*, III, p. 153, n. 71.

[39] S. C. de Rel., decr. 5 apr. 1910, II, IV—*Periodica*, V (1910), 98, 99, 123.

the term in canon 544, § 3, between the terms "seminary" and "postulancy and novitiate," as though intended to designate an institute of the same type.

Thus the major superioress in granting admissions to the novitiate may feel safe in following the practice of seeking testimonials, not excluding, of course, the major superioress of an institute in which the candidate previously spent some time as a postulant or as a novice, solely from the superioress of a "college" in which the candidate lived as an aspirant to receive training to enter some form of religious life in the future. In the United States "colleges" of this type are not common for women.

If these testimonials are legitimately requested, the superioress authorized by law to issue them is obliged to comply with the request, and to testify under oath to the truth of what she states.[40]

The Sacred Congregation of Religious, on being asked to recommend the applicable remedy to be invoked when superiors refuse to testify under oath to these testimonial letters, replied that the prescription of the canon is to be observed. If a superioress refuses to follow this prescription, the local ordinary, if the case is linked with a diocesan or lay institute, shall compel obedience to the law by means of penalties, not excluding deprivation of office. If after such action the sworn testimony cannot be obtained, the matter should be referred to the Sacred Congregation.[41]

Besides the obligation imposed on the major superioress when she admits a candidate to the novitiate, namely, of obtaining specific testimonial letters, the Code confers a right on her to exact any other testimonials that seem necessary or opportune.[42] This concession is especially helpful to her in the fulfilling of her obligation to make a thorough investigation into the character and morals of every candidate.[43]

---

[40] The following formula is offered as an example of the oath required in the issuing of testimonials. I, N. N. Provincial of .... at ....
do hereby testify and swear that the information herein contained is to the best of my knowledge true. So help me God. Seal, date.   Signature.

[41] *Circa testimoniales iuratas,* 21 nov. 1919—*AAS,* XII (1920), 17.

[42] Canon 544, § 6.

[43] Canon 544, § 7.

It may also be used not only to make certain that the applicant is acting of her own free will, but also to ascertain that financial obligations or other impediments do not stand in the way of admission. Through its use it may further be certified that the parents do not object, and that there is no danger of civil entanglements consequent upon such an objection.

Every superioress who is approached for the requisite testimonials must send them signed and sealed, gratuitously, and within three months from the time that the request for them was made.[44] If the superioress to whom the request was sent judges that grave reasons prohibit her from complying with it, she must within the same three month period transmit these reasons to the Holy See.[45]

Examples of such reasons could be verified in a prohibition of the civil law, or in threats of personal violence, or in various forms of sinister intimidation.[46] If the superioress replies that the person who was previously a subject and about whom information is being sought is not sufficiently known to her, her obligation will be fulfilled, and the one seeking the information must resort to other trustworthy means of obtaining it; on the contrary, if the superioress to whom the request is sent does not answer at all, the petitioner should inform the Holy See of her failure.[47]

The content matter of these testimonial letters must under grave obligation be the fruit of a diligent investigation. It will vary with individual requests, but in general it may be said that they should contain: (a) the complete date of birth; (b) the name of the parents of the applicant, mention of the state of their health, and of their religious affiliations; (c) a description of the character of the candidate in question, including an evaluation of her piety and moral life, on the actual presence or great probability of any accusations against her, on any probable canonical impediments in the case, on the person's mental ability, and on the state of her physical health; (d)

---

[44] Canon 545, § 1.

[45] Canon 545, § 2.

[46] Fanfani, *De Iure Religiosorum*, p. 208, n. 184.

[47] Cf. canon 545, § 3.

the reasons for the dismissal or for the voluntary departure from the institute, if the candidate was a postulant or a novice.[48]

All who receive the information communicated in testimonial letters are bound to keep secret not only the details learned, but also the names of the persons who have supplied them.[49] This obligation binds in justice, and is obviously a grave obligation if the matter involved is serious.[50] The major superioress who admits the candidate to the novitiate must present some of this information to her council that they may have the knowledge necessary to pass judgment on the candidate. They, too, then become bound to this secret.[51] Any information not pertinent to the question of admission should not be revealed even to the council.

Canon 561, § 1, states that the care and training of the novices is to be confided to one specially appointed for this work. It further adds that no one else may interfere with it in any way, except superioresses so authorized by the constitutions, including those who are charged with the canonical visitation. Finally, it determines that in matters of discipline which pertain to the whole house both the novice mistress and the novices are subject to the local superioress. Canon 561, § 1, leaves room for further clarification in the constitutions regarding the specific rights of the superioresses involved. It may be said, however, that unless the constitutions permit it, no superioress should attempt to assert any authority in matters that concern the internal direction of the novitiate.[52]

It is not easy to determine what matters pertain to the universal discipline of the house. Authors list as belonging to it the acts which are performed outside the novitiate proper. These acts would include the penances performed in the refectory, the permissions to see visitors in the parlor, the various forms of recreation and exer-

---

[48] Cf. canon 545, § 4; Schaefer, *De Religiosis*, pp. 498-499, n. 226; Geser, *The Canon Law Governing Communities of Sisters*, p. 208, q. 652.

[49] Canon 546.

[50] Schaefer, *De Religiosis*, p. 488, n. 266.

[51] Creusen-Garesché-Ellis, *Religious Men and Women in the Code*, p. 142, n. 183; Fanfani, *De Iure Religiosorum*, p. 209, n. 186.

[52] Schaefer, *De Religiosis*, p. 532, n. 245; Coronata, *Institutiones*, I, p. 740, n. 585.

cise undertaken in common, the departure from the convent, etc.[53] In these acts, then, and others like them, the local superioress is . the competent authority to make decisions and to execute regulations for the novices as well as for the other subjects placed under her charge.

The Code makes it adequately clear that the major superioress should assign only sisters of exemplary character as associates and instructors of the novices.[54] It requires, moreover, that the mistress of novices report to the chapter or the major superioress at least once a year on the conduct of each novice.[55] Canon 563 clearly authorizes the constitutions to determine the frequency of these reports, and to specify the precise superioress or chapter to whom they are to be made.[56]

The novitiate begins either with the putting on of the habit or with some other act designated by the constitutions as marking the start of the novitiate.[57] In admitting the novice the major superioress may not by her own authority change the way prescribed by the constitutions of her institute.[58] At the end of the novitiate the major superioress may for the sake of further observation add six months to the minimum of the full year prescribed by the Code.[59]

Canon 556, § 3, states that the superioress must not grant a novice permission to remain outside the novitiate without a just cause. The Code does not specify which superioress is authorized to give this permission, but it seems that in accord with her usual authority to grant permissions to leave the convent the local superioress would be competent to permit novices to remain outside the novitiate when a sufficient cause warrants this absence. Both the local superioress and the major superioress must take care that the

---

[53] Coronata, *op. cit.*, I, pp. 740-741, n. 585; Schaefer, *op. cit.*, p. 533, n. 245; Creusen-Garesché-Ellis, *Religious Men and Women in the Code*, p. 155, n. 205.

[54] Canon 554, § 3.

[55] Canon 563.

[56] Cf. Schaefer, *De Religiosis*, p. 533, n. 245; Vermeersch-Creusen, *Epitome*, I, p. 507, n. 711.

[57] Canon 553.

[58] Creusen-Garesché-Ellis, *Religious Men and Women in the Code*, p. 148, n. 192.

[59] Canon 571, § 2.

year of novitiate is continuous and uninterrupted in order that it may be valid. If a competent superioress dismisses a novice, and the novice in turn leaves the convent, the novitiate is interrupted and the time already served is henceforth reckoned as nothing.[60]

The same interruption occurs if any superioress permits a novice to spend beyond thirty days outside the novitiate house, regardless of the fact that these days do or do not run continuously.[61] In other cases of absence the law presents two possibilities. If a superioress permits a novice to remain outside the novitiate house, but not for more than fifteen days, whether continuous or non-continuous, the major superioress, as she sees fit, may or may not require an additional fifteen days at the expiration of the regular year.[62] If, however, the permission which was granted for the novice's absence from the novitiate includes a stay of more than fifteen days but not beyond thirty, the same option is no longer available for the major superioress, for she must require that these days of absence from the novitiate be supplied.[63]

Canon 556, § 4, states that if the major superioress gives permission for a transfer from one novitiate to another, the novitiate is not thereby interrupted. It must be added, however, that the rules stated above regarding interruptions and the necessity for supplying the days of absence must be followed even when the absence is due to time lost in making a transfer. Thus, if more than thirty days are spent in passing from one novitiate to another, the novitiate is interrupted and must be entirely repeated.[64]

One exception is made to the law which requires every novice to spend at least a full year in the novitiate before she is permitted to make profession.[65] When a candidate who has actually begun her postulancy or her novitiate becomes gravely ill, and in the doctor's opinion is at the point of death, her profession may be received in accord with the rules and the constitutions, either by the major

[60] Canon 556, § 1.

[61] Canon 556, § 1.

[62] Canon 556, § 2.

[63] Canon 556, § 2.

[64] P. C. I., 13 iul. 1930—*AAS,* XXII (1930), 365.

[65] S. C. de Rel., decr., *De professione religiosa in articulo mortis movitiis vel postulantibus permissa,* 30 dec. 1922—*AAS,* XV (1923), 156.

superioress who has the ordinary right to receive the profession, or by any religious who is actually the superioress of the monastery or of the house of novitiate or probation, and by their delegates. Should the person so professed recover, she must return to her original status, retaining the right to leave the institute without any obligations under her profession. On the other hand, she is subject to dismissal by the major superioress without formalities other than those required in the case of any other novice. The Sacred Congregation permits the foregoing provisions to be added to the constitutions apart from every obligation to submit any petition to Rome for making this addition.

If a novice proves unsatisfactory, the superioress may in accord with the constitutions dismiss her for any just cause, and is in no way bound to explain her action to the novice.[66] It is advisable, however, in the interest of future convenient reference, to keep records of the reason for the dismissal. Such an interest would be served, for example, in the case of a future request for testimonials, or in the case of the ex-novice's recourse to the Holy See against the decree of her dismissal. If the constitutions are silent with regard to the particular superioress who is authorized to dismiss the novice, then by analogy with the law which governs the factor of competency in the admission of candidates to the novitiate, the right to dismiss the novice seems to belong to the major superioress who had the right to admit her as an aspirant to the novitiate.[67]

ARTICLE 3. PROFESSION

Profession in its use as a term to describe that act by which one embraces the religious state means the public taking of the three vows of poverty, chastity, and obedience in an approved religious institute, and, in turn, the acceptance of that person by the institute according to its rule and constitutions.[68] Profession may

---

[66] Canon 571, § 1.

[67] Cf. canon 543; Schaefer, *De Religiosis*, p. 558, n. 259.

[68] Cf. Creusen-Garesché-Ellis, *Religious Men and Women in the Code*, p. 170, n. 222; Schaefer, *De Religiosis*, p. 565, n. 263; Geser, *The Canon Law Governing Communities of Sisters*, pp. 244-245, q. 775.

be temporary, thus leaving the person free after the expiration of the set time, or perpetual, and thus binding the person for life. In either case two distinct functions belong to the superioress. They are the admission of the candidate to profession and the actual reception of the profession in the name of the community. Admission is an act by which the superioress decides that a novice may and should become affiliated with the religious family; reception of the profession is the actual act of affiliation.[69]

The competent superioress for admitting a novice to profession is the one who is so designated by the constitutions.[70] She must be a major superioress.[71] Thus the Code clearly specifies the requisite kind of superioress, and does not leave it to the constitutions to designate any other superior to admit novices to profession than a major superioress of the institute. To act validly in the case of admission to the first temporary profession, this superioress must have the consent of her council or of the chapter expressed in a decisive vote; in the case of perpetual profession, she may act after a consultative vote.[72] The Code does not make any regulation for the type of vote that is needed when the profession, while being temporary, implies merely a renewal after the first profession. It may safely be concluded, however, that a decisive vote is not required in this case unless the constitutions determine otherwise.[73] When a religious who is professed with perpetual vows has transferred from one religious institute to another, as she is permitted to do according to canon 634, and is now to make her perpetual profession in the new institute, the vote of the council is decisive in character.[74]

The consent of the local ordinary for the admission of a novice to temporary profession, or of a religious to perpetual profession, is not necessary, but as in the case of admission to the novitiate, the

[69] Wernz-Vidal, *Ius Canonicum*, III, p. 271, n. 303.

[70] Canon 572, § 1, 2°.

[71] Canon 543.

[72] Canon 575, § 2.

[73] Schaefer, *De Religiosis*, p. 570, n. 265; Coronata, *Institutiones*, I, p. 753, n. 591.

[74] P. C. I., 14 iul. 1922—*AAS*, XIV (1922), 582.

major superioress must notify him at least two months in advance of the approaching admission of candidates to profession.[75]

Before an otherwise competent superioress may admit a candidate to profession, she must take care that the following conditions prescribed for validity are fulfilled. The candidate must have attained the legitimate age, that is, the age of sixteen years in the case of her first temporary profession, and of twenty-one years in the case of her perpetual profession.[76] Secondly, she must have made a valid novitiate.[77] Thirdly, she must be free from violence, grave fear, and error induced by fraud.[78] Fourthly, if the profession is to be perpetual, the candidate must have previously spent at least three years in temporary profession.[79]

In order to preclude all likelihood of any defective consent on the part of the candidate, there rests on the major superioress the obligation to instruct the candidates fully on the nature of the step that they are about to take, and to supply sufficient knowledge that they may adequately understand the meaning and the nature of the vows they propose to take.[80] An excommunication is automatically incurred by anyone who forces another to make profession of temporary or perpetual vows in religion.[81]

Canon 571, § 1, prescribes that there should be no interruption or delay even of one day in the renewal of the profession. The major superioress, however, must remember that the required three years of temporary profession before a religious may make her perpetual profession must be three complete years. Canon 577, § 2, grants the major superioress the right to permit anticipation even up to a month in the renewal of temporary profession. This faculty may not be used in reference to perpetual profession. Moreover, if it has been used during the course of the three years of temporary profession, those periods which have been omitted from the three

[75] Canon 522, § 1.

[76] Canon 572, § 1, 2°; canon 573.

[77] Canon 572, § 1, 3°; canon 555.

[78] Canon 572, § 1, 4°.

[79] Canon 572, § 2.

[80] Cf. Geser, *The Canon Law Governing Communities of Sisters*, p. 247, q. 784.

[81] Canon 2352.

years must be supplied at the end of the year prior to perpetual profession.[82]

Canon 575, § 1, prescribes that after the period of temporary profession has elapsed, the religious, provided that she has attained the proper age, and the institution is one in which the members take perpetual vows, should either make her perpetual profession or return to the world. For a just cause the major superioress may permit instead of perpetual profession, a renewal of temporary vows, but never for a period in excess of three years.[83]

Authors disagree with regard to the proper interpretation of the text of canon 574, § 2, in which authorization for this extension is found. Some assert that the extended period may be computed from the end of the actual period of temporary profession, whether it has been composed of three years, or, when at her first profession the novice's age was under eighteen complete years, of the three years plus an additional year or two as determined by the novice's age of seventeen or sixteen years at the time of her first temporary profession.[84] Others teach that the maximum time of temporary profession may not, without conflicting with the Code, be extended beyond six years, and that the three additional years permitted by the law for a just cause must be reckoned as an interval to be added to the three year period of temporary profession, that is, to the three years which the law requires when it abstracts from the age requirement for perpetual profession.[85]

An incontrovertible solution cannot be given to this question. Until further instruction is received from the Holy See, the broader interpretation, so it seems, may be followed, and recourse to the Holy See would not be necessary if a major superioress desired to extend the period of temporary profession for three years after a four or five year period of temporary profession had elapsed. The competent superioress for the extension of the period of temporary

---

[82] Cf. Creusen-Garesché-Ellis, *Religious Men and Women in the Code*, p. 179, n. 236; Schaefer, *De Religiosis*, p. 593, n. 269.

[83] Canon 574, § 2.

[84] Schaefer, *De Religiosis*, p. 588, n. 268, nota 110; Coronata, *Institutiones*, I, p. 757, n. 592; Augustine, *Commentary*, III, 260.

[85] Vermeersch-Creusen, *Epitome*, I, p. 523, n. 726; Oesterle, *Praelectiones Iuris Canonici*, p. 318.

profession is ordinarily to one who possesses the right to admit candidates to profession, but the constitutions could direct otherwise.[86]

Just as for the admission of the candidate to profession, so too for the reception of the profession, the common law leaves the designation of the superioress to the constitutions. It further permits this authorized superioress in the act of receiving the profession to act personally or through a delegate.[87] Under the constitutions the right to accept the profession may be reserved to the local ordinary. In institutes of women religious of pontifical approval, if the constitutions are not explicit in regard to this reservation, and the formula for profession mentions only the local ordinary or his delegate, the latter must be considered as exclusively authorized to receive the vows.[88]

Schaefer holds that the response of the Pontifical Commission for the Interpretation of the Code, in which the exclusive authority of the local ordinary was thus indicated, refers only to those congregations which are specifically mentioned in the response, namely, those of women religious of pontifical approval. He bases this opinion on the grounds that the response should be strictly interpreted, inasmuch as the act of receiving the profession is of itself something that pertains to the internal superiors.[89] Creusen-Garesché-Ellis, though admitting that only congregations of women religious of pontifical approval are mentioned in this response, assert that the decision of the Pontifical Commission may be applied to diocesan congregations in which the formula of profession makes no mention of the superioress, but only mentions the bishop or his delegate.[90] In so important a matter, one in which the validity of the profession is involved, it does not seem prudent to extend the response of the Pontifical Commission to other congregations than those specifically named in it. It would seem far better for diocesan con-

---

[86] Creusen-Garesché-Ellis, *Religious Men and Women in the Code*, p. 175, n. 230.

[87] Canon 572, § 1, 6°.

[88] P. C. I., 1 mart. 1921—*AAS*, XIII (1921), 178.

[89] *De Religiosis*, p. 579, n. 266; cf. Maroto, "Annotationes," *CpR*, II (1921), 162-164.

[90] *Religious Men and Women in the Code*, p. 174, n. 227.

gregations whose constitutions are not specific as to who is competent for the receiving of the professions to petition the proper authority for permission to make their constitutions specific in this matter.

When the constitutions provide that she who is to receive the act of profession be a member of the community, they usually designate the same person who is authorized to admit novices to profession, but it is not required that they should.[91] The superioress who under the constitutions possesses the right to receive the profession may do so personally, she may delegate another to receive it, or she may, in accepting it herself, provide that it should be made before another who enjoys a precedence of dignity, for example, before the priest who celebrates the Mass of the day.[92]

The elements of the ceremony of profession are to be designated by the constitutions.[93] No specific hour is set by the common law for the ceremony of the profession. As to the place where the profession is to be made, the common law is specific only with reference to the first temporary profession, which is to be made in the novitiate.[94] Regarding the form of the religious profession, the common law prescribes only that it should be express and external, whether oral, written or indicated by some sign.[95] Witnesses are not required, but after the ceremony a document attesting to the fact of the profession must be signed by the newly professed and by the one who officially accepted the profession.[96] If the one who accepts the profession, functions as a delegate, it would be most prudent to note this fact, and also the fact that the delegation had been validly granted for the act performed. A copy of this document should be kept in the archives of the religious institute. If the profession was solemn, notification of it should also be sent to

---

[91] Schaefer, *De Religiosis,* p. 578, n. 266; Coronata, *Institutiones,* I, p. 756, n. 591, nota 2; Vermeersch-Creusen, *Epitome,* I, p. 520, n. 723.

[92] Creusen-Garesché-Ellis, *Religious Men and Women in the Code,* p. 173, n. 226; Berutti, *Institutiones Iuris Canonici,* III, p. 199, n. 87.

[93] Canon 576, § 1.

[94] Canon 574, § 1.

[95] Cf. canon 572, § 1; Coronata, *Institutiones,* I, pp. 754-755, n. 592.

[96] Canon 576, § 2.

the parish of the baptism of the professed to be recorded in the register there.[97]

Besides the many effects that profession produces relative to the religious herself, the Code in several canons points out certain rights conferred and certain duties imposed by it on major superioresses. Canon 569 decrees that, unless the constitutions make other provision, the novice must before making her profession dispose of the use and income of her personal property for the period contemplated by the terms of her profession. Canon 580, § 3, states that she may not, unless constitutions rule otherwise, change this arrangement without the consent of the superioress general.

This faculty is enjoyed only by the supreme moderator, not by subordinate superioresses, although it seems that the faculty could be delegated to them.[98] According to canon 580, § 3, nuns must have also the authorization of the local ordinary and of their regular superior, if they are subject to the superior of an order of men religious. Permission of the Holy See is needed by all communities if the change affects a notable part of the property in favor of the religious institute.[99]

Authors estimate a notable part of the property of the religious as consisting of one-third or one-fourth of it.[100] Vermeersch taught that if the major superioress, by the entirely voluntary appointment of the novice, had been made the administrator of the novice's property, and had been given the right to make changes in its use and in the distribution of its income as circumstances required, she is authorized when circumstances warrant this act to make these changes even to the point of designating the distribution of a notable part of the benefits in favor of the religious institute without recourse to Rome.[101]

---

[97] Canon 576, § 2.

[98] Larraona, "De paupertate simplici," *CpR*, II (1921), 43; Schaefer, *De Religiosis*, p. 596, n. 270.

[99] P. C. I., 15 mart. 1936—*AAS*, XXVIII (1936), 210.

[100] Cf. Schaefer, *De Religiosis*, p. 598, n. 270; Creusen-Garesché-Ellis, *Religious Men and Women in the Code*, p. 184, n. 243.

[101] "De renuntiatione bonorum. Species facti," *Periodica*, XI (1922-1923), (158).

To grant authorization for changes in the last wills and testaments of novices and of professed religious is not within the competence of even the superioress general, but is reserved to the Holy See, unless the case is an urgent one and the time available is not adequate to permit the obtaining of permission from the Holy See. Under these circumstances the major superioress may grant permission, and if she cannot be reached, then the local superioress.[102] The permission of the Holy See would not be needed to make changes required by events unforeseeable at the time the will was written. Thus, the Holy See would not have to be approached if a will became invalid or one of the beneficiaries died. In such cases the necessary modifications could be made freely by the religious.[103]

After the expiration of the temporary vows the religious, unless she has not attained the legitimate age, or unless her institute can allow her to follow another procedure, pronounces her perpetual vows. The institute is not free to dismiss her without a just and reasonable cause.[104] Examples of just and reasonable causes are serious doubt concerning her fitness to perform her duties as a religious, the lack of a religious spirit, the obvious want of a vocation.[105]

The Code does not designate the superioress who possesses the right of dismissing a religious who has made temporary profession, but canon 543 seems to supply a sufficient norm. In that canon the right to admit a novice to temporary, and a religious to perpetual, profession is granted to the major superioress as determined by the constitutions. Since the right to grant admission includes the right to deny admission, it may be said that the competent superioress is the one thus named by the constitutions.[106]

Again, under canon 543 it seems that the major superioress should approach her council in acting on the dismissal of a religious who has made temporary profession. The vote to be obtained in this case should be decisive or consultative according as

---

[102] Canon 583, § 3.

[103] Cf. Coronata, *Institutiones*, I, p. 762, n. 593; Creusen-Garesché-Ellis, *Religious Men and Women in the Code*, p. 185, n. 243.

[104] Canon 637.

[105] Cf. Fanfani, *De Iure Religiosorum*, p. 481, n. 477.

[106] Cf. Coronata, *Institutiones*, I, p. 854, n. 639, nota 1.

the constitutions determine. If these are silent on the matter, a consultative vote seems sufficient.[107]

ARTICLE 4. DISMISSAL

Dismissal from a religious institute is a mandate to withdraw, given to a religious by the competent authority for reasons sanctioned by law, usually because of some serious fault or crime.[108] Two forms of dismissal exist, namely, that which is automatically imposed by law, and that which is executed by the decree or sentence of a superior.[109] In the second instance the formalities differ with the varying type of vows pronounced by the religious in question.

Canon 646, § 1, states that any religious who is guilty of public apostasy from the Catholic faith, who has run away with a person of the other sex, or who has contracted or attempted marriage, is thereby dismissed from her religious institute. For the validity of this dismissal no formalities are required; once the crime has been committed the effect is automatically produced. The declaration of fact required by canon 646, § 2, is not necessary for the validity of the dismissal.[110]

It is an obligation imposed in the Code on the major superioress, namely, that she meet with the chapter or her council, producing for their consideration all the evidence of the crime, and over her signature and theirs make a declaration of the crime. The evidence must be kept in the registers of the convent. The superioress may be any major superioress, general or provincial, unless the constitutions make specific designation of the superioress entrusted with this function.[111]

The constitutions can not only determine the latter authority, but they can also specify whether the superioress must have the

---

[107] Cf. canon 575, § 2.

[108] Cf. Schaefer, *De Religiosis*, p. 984, n. 574; Wernz-Vidal, *Ius Canonicum*, III, pp. 470-471, n. 434.

[109] In other forms of departure from religious institutes consequent upon indults of secularization or of exclaustration, the formalities are handled mainly by authorities outside the community, and hence have not been treated here.

[110] P. C. I., 30 iul. 1934—*AAS*, XXVI (1934), 494.

[111] Cf. Fanfani, *De Iure Religiosorum*, p. 495, n. 497.

decisive vote or only the consultative vote of her council for the sake of declaring the crime as a fact. If the constitutions are silent, the superioress seems to be able to proceed with merely the consultative vote of her council.[112]   Thus, in the latter case she could proceed even if the council was not satisfied that the evidence warranted the declaration.

Prudence, in most cases, seems to dictate that a declaration of the fact of the crime be not made unless there was agreement by the superioress and her council that the crime was certain.   The superioress and the members of the council should always remember when reviewing the evidence that they are dealing with penal matters and therefore a strict interpretation must be followd, that is, one which looks to the innocence of the religious until her guilt is proved.[113]

As previously noted, the formalities for the dismissal of a religious differ according to the nature of the vows she has pronounced.   For the dismissal of a religious with temporary vows the common law provides only a summary procedure, which varies with the type of institute to which the religious belongs.[114]

In pontifically approved institutes the competent superior for the dismissal of a religious who has made temporary profession is the superioress general.[115]   She may not act, however, without the consent of her council expressed in a secret vote.   If the vote favors dismissal, she may then issue the decree personally without approaching any higher authority.

The competent authority for the dismissal of a member of a monastery of nuns who has made temporary profession is the local ordinary of the diocese in which the monastery is located.   A difficulty arises when the monastery is subject to the regular superior of an order of men religious.   Canon 647, § 1, states that when the monastery is so subject, the competent superior for dismissal is the regular superior of the order of men religious to whom the monastery is subject.   But it does not make clear whether this reservation

---

[112] Coronata, *Institutiones*, I, p. 867, n. 646, nota 8.
[113] Canon 19.
[114] Canon 647.
[115] Canon 647, § 1.

means that both the local ordinary and the regular superior are equally competent and that either may act,[116] whether it signifies that they should concur on the matter and act jointly,[117] or finally whether it determines that the regular superior alone is capable of effecting the dismissal.[118]

Until the law is clarified by an authentic interpretation, the accepted practice in a given place may be followed. On another provision, however, canon 647, § 1, is clear, i. e., that the competent superior for the dismissal of nuns who have made temporary profession may not act before the major superioress, acting with the consent of her council, has attested in writing the reasons for the dismissal.

The competent superior for the dismissal of a religious who has made temporary profession in a diocesan institute is the ordinary of the diocese in which the convent of the religious in question is situated. He may not act, however, without the knowledge of the major superioress, or against her will when she justly disagrees with his opinion. If he, nevertheless, proceeds with the dismissal, she has a right to make recourse to the Holy See.[119] This recourse arrests the decree of dismissal, and no further action may be taken by the bishop until the Holy See has given its opinion on the merits of the case.[120]

Should a need for dismissal arise, the major superioress designated by the constitutions in a community of diocesan approval, or if the constitutions are silent in the matter, the superioress general, should petition the local ordinary to take action. This procedure

---

[116] Augustine, *Commentary*, III, 388.

[117] Coronata, *Institutiones*, I, p. 868, n. 647, nota 6; Berutti, *Institutiones Iuris Canonici*, III, p. 341, n. 159; Fanfani, *De Iure Religiosorum*, p. 500, n. 501; Vermeersch-Creusen, *Epitome*, I, p. 598, n. 808.

[118] Schaefer, *De Religiosis*, pp. 991-992, n. 578; Pejška, *Ius Canonicum Religiosorum*, p. 190; O'Neil, *The Dismissal of Religious in Temporary Vows*, The Catholic University of America Canon Law Studies, n. 166 (Washington, D. C.: The Catholic University of America Press, 1942), p. 97.

[119] Creusen-Garesché-Ellis, *Religious Men and Women in the Code*, p. 267, n. 347.

[120] Canon 498.

is likewise applied by the Code to communities whose members live in common without vows.[121]

The common law states that even a religious in temporary vows should be dismissed only for grave causes.[122] It adds further that these causes may exist either on the side of the institute or on the side of the religious.[123] As an example, it cites the lack of a religious spirit with a consequent scandal to others, provided that repeated warnings have been given and salutary penances imposed without effect. Other causes may certainly warrant dismissal, and as cases arise the competent superior must decide on their adequacy. The duty of the superior is twofold: it extends to the institute as well as to the religious. Charity must always be shown to the religious, but there must also be justice for the institute.

Before dismissal the religious who is professed with temporary vows must be warned and punished at least twice. These warnings are not strictly canonical admonitions; rather, they are benevolent corrections.[124] It would be most useful for future proof, however, if the warning were issued in writing or before two witnesses.[125] The law does not require that the warnings be given by the superior who is competent to effect the dismissal, that is, at her personal command, or even by a higher superioress.[126]

While it is true that the dismissal of one who is in temporary vows does not require a formal trial, and that the causes on which it is based do not have to be proved according to the technical forms in use before a formal tribunal, still the superioress must be morally certain of the existence and of the adequacy of the reasons for the dismissal, and must make them known to the accused religious to provide her an opportunity of answering them.[127]

Further, the responses given in defense by the religious in temporary vows whose dismissal is contemplated must always be sent

---

[121] Canons 673 and 771.

[122] Canon 647, § 2, 1°.

[123] Canon 647, § 2, 2°.

[124] Fanfani, *De Iure Religiosorum*, p. 499, n. 500.

[125] Creusen-Garesché-Ellis, *Religious Men and Women in the Code*, p. 268, n. 349.

[126] Schaefer, *De Religiosis*, pp. 993-994, n. 579.

[127] Canon 647, § 2, 3°.

to the one competent to dismiss her. Specific methods of carrying out these prescriptions are not given in the Code, and therefore the superioress may choose the method that she deems most effective. As with all regulations in regard to dismissal, there is a grave obligation to follow these which provide for a just defense and establish a moral certainty regarding the adequacy of the cause of dismissal.

Every religious in temporary vows when dismissed by a superior has a right to take recourse to the Holy See, and once this step is taken, the effect of the dismissal is suspended until notification has been received of its confirmation.[128] The Sacred Congregation of Religious in response to a question regarding the time allowed to the religious for making this recourse answered that it is established as ten days from the date of the receipt by the religious of the decree of dismissal.[129]

The Congregation added further that, as proof that this recourse has been made, an authentic document or at least the testimony of two trustworthy persons is requisite and sufficient. In reference to the time allotted, it noted that the ten days commence only when the religious knows of her right to make recourse and is able to do so. Consequently superiors are directed, when issuing the decree of dismissal, to advise the dismissed religious of her right to invoke a recourse and of the time limit within which it must be made. The Sacred Congregation declared further that while the recourse is pending the dismissed person remains a religious with all her former rights and obligations. She has a right and duty to remain in her convent, and is subject to her superioresses.

Passing now to the case of the dismissal of a religious in perpetual vows, one notes that before a religious who has emitted perpetual vows, whether they be solemn or simple, may be dismissed, the common law demands that there be grave exterior causes coupled with an incorrigibility fully demonstrated, in the judgment of the major superioress, by the failure of the efforts to bring about re-

---

[128] Canon 647, § 2, 4°.

[129] *De recursu contra decretum dimissionis religiosi professi a votis temporariis,* 30 iul. 1923—*AAS,* XV (1923), 457.

pentance and amendment.[130] Without being specific as to numbers or even species, the law simply requires grave exterior causes to justify such a dismissal. There seems to be no doubt that delicts in the canonical meaning of the word are not necessary. Rather, any moral defect of a serious nature would suffice.

Examples of the kind of fault required are an unwillingness on the part of the religious to live the common life, or a continual disturbance by her of the peace and harmony of the community.[131] Coronata is of the opinion that the offense must be theologically grave.[132] Others say that this is not necessary.[133] While it cannot be said with absolute certainty that either view is correct, it is difficult to imagine that a religious would not be sinning gravely against her state of life, if she constantly showed herself unwilling to strive to attain the perfection to the achievement of which she has dedicated her life.

Besides being grave, these causes for dismissal must be exterior, i.e., capable of being proved juridically, of being established in the external forum.[134] This does not mean, however, that they must be public as opposed to occult.[135] They could be known to a few prudent persons who would not divulge them further,[136] and still be sufficient as causes for dismissal.

Further, the element of incorrigibility must be found in these grave exterior faults that form the basis for the dismissal. Those in authority must have discovered from repeated efforts that no hope exists for a change of attitude on the part of the religious. Unlike the prescriptions for the dismissal of men religious in perpetual vows,[137] the Code does not require in the case of women

---

[130] Canon 651, § 1.

[131] Wernz-Vidal, *Ius Canonicum*, III, p. 480, n. 442; Berutti, *Institutiones Iuris Canonici*, III, p. 347, n. 166.

[132] *Institutiones*, I, p. 873, n. 651.

[133] Schaefer, *De Religiosis*, p. 1004, n. 584; Vermeersch-Creusen, *Epitome*, I, p. 600, n. 810; Battandier, *Guide Canonique*, p. 271, n. 320.

[134] Fanfani, *De Iure Religiosorum*, p. 512, n. 513.

[135] Cocchi, *Commentarium*, IV, p. 277, n. 150; Schaefer, *De Religiosis*, p. 1004, n. 584.

[136] Cf. canon 2197; Ayrinhac-Lydon, *Penal Legislation*, p. 4, n. 6.

[137] Cf. canon 649.

religious three offenses and two admonitions.[138]   Schaefer[139] and
Coronata[140] remark, however, that in the jurisprudence of the Holy
See a dismissal is not confirmed unless this norm is followed.   Certainly it must be said that the major superioress has an obligation
to see that the wayward religious is warned, threatened, exhorted,
and that penances have been imposed upon her before thought be
given to her dismissal.   Thus it is necessary for the major superioress
to fulfill her obligation of establishing that, in spite of efforts to
bring about the amendment of the religious, there is no hope of
repentance.   No reason seems to prevent the local superioress from
participating in or carrying out entirely this attempt at reform.[141]

However, since the judgment that no hope of amendment exists
will have to be made by the superioress general, the latter should keep
herself informed on all efforts made in this direction, and be satisfied in her own mind that enough has been done to reach an honest
and morally certain decision.   The superioress general must see,
too, that the accused religious is given an opportunity to answer the
charges made against her, for the Code places an obligation on this
superioress to keep these responses on record, and to include them
in the acts of dismissal when she forwards them to the higher
authority.[142]

The competent authority to effect the dismissal of those who
are in perpetual vows, just as with the dismissal of those who are
in temporary vows, differs with the various types of religious institutes.   When dismissal concerns a member of a diocesan institute,
the local ordinary of the diocese in which the religious is assigned
examines the causes and issues the decree of dismissal.[143]   He must
have evidence of the adequacy of the causes, and also the statement
of the superioress that after sufficient efforts made by her to effect
an amendment, there is in her judgment, no hope of repentance

---

[138] Creusen-Garesché-Ellis, *Religious Men and Women in the Code*, p. 272,
n. 356.

[139] *De Religiosis*, p. 1005, n. 584.

[140] *Institutiones*, I, p. 874, n. 651, nota 3.

[141] Cf. Creusen-Garesché-Ellis, *Religious Men and Women in the Code*, p.
272, n. 356.

[142] Canon 651, § 2.

[143] Canon 652, § 1.

on the part of the religious.[144]   The law does not designate the superioress from whom he is to receive this evidence.   In view of the fact that in pontifically approved institutes the superioress general is designated as authorized to perform this function in relation to the Sacred Congregation of Religious,[145] the duty would likewise seem that of the superioress general of the diocesan institute in relation to the local ordinary.

The competent superior to effect the dismissal of nuns is the Sacred Congregation of Religious, which is to be supplied with the opinion of the local ordinary and of the regular superior of the order of men religious to which the monastery of nuns may be subject.   After receiving the evidence from the superioress of the monastery, the local ordinary must transmit all the acts and documents, including the opinions just indicated, to the Sacred Congregation.[146]

In congregations of pontifical approval all acts and documents must likewise be transmitted to the Holy See for a final decision. As just noted, this function belongs to the office of the superioress general.   She does not add her own opinion.[147]   Indeed, her opinion would seem superfluous, inasmuch as it is not likely that a superioress would send a case to Rome enclosing her own judgment that there is no hope of repentance, and yet not be in favor of the dismissal.

Authors discuss the question whether the superioress in forming her judgment and in sending the acts to the competent authority must antecedently approach her council.   Coronata [148] and Creusen-Garesché-Ellis [149] hold that consultation on so important a matter would certainly be most prudent.   Schaefer [150] and Larraona [151] report that it is the practice of the Holy See to demand this consultation before accepting a case.   Certainly the obligation is not explicitly or implicitly stated in the Code.

[144] Canon 652, § 2.

[145] Cf. canon 652, § 2.

[146] Canon 652, § 2.

[147] Schaefer, *De Religiosis*, p. 1006, n. 585; Coronata, *Institutiones*, I, p. 876, n. 652.

[148] *Op. cit.*, I, p. 874, n. 651.

[149] *Religious Men and Women in the Code*, p. 273, n. 357.

[150] *Op. cit.*, p. 1007, n. 581.

[151] "Consultationes," *CpR*, II (1921), 364-366.

An extraordinary type of dismissal is provided by the Code in canon 653, which cites two causes that can warrant the use of this method. They are grave exterior scandal and most grave and imminent harm threatening the community as a consequence of the delinquency of the religious who deserves to be dismissed. The scandal which forms the basis for the extraordinary method of dismissal must have spread outside the religious house,[152] or be one that certainly will become publicly known.[153] The harm threatening must involve the community and not merely an individual religious.[154]

Authors do not define the precise meaning of the term *"communitas"* as used in canon 653, but the fact that in the canon it is not capitalized shows that the legislator did not intend the term as synonymous with the words "institute" or "congregation." Therefore it seems sufficient for the invoking of the extraordinary method of dismissal mentioned in canon 653 that the grave and imminent harm threatens an individual religious house or province. Claeys Bouuaert-Simenon remark that the extraordinary method of dismissal may also be used if the harm threatens a superioress, for then, at least indirectly, the whole community is touched.[155]

In these cases the religious may be sent without further delay into the world by the major superioress acting with the consent of her council, and if time does not permit the approach even to the major superioress, by the local superioress, provided that she has the consent of her council and of the local ordinary.[156] In all instances in which resort is taken to this extraordinary form of dismissal, the whole matter must be referred to the Holy See without delay either by the local ordinary or by the major superioress.[157]

Wernz-Vidal exclude the major superioress of communities of nuns and of diocesan institutes from the ambit of this right, asserting

---

[152] Fanfani, *De Iure Religiosorum*, p. 495, n. 498.

[153] Berutti, *Institutiones Iuris Canonici*, III, p. 349, n. 168; Vermeersch-Creusen, *Epitome*, I, p. 601, n. 813.

[154] Schaefer, *De Religiosis*, p. 1008, n. 586; Coronata, *Institutiones*, I, p. 876, n. 652.

[155] *Manuale Iuris Canonici ad usum Seminariorum* (3 vols., Vol. I, 3. ed., 1930; Vol. II, 1931; Vol. III, 3. ed., 1931, Gandae et Loedii), II, p. 390, n. 695.

[156] Canon 653.

[157] Canon 653.

that it belongs exclusively in these instances to the local ordinary.[158] Canon 653 simply states, without distinction as to the type of institute involved, that the major superioress may act, and unless further authentic interpretation is forthcoming, there does not seem to be any reason why the superioress of a monastery and the major superioresses of diocesan institutes should be excluded from the general class so designated.[159]

Since canon 653 is placed in the Code under the chapter which deals with the dismissal of religious in perpetual vows, the extraordinary procedure for dismissal which it provides obviously embraces the dismissal of those in perpetual vows. However, authors agree that, should grave exterior scandal or most grave and imminent harm threaten the community as contemplated by canon 653, the summary procedure of extraordinary dismissal may be followed also in the dismissal of religious in temporary vows.[160]

[158] *Ius Canonicum*, III, p. 490, n. 459.

[159] Cf. Schaefer, *De Religiosis*, pp. 1007-1008, n. 586; Gallik, *The Rights and Duties of Bishops Regarding Diocesan Sisterhoods*, p. 122; Vermeersch-Creusen, *Epitome*, I, p. 602, n. 815.

[160] Fanfani, *De Iure Religiosorum*, p. 497, n. 499; Coronata, *Institutiones*, I, p. 876, n. 652; O'Neil, *The Dismissal of Religious in Temporary Vows*, p. 101.

CONCLUSIONS

1. The office of superioress dates from the establishment of the first communities of women religious. (pp. 1-2)

2. From the beginning of the Church her common law has forbidden women to exercise ecclesiastical jurisdiction, but there is evidence to support the belief that superioresses by special privilege have enjoyed this prerogative to a limited extent. (pp. 22, 30-31)

3. The full development in the office of superioress came with the approval given in the *"Normae of* 1901" to the office of provincial and to the office of superioress general. (p. 42)

5. The practice of not reckoning the years spent in completing a partially fulfilled term of a predecessor for computing the tenure of office, while permissible in reference to minor superioresses, is not permissible in reference to major superioresses. (pp. 54-56)

5. The designation of the local ordinary of the diocese in which the election of the superioress general of diocesan institutes is to be held as the one enjoying the right to preside at the election and to confirm it, offers a norm for all relations between this office in such an institute and the higher authority when the situation is not specifically regulated in the common law. (pp. 60, 62, 135)

6. The impediment of illegitimacy which disqualifies one for the office of major superioress is removed by all forms of juridic legitimation with the exception of that obtained through a particular rescript. (pp. 72-74)

7. The dominative power that a superioress possesses has its root in the very nature of a society, and therefore extends as a derived natural right over all persons who by profession or contract make themselves members of the society which she governs. (pp. 76-77)

BIBLIOGRAPHY

SOURCES

Acta Apostolicae Sedis, Commentarium Officiale, Romae (Civitate Vaticana), 1909—

Acta Sanctae Sedis, 41 vols., Romae, 1865-1908.

Bullarum Diplomatum et Privilegiorum Sanctorum Romanorum Pontificum Taurienensis Editio, 25 vols., Augustae Taurinorum, 1857-1885.

Codex Iuris Canonici Pii X Pontificis Maximi iussu digestus Benedicti XV auctoritate promulgatus, Romae: Typis Polyglottis Vaticanis, 1917.

Codicis Iuris Canonici Fontes Cura Emi Petri Card. Gasparri editi, 9 vols., Romae (postea Civitate Vaticana): Typis Polyglottis Vaticanis, 1923-1939. Vols. VII-IX, ed. cura et studio Emi Iustiniani Card. Serédi.

Collectanea in Usum Secretariae Sacrae Congregationis Episcoporum et Regularium, 2. ed. Bizzarri, Romae, 1885.

Concilium Tridentinum Diariorum, Actorum, Epistolarum, Tractatuum, Nova Collectio, Edidit Societas Goerresiana, 13 vols., Friburgi Brisgoviae: B. Herder, 1901-1938.

Corpus Iuris Canonici, editio Lipsiensis secunda post Aemilii Richteri curas . . . instruxit Aemilius Friedberg, 2 vols., Lipsiae, 1879-1881.

Corpus Iuris Civilis, 3 vols., Vol. I, ed. stereotypa 15., *Institutiones,* quas recognovit P. Kreuzer: *Digesta,* quae recognovit. T. Mommsen et retractavit P. Kreuger; Vol. II, ed. stereotypa 10., *Codex Iustinianus,* quem recognovit et retractavit P. Kreuger; Vol. III, ed. stereotypa 5., *Novellae,* quas recognovit R. Schoell, et absolvit G. Kroll, Berolini: Apud Weidmannos, 1928-1929.

Corpus Scriptorum Ecclesiasticorum Latinorum, ed. consilio et impensis Academiae Litterarum Caesariae Vindobonensis, Vindobonae, 1866—.

Decretales D. Gregorii Papae IX, una cum Glossis Restitutae, Romae, 1582.

Decisiones Sacrae Rotae Romanae coram Dunozati, 2 vols., Romae, 1668.

Decisiones Sacrae Rotae Romanae coram Molines, 5 vols., Romae, 1718.

Decretum Gratiani, emendatum et nationibus illustratum una glossis, Gregorii XIII, Pont. Max., iussi editum, 2 vols., Romae, 1582.

Jaffé, Philippus, *Regesta Pontificum Romanorum ab condita Ecclesia ad annum post Christum natum MCXCVIII (1198), 2.* ed. cura Wattenbach, Kaltenbrunner (ad annum 590), Ewald (590-882), et Loewenfeld (882-1198), 2 vols in 1, Lipsiae, 1885-1888.

Hardouin, Jean, *Acta Conciliorum et Epistolae Decretales ac Constitutiones Summorum Pontificum,* 12 vols., Parisiis, 1714-1715.

Liber Sextus Decretalium, una cum Clementinis et Extravagantibus Earumque Glossis Restitutis, Romae, 1852.

Mansi, J. D., *Sacrorum Conciliorum Nova et Amplissima Collectio,* 53 vols. in 60, Paris, Leipzig, Arnhem, 1901-1927.

Monumenta Germaniae Historica, Legum Sectio II, *Capitularia Regum Francorum,* Tom. I, ed. A. Boretius, Hannoveriae, 1883.

Monumenta Germaniae Historica, Legum Sectio III, *Concilia Aevi Karolini I,* Tom. II, Pars 1, ed. A. Werminghoff, Hannoverae: Lipsiae, 1908.

Normae secundum quas S. Cong. Ep. et Reg. procedere solet in approbandis Novis Institutis Votorum Simplicium, Romae: Typis S. Cong. de Propaganda Fide, 1901.

Pallottini, Salvator, *Collectio omnium conclusionum et resolutionum quae in causis propositis apud S. Cong. Cardinalium S. Concilii Tridentini Interpretum prodierunt anno 1564 ad annum 1860,* 18 vols., Romae, 1868-1895.

Potthast, Augustus, *Regesta Pontificum Romanorum inde ab anno post Christum natum MCXCVIII (1198) ad annum MCCCIV (1304),* 2 vols., Berolini, 1874-1875.

Rotae Auditorum Decisiones Novae, Antiquae, et Antiquiores, Venetiis, 1570.

Schroeder, Henry J., *Canons and Decrees of the Council of Trent,* St. Louis: Herder, 1941.

REFERENCE WORKS

Alzog, John, *Manual of Universal Church History,* 4 vols., Dublin: M. H. Gill & Son, 1879.

Augustine, Charles, *A Commentary on the New Code of Canon Law,* 8 vols., Vol. III, 5. ed., 1938; Vol. VI, 3. ed., 1931, St. Louis: Herder.

Ayrinhac, H. A.-Lydon, P. J., *Marriage Legislation in the New Code of Canon Law,* New, Revised Ed., New York: Benziger Brothers, Inc., 1943.

——, *Penal Legislation in the New Code of Canon Law,* New York: Benziger Brothers, 1936.

Bachofen, Augustinus, *Compendium Juris Regularium,* New York: Benziger Brothers, 1903.

Bakalarczyk, R., *De Novitiatu,* The Catholic University of America Canon Law Studies, n. 36, Washington, D. C.: The Catholic University of America, 1927.

Balmès, Hilaire, *Les Religieux à Voeux Simples d'après le Code,* Bruxelles: Action Catholique, 1921.

Barbosa, Augustinus, *Collectanea Doctorum in Ius Pontificium Universum,* 3 vols. in 6, Lugduni, 1656.

——, *Collectanea eorum Doctorum qui in suis operibus Concilii Tridentini loca referentes illorum materiam incidenter tractarunt,* Lugduni, 1657.

Bastien, Pierre, *Directoire Canonique a l'Usage des Congrégations à voeux simples,* 3. ed., Bruges: Beyaert, 1923.

Battandier, Albert, *Guide canonique pour les constitutions des instituts à voeux simples,* 6. ed., Paris, 1923.

Berutti, Christophorus, *Institutiones Iuris Canonici,* 6 vols., Vol. III, Taurini-Romae: Marietti, 1936.

Beste, Udalricus, *Introductio in Codicem,* ed. altera, Collegeville, Minn.: St. John's Abbey Press, 1944.

Bouix, D., *Tractatus de Jure Regularium,* 3. ed., 2 vols., Parisiis, 1882.

Bouscaren, T. Lincoln, *The Canon Law Digest,* 2 vols., Milwaukee: Bruce, 1934-1943.

Butler, Cuthbert, *Benedictine Monasticism,* 2. ed., London: Longmans, Green & Company, 1924.

————, *The Lausiac History of Palladius,* Texts and Studies, VI, 2 vols., Cambridge, 1898-1904.

Cambridge Medieval History, The, 8 vols., Reprint, New York: Macmillan, 1936.

Cappello, Felix, *Tractatus Canonico-Moralis de Sacramentis,* 3 vols. in 6, Vol. III, 4. ed., Romae: Apud Aedes Universitatis Gregorianae, 1939.

Chelodi, Ioannes, *Ius de Personis iuxta Codicem Iuris Canonici,* ed. altera a Sac. Ernesto Bertagnolli recognita et aucta, Tridentini: Libr. Edit. Tridentum, 1927.

Chrysostom, John, *On the Priesthood,* transl. by Boyle, Westminster, Md.: Newman Book Shop, 1943.

Claeys-Bouuaert, F.-Simenon, G., *Manuale Juris Canonici ad usum Seminariorum,* 3 vols., Vol. I, 3. ed., 1930; Vol. II, 1931; Vol. III, 3. ed., 1931, Gandae et Leodii.

Clancy, Patrick M., *The Local Religious Superior,* The Catholic University of America Canon Law Studies, n. 175, Washington, D. C.: The Catholic University of America Press, 1943.

Cocchi, Guidus, *Commentarium in Codicem Iuris Canonici ad Usum Scholarum,* 8 vols. in 5, Vol. IV, 3. ed., Taurinorum Augustae: Marietti, 1932.

Coronata, Mattheus Conte a, *Institutiones Iuris Canonici ad Usum Utriusque Cleri et Scholarum,* 5 vols., Vol. I, 2. ed., Taurini: Marietti, 1939.

Creusen, I.-Garesché, Edward-Ellis, Adam, *Religious Men and Women in the Code,* 5. ed., Milwaukee, Wis.: The Bruce Publishing Co., 1940.

De Luca, Joannes Baptista Cardinalis, *Theatrum Veritatis et Justitiae,* 15 vols. in 8, Coloniae Agrippinae, 1706.

Dictionnaire d'Archéologie Chrétienne et de Liturgie, 16 vols., Paris: Librairie Letouzey et Ané, 1907-1939.

Fagnanus, Prosper, *Commentaria in Librum Decretalium,* 5 vols., Venetiis, 1696.

Fanfani, Ludovicus, *De Iure Religiosorum ad Normam Codicis Iuris Canonici,* 2. ed., Taurini-Romae: Marietti, 1925.

Farrell, Benjamin F., *The Rights and Duties of the Local Ordinary Regarding Congregations of Women Religious of Pontifical Approval,* The Catholic University of America Canon Law Studies, n. 128, Washington, D. C.: The Catholic University of America Press, 1941.

Ferraris, Lucius, *Prompta Bibliotheca Canonica, Iuridica, Moralis, Theologica, nec non Ascetica, Polemica, Rubricistica, Historica,* 8 vols., Romae, 1885-1892. Supplementum ed. I. Bucceroni, Romae, 1899.

Ferreres, Ioannes, *Institutiones Canonicae*, 2. ed., 2 vols., Barcinonae: Subirana, 1920.

Flanagan, Bernard J., *The Canonical Erection of Religious Houses*, The Catholic University of America Canon Law Studies, n. 179, Washington, D. C.: The Catholic University of America Press, 1943.

Gallik, George A., *The Rights and Duties of Bishops Regarding Diocesan Sisterhoods*, St. Paul, Minnesota: Wanderer Printing Co., 1939.

Gasquet, F. A., *English Monastic Life*, 2. ed. rev., New York, 1904.

Geser, Fintan, *The Canon Law Governing Communities of Sisters*, St. Louis, Mo., B. Herder Book Co., 1939.

Harrigan, Robert J., *The Radical Sanation of Invalid Marriages*, The Catholic University of America Canon Law Studies, n. 116, Washington, D. C.: The Catholic University of America, 1938.

Hostiensis, Cardinalis (Henricus de Segusio), *Commentaria in Quinque Decretalium Libros*, 5 vols. in 3, Venetiis, 1581.

Laymann, Paulus, *Theologia Moralis in Quinque Libros Partita*, Venetiis, 1719.

Levy-Bruhl, Henri, *Études sur les Élections Abbatiales en France*, Paris, 1913.

Lewis, Gordian, *Chapters in Religious Institutes*, The Catholic University of America Canon Law Studies, n. 181, Washington, D. C.: The Catholic University of America Press, 1943.

Martène, Edmond, *Tractatus de Antiqua Ecclesiae Disciplina in Divinis Celebrandis Officiis*, Lugduni, 1706.

——, *De Antiquis Ecclesiae Ritibus*, 4 vols., Rotomagi, 1700.

McDevitt, Gilbert J., *Legitimacy and Legitimation*, The Catholic University of America Canon Law Studies, n. 138, Washington, D. C.: The Catholic University of America Press, 1941.

McManus, James E., *The Administration of Temporal Goods in Religious Institutes*, The Catholic University of America Canon Law Studies, n. 109, Washington, D. C.: The Catholic University of America, 1937.

Migne, J. P., *Patrologiae Cursus Completus, Series Graeca*, 162 vols., Parisiis, 1857-1866.

——, *Patrologiae Cursus Completus, Series Latina*, 221 vols., Parisiis, 1844-1864.

Montalembert, Count de, *The Monks of the West*, 2 vols., New York: P. J. Kenedy & Sons, 1905.

Mothon, Joseph, *Institutions Canoniques*, 3 vols., Paris: Desclée, 1922-1924.

Navarrus (Martinus de Azpilcueta), *Opera Omnia*, 6 vols., Venetiis, 1618-1621.

Noval, Joseph, *Commentarium Codicis Iuris Canonici*, Lib. IV, *De Processibus*, 2 vols., Romae: Marietti, 1920-1932.

O'Brien, Joseph D., *The Exemption of Religious in Church Law*, Milwaukee: The Bruce Publishing Company, 1943.

Oesterle, Gerardus, *Praelectiones Iuris Canonici*, Romae: In Collegio S. Anselmi, 1931.

O'Neil, Francis J., *The Dismissal of Religious in Temporary Vows*, The Catholic University of America Canon Law Studies, n. 166, Washington, D. C.: The Catholic University of America Press, 1942.

Orth, Clement R., *The Approbation of Religious Institutes*, The Catholic University of America Canon Law Studies, n. 71, The Catholic University of America, 1931.

Ottaviani, Alaphridus, *Compendium Iuris Publici Ecclesiastici ad Usum Auditorum S. Theologiae*, Typis Polyglottis Vaticanis, 1936.

Panormitanus, Abbas (Nicolaus de Tudeschis), *Commentaria in Quinque Libros Decretalium*, 5 vols. in 7, Venetiis, 1588.

Parsons, Anscar, *Canonical Elections*, The Catholic University of America Canon Law Studies, n. 118, Washington, D. C.: The Catholic University of America Press, 1939.

Pellizzarius, Franciscus, *Tractatio de Monialibus*, 3. ed., Venetiis, 1631.

Pejška, Josephus, *Ius Canonicum Religiosorum*, 3. ed., Friburgi-Brisgoviae: Herder & Co., 1927.

Petra, Vincentius Cardinalis, *Commentaria ad Constitutiones Apostolicas*, 5 vols. in 2, Venetiis, 1729.

Pirhing, Ernricus, *Jus Canonicum Nova Methodo Explicatum*, 5 vols. in 4, Dillingae, 1674-1678.

Reiffenstuel, Analectus, *Ius Canonicum Universum*, 5 vols. in 7, Parisiis, 1864-1870.

Reilly, Thomas F., *The Visitation of Religious*, The Catholic University of America Canon Law Studies, n. 112, Washington, D. C.: The Catholic University of America, 1938.

Rodericus, Emanuelis, *Resolutiones Questionum Regularium*, Lugduni, 1634.

Sandeus, Felinus, *Commentaria Iuris Canonici in Quinque Libros Decretalium*, 3 vols., Venetiis, 1570.

Schaefer, Timotheus, *De Religiosis ad Normam Codicis Iuris Canonici*, 3. ed., Romae: Typis Polyglottis Vaticanis, 1940.

Schmalzgrueber, Franciscus, *Ius Ecclesiasticum Universum*, 5 vols. in 12, Romae, 1843-1845.

Smith, Mariner, *The Penal Law for Religious*, The Catholic University of America Canon Law Studies, n. 98, Washington, D. C.: The Catholic University of America, 1935.

Suarez, Franciscus, *Opera Omnia*, 26 vols., Parisiis, 1856-1878.

Tamburini, Ascanius, *De Jure Abbatum et Aliorum Praelatorum*, 3 vols. in 2, Coloniae Agrippinae, 1691.

Thomassinus, Ludovicus, *Vetus et Nova Ecclesiae Disciplina circa Beneficia et Beneficiarios*, 10 vols., Moguntiae, 1787.

Van Hove, A., *Commentarium Lovaniense in Codicem Iuris Canonici*, Vol. I, Tom. II, *De Legibus Ecclesiasticis*, Mechliniae-Romae: Dessain, 1930.

Vermeersch, A.-Creusen, I., *Epitome Iuris Canonici cum Commentariis ad Scholas et ad Usum Privatum*, 3 vols., Vol. I, 6. ed., 1937; Vol. II, 5. ed., 1934; Vol. III, 5. ed., 1936, Mechliniae et Romae: H. Dessain.

Vromant, G., *De Bonis Ecclesiae Temporalibus*, Louvain: Desbarax, 1927.

Wernz, F.-Vidal, P., *Ius Canonicum ad Codicis Normam Exactum*, 7 vols. in 8, Vol. III, *De Religiosis*, Romae: Universitas Gregoriania, 1933.

Principal Articles

Goyeneche, S., "Consultationes"—*CpR.*, III (1922), 139-146.

———, "Consultationes"—*CpR*, III (1922), 215-224.

———, "Consultationes"—*CpR*, V (1924), 26-31.

———, "Consultationes"—*CpR*, VII (1926), 249-254.

———, "Consultationes"—*CpR*, VIII (1927), 31-35.

Larraona, Arcadius, "Consultationes"—*CpR*, I (1920), 30-32; 179-183.

———, "Commentarium Codicis"—*CpR*, II (1921), 135-139.

———, "De paupertate simplici"—*CpR*, II (1921), 40-45.

———, "Consultationes"—*CpR*, II (1921), 361-366.

———, "Commentarium Codicis"—*CpR*, IV (1923), 39-46.

———, "Commentarium Codicis"—*CpR*, V (1924), 324-334; 417-436.

———, "Commentarium Codicis"—*CpR*, VII (1926), 93-98; 239-248; 296-300; 376-389.

———, "Ad can. 518 et 519 seu de regularium confessionibus"—*CpR*, VIII (1927), 359-374.

———, "Commentarium Codicis"—*CpR*, VIII (1927), 275-283.

———, "Commentarium Codicis"—*CpR*, IX (1928), 23-31.

———, "Commentarium Codicis"—*CpR*, X (1929), 33-38.

———, "De Visitatorum potestate applicandi poenas in can. 2413 statutas"—*CpR*, X (1929), 368-377.

———, "Commentarium Codicis"—*CpR*, XI (1930), 20-30.

———, "Commentarium Codicis"—*CpR*, XII (1931), 353-359; 435-442.

———, "Commentarium Codicis"—*CpR*, XIII (1932), 24-35; 353-362.

Maroto, Philippus, "Annotationes"—*CpR*, II (1921), 3-8; 60-70; 162-168.

Vermeersch, Arthurus, "De variis litteris exigendis ante ingressum"—*Periodica*, IX (1920), (5)-(7).

———, "Annotationes"—*Periodica*, X (1922-1923), 35-36.

———, "Annotationes"—*Periodica*, XI (1922-1923), 31-32.

———, "De renuntiatione bonorum, species facti"—*Periodica*, XI (1922-1923), (158)-(159).

———, "De consiliariis superiorum"—*Periodica*, XV (1926-1927), (61)-(63).

Van de Kerckhove, M., "De notione jurisdictionis apud decretistas et priores decretalistae"—*JP*, XVIII (1938), 10-14.

PERIODICALS

Commentarium pro Religiosis (ab anno 1935: *Commentarium pro Religiosis et Missionariis*), Romae, 1920—

Jus Pontificium, Romae, 1921—

Periodica de Religiosis et Missionariis, Brugis, 1905-1919; *Periodica de Re canonica et Morali utilia praesertim Religiosis et Missionariis*, Brugis, 1920-1927; *Periodica de Re Morali, Canonica, Liturgica*, Brugis, 1927-1936 et Romae, 1937—

ABBREVIATIONS

AAS—Acta Apostolicae Sedis.

ASS—Acta Sancta Sedis.

Bull. Rom. Taur.—Bullarum Romanorum Pontificum Tauriensis Editio.

Coll. S. C. Ep. et Reg.—Collectanea Sacrae Congregationis Episcoporum et Regularium.

CpR—Commentarium pro Religiosis.

CpRM—Commentarium pro Religiosis et Missionariis.

CSEL—Corpus Scriptorum Ecclesiasticorum Latinorum.

DACL—Dictionnaire d'Archéologie Chrétienne et de Liturgie.

Ferraris—*Prompta Bibliotheca.*

Fontes—Codicis Iuris Canonici Fontes cura. . . . *Gasparri editi.* . . .

Hardouin—*Acta Conciliorum,* etc.

JE—Jaffé, *Regesta Pontificum Romanorum* (edited by Ewald).

JK—Jaffé, *op. cit.* (edited by Kaltenbrunner).

JL—Jaffé, *op. cit.* (edited by Loewenfeld).

Mansi—*Sacrorum Conciliorum Nova et Amplissima Collectio.*

*MPL—*Migne, *Patrologia Latina.*

MGH—Monumenta Germaniae Historica.

Periodica—Periodica de Re Canonica, Morali, etc.

P. C. I.—*Pontificia Commissio ad Codicis Canones authentice interpretandos.*

Potthast—Potthast, *Regesta Pontificum Romanorum.*

S. C. de Rel.—*Sacra Congregatio de Religiosis.*

ALPHABETICAL INDEX

BIOGRAPHICAL NOTE

THOMAS JOSEPH BOWE was born on February 4, 1916, at San Francisco, California. His grammar school education was received at St. Paul's and St. Monica's Schools in San Francisco. After completing six years at St. Joseph's Junior Seminary, Mountain View, California, he entered St. Patrick's Seminary, Menlo Park, California, in September, 1937. He received the B.A. degree in 1939, and was ordained to the sacred priesthood at San Francisco, March 20, 1943. In September of 1943 he entered the Catholic University of America to pursue a graduate course of studies in Canon Law. From this Institution he received the degree of Baccalaureate in Canon Law in May, 1944, and the degree of Licentiate in Canon Law in May, 1945.

CANON LAW STUDIES *

1. FRERIKS, REV. CELESTINE A., C.PP.S., J.C.D., Religious Congregations in Their External Relations, 121 pp., 1916.
2. GALLIHER, REV. DANIEL M., O.P., J.C.D., Canonical Elections, 117 pp., 1917.
3. BORKOWSKI, REV. AURELIUS L., O.F.M., J.C.D., De Confraternitatibus Ecclesiasticis, 136 pp., 1918.
4. CASTILLO, REV. CAYO, J.C.D., Disertacion Historico-Canonica sobre la Potestad del Cabildo en Sede Vacante o Impedida del Vicario Capitular, 99 pp., 1919 (1918).
5. KUBELBECK, REV. WILLIAM J., S.T.B., J.C.D., The Sacred Penitentiaria and Its Relation to Faculties of Ordinaries and Priests, 129 pp., 1918.
6. PETROVITS, REV. JOSEPH, J.C., S.T.D., J.C.D., The New Church Law on Matrimony, X-461 pp., 1919.
7. HICKEY, REV. JOHN J., S.T.B., J.C.D., Irregularities and Simple Impediments in the New Code of Canon Law, 100 pp., 1920.
8. KLEKOTKA, REV. PETER J., S.T.B., J.C.D., Diocesan Consultors, 179 pp., 1920.
9. WANENMACHER, REV. FRANCIS, J.C.D., The Evidence in Ecclesiastical Procedure Affecting the Marriage Bond, 1920 (Printed 1935).
10. GOLDEN, REV. HENRY FRANCIS, J.C.D., Parochial Benefices in the New Code, IV-119 pp., 1921 (Printed 1925).
11. KOUDELKA, REV. CHARLES J., J.C.D., Pastors, Their Rights and Duties According to the New Code of Canon Law, 211 pp., 1921.
12. MELO, REV. ANTONIUS, O.F.M., J.C.D., De Exemptione Regularium, X-188 pp., 1921.
13. SCHAAF, REV. VALENTINE THEODORE, O.F.M., S.T.B., J.C.D., The Cloister, X-180 pp., 1921.
14. BURKE, REV. THOMAS JOSEPH, S.T.D., J.C.D., Competence in Ecclesiastical Tribunals, IV-117 pp., 1922.
15. LEECH, REV. GEORGE LEO, J.C.D., A Comparative Study of the Constitution "Apostolicae Sedis" and the "Codex Juris Canonici," 179 pp., 1922.
16. MOTRY, REV. HUBERT LOUIS, S.T.D., J.C.D., Diocesan Faculties According to the Code of Canon Law, II-167 pp., 1922.
17. MURPHY, REV. GEORGE LAWRENCE, J.C.D., Delinquencies and Penalties in the Administration and the Reception of the Sacraments, IV-121 pp., 1923.
18. O'REILLY, REV. JOHN ANTHONY, S.T.B., J.C.D., Ecclesiastical Sepulture in the New Code of Canon Law, II-129 pp., 1923.

---

* From nn. 1-100 inclusive only nn. 25 and 57 are still obtainable.

From n. 101 onward all numbers are available except the following: nn. 101-118 inclusive, and also n. 122.

19. MICHALICKA, REV. WENCESLAS CYRILL, O.S.B., J.C.D., Judicial Procedure in Dismissal of Clerical Exempt Religious, 107 pp., 1923.
20. DARGIN, REV. EDWARD VINCENT, S.T.B., J.C.D., Reserved Cases According to the Code of Canon Law, IV-103 pp., 1924.
21. GODFREY, REV. JOHN A., S.T.B., J.C.D., The Right of Patronage According to the Code of Canon Law, 153 pp., 1924.
22. HAGEDORN, REV. FRANCIS EDWARD, J.C.D., General Legislation on Indulgences, II-154 pp., 1924.
23. KING, REV. JAMES IGNATIUS, J.C.D., The Administration of the Sacraments to Dying Non-Catholics, V-141 pp., 1924.
24. WINSLOW, REV. FRANCIS JOSEPH, O.F.M., J.C.D., Vicars and Prefects Apostolic, IV-149 pp., 1924.
25. CORREA, REV. JOSE SERVELION, S.T.L., J.C.D., La Potestad Legislativa de la Iglesia Catolica, IV-127 pp., 1925.
26. DUGAN, REV. HENRY FRANCIS, A.M., J.C.D., The Judiciary Department of the Diocesan Curia, 87 pp., 1925.
27. KELLER, REV. CHARLES FREDERICK, S.T.B., J.C.D., Mass Stipends, 167 pp., 1925.
28. PASCHANG, REV. JOHN LINUS, J.C.D., The Sacramentals According to the Code of Canon Law, 129 pp., 1925.
29. PIONTEK, REV. CYRILLUS, O.F.M., S.T.B., J.C.D., De Indulto Exclaustrationis necnon Saecularizationis, XIII-289 pp., 1925.
30. KEARNEY, REV. RICHARD JOSEPH, S.T.B., J.C.D., Sponsors at Baptism According to the Code of Canon Law, IV-127 pp., 1925.
31. BARTLETT, REV. CHESTER JOSEPH, A.M., LL.B., J.C.D., The Tenure of Parochial Property in the United States of America, V-108 pp., 1926.
32. KILKER, REV. ADRIAN JEROME, J.C.D., Extreme Unction, V-425 pp., 1926.
33. McCORMICK, REV. ROBERT EMMETT, J.C.D., Confessors of Religious, VIII-266 pp., 1926.
34. MILLER, REV. NEWTON THOMAS, J.C.D., Founded Masses According to the Code of Canon Law, VII-93 pp., 1926.
35. ROELKER, REV. EDWARD G., S.T.D., J.C.D., Principles of Privilege According to the Code of Canon Law, XI-166 pp., 1926.
36. BAKALARCZYK, REV. RICHARDUS, M.I.C., J.U.D., De Novitiatu, VIII-208 pp., 1927.
37. PIZZUTI, REV. LAWRENCE, O.F.M., J.U.L., De Parochis Religiosis, 1927. (Not Printed.)
38. BLILEY, REV. NICHOLAS MARTIN, O.S.B., J.C.D., Altars According to the Code of Canon Law, XIX-132 pp., 1927.
39. BROWN, MR. BRENDAN FRANCIS, A.B., LL.M., J.U.D., The Canonical Juristic Personality with Special Reference to its Status in the United States of America, V-212 pp., 1927.
40. CAVANAUGH, REV. WILLIAM THOMAS, C.P., J.U.D., The Reservation of the Blessed Sacrament, VIII-101 pp., 1927.

41. DOHENY, REV. WILLIAM J., C.S.C., A.B., J.U.D., Church Property: Modes of Acquisition, X-118 pp., 1927.

42. FELDHAUS, REV. ALOYSIUS H., C.PP.S., J.C.D., Oratories, IX-141 pp., 1927.

43. KELLY, REV. JAMES PATRICK, A.B., J.C.D., The Jurisdiction of the Simple Confessor, X-208 pp., 1927.

44. NEUBERGER, REV. NICHOLAS J., J.C.D., Canon 6 or the Relation of the Codex Juris Canonici to the Preceding Legislation, V-95 pp., 1927.

45. O'KEEFE, REV. GERALD MICHAEL, J.C.D., Matrimonial Dispensations, Powers of Bishops, Priests, and Confessors, VIII-232 pp., 1927.

46. QUIGLEY, REV. JOSEPH A. M., A.B., J.C.D., Condemned Societies, 139 pp., 1927.

47. ZAPLOTNIK, REV. JOHANNES LEO, J.C.D., De Vicariis Foraneis, X-142 pp., 1927.

48. DUSKIE, REV. JOHN ALOYSIUS, A.B., J.C.D., The Canonical Status of the Orientals in the United States, VIII-196 pp., 1928.

49. HYLAND, REV. FRANCIS EDWARD, J.C.D., Excommunication, Its Nature, Historical Development and Effects, VIII-181 pp., 1928.

50. REINMANN, REV. GERALD JOSEPH, O.M.C., J.C.D., The Third Order Secular of Saint Francis, 201 pp., 1928.

51. SCHENK, REV. FRANCIS J., J.C.D., The Matrimonial Impediments of Mixed Religion and Disparity of Cult, XVI-318 pp., 1929.

52. COADY, REV. JOHN JOSEPH, S.T.D., J.U.D., A.M., The Appointment of Pastors, VIII-150 pp., 1929.

53. KAY, REV. THOMAS HENRY, J.C.D., Competence in Matrimonial Procedure, VIII-164 pp., 1929.

54. TURNER, REV. SIDNEY JOSEPH, C.P., J.U.D., The Vow of Poverty, XLIX-217 pp., 1929.

55. KEARNEY, REV. RAYMOND A., A.B., S.T.D., J.C.D., The Principles of Delegation, VII-149 pp., 1929.

56. CONRAN, REV. EDWARD JAMES, A.B., J.C.D., The Interdict, V-163 pp., 1930.

57. O'NEILL, REV. WILLIAM H., J.C.D., Papal Rescripts of Favor, VII-218 pp., 1930.

58. BASTNAGEL, REV. CLEMENT VINCENT, J.U.D., The Appointment of Parochial Adjutants and Assistants, XV-257 pp., 1930.

59. FERRY, REV. WILLIAM A., A.B., J.C.D., Stole Fees, V-136 pp., 1930.

60. COSTELLO, REV. JOHN MICHAEL, A.B., J.C.D., Domicile and Quasi-Domicile, VII-201 pp., 1930.

61. KREMER, REV. MICHAEL NICHOLAS, A.B., S.T.B., J.C.D., Church Support in the United States, VI-136 pp., 1930.

62. ANGULO, REV. LUIS, C.M., J.C.D., Legislation de la Iglesia sobre la intencion en la application de la Santa Misa, VII-104 pp., 1931.

63. FREY, REV. WOLFGANG NORBERT, O.S.B., A.B., J.C.D., The Act of Religious Profession, VIII-174 pp., 1931.

64. ROBERTS, REV. JAMES BRENDAN, A.B., J.C.D., The Banns of Marriage, XIV-140 pp., 1931.
65. RYDER, REV. RAYMOND ALOYSIUS, A.B., J.C.D., Simony, IX-151 pp., 1931.
66. CAMPAGNA, REV. ANGELO, PH.D., J.U.D., Il Vicario Generale del Vescovo, VII-205 pp., 1931.
67. COX, REV. JOSEPH GODFREY, A.B., J.C.D., The Administration of Seminaries, VI-124 pp., 1931.
68. GREGORY, REV. DONALD J., J.U.D., The Pauline Privilege, XV-165 pp., 1931.
69. DONOHUE, REV. JOHN F., J.C.D., The Impediment of Crime, VII-110 pp., 1931.
70. DOOLEY, REV. EUGENE A., O.M.I., J.C.D., Church Law on Sacred Relics, IX-143 pp., 1931.
71. ORTH, REV. CLEMENT RAYMOND, O.M.C., J.C.D., The Approbation of Religious Institutes, 171 pp., 1931.
72. PERNICONE, REV. JOSEPH M., A.B., J.C.D., The Ecclesiastical Prohibition of Books, XII-267 pp., 1932.
73. CLINTON, REV. CONNELL, A.B., J.C.D., The Paschal Precept, IX-108 pp., 1932.
74. DONNELLY, REV. FRANCIS B., A.M., S.T.L., J.C.D., The Diocesan Synod, VIII-125 pp., 1932.
75. TORRENTE, REV. CAMILO, C.M.F., J.C.D., Las Procesiones Sagradas, V-145 pp., 1932.
76. MURPHY, REV. EDWIN J., C.PP.S., J.C.D., Suspension Ex Informata Conscientia, XI-122 pp., 1932.
77. MACKENZIE, REV. ERIC F., A.M., S.T.L., J.C.D., The Delict of Heresy in its Commission, Penalization, Absolution, VII-124 pp., 1932.
78. LYONS, REV. AVITUS E., S.T.B., J.C.D., The Collegiate Tribunal of First Instance, XI-147 pp., 1932.
79. CONNOLLY, REV. THOMAS A., J.C.D., Appeals, XI-195, pp., 1932.
80. SANGMEISTER, REV. JOSEPH V., A.B., J.C.D., Force and Fear as Precluding Matrimonial Consent, V-211 pp., 1932.
81. JAEGER, REV. LEO A., A.B., J.C.D., The Administration of Vacant and Quasi-Vacant Episcopal Sees in the United States, IX-229 pp., 1932.
82. RIMLINGER, REV. HERBERT T., J.C.D., Error Invalidating Matrimonial Consent, VII-79 pp., 1932.
83. BARRETT, REV. JOHN D. M., S.S., J.C.D., A Comparative Study of the Third Plenary Council of Baltimore and the Code, IX-221 pp., 1932.
84. CARBERRY, REV. JOHN J., PH.D., S.T.D., J.C.D., The Juridical Form of Marriage, X-177 pp., 1934.
85. DOLAN, REV. JOHN L., A.B., J.C.D., The Defensor Vinculi, XII-157 pp., 1934.
86. HANNAN, REV. JEROME D., A.M., S.T.D., LL.B., J.C.D., The Canon Law of Wills, IX-517 pp., 1934.

87. LEMIEUX, REV. DELISE A., A.M., J.C.D., The Sentence in Ecclesiastical Procedure, IX-131 pp., 1934.

88. O'ROURKE, REV. JAMES J., A.B., J.C.D., Parish Registers, VII-109 pp., 1934.

89. TIMLIN, REV. BARTHOLOMEW, O.F.M., A.M., J.C.D., Conditional Matrimonial Consent, X-381 pp., 1934.

90. WAHL, REV. FRANCIS X., A.B., J.C.D., The Matrimonial Impediments of Consanguinity and Affinity, VI-125 pp., 1934.

91. WHITE, REV. ROBERT J., A.B., LL.B., S.T.B., J.C.D., Canonical Ante-Nuptial Promises and the Civil Law, VI-152 pp., 1934.

92. HERRERA, REV. ANTONIO PARRA, O.C.D., J.C.D., Legislacion Ecclesiastica sobra el Ayuno y la Abstinencia, XI-191 pp., 1935.

93. KENNEDY, REV. EDWIN J., J.C.D., The Special Matrimonial Process in Cases of Evident Nullity, X-165 pp., 1935.

94. MANNING, REV. JOHN J., A.B., J.C.D., Presumption of Law in Matrimonial Procedure, XI-111 pp., 1935.

95. MOEDER, REV. JOHN M., J.C.D., The Proper Bishop for Ordination and Dismissorial Letters, VII-135 pp., 1935.

96. O'MARA, REV. WILLIAM A., A.B., J.C.D., Canonical Causes for Matrimonial Dispensations, IX-155 pp., 1935.

97. REILLY, REV. PETER, J.C.D., Residence of Pastors, IX-81 pp., 1935.

98. SMITH, REV. MARINER T., O.P., S.T.Lr., J.C.D., The Penal Law for Religious, VIII-169 pp., 1935.

99. WHALEN, REV. DONALD W., A.M., J.C.D., The Value of Testimonial Evidence in Matrimonial Procedure, XIII-297 pp., 1935.

100. CLEARY, REV. JOSEPH F., J.C.D., Canonical Limitations on the Alienation of Church Property, VIII-141 pp., 1936.

101. GLYNN, REV. JOHN C., J.C.D., The Promoter of Justice, XX-337 pp., 1936.

102. BRENNAN, REV. JAMES H., S.S., M.A., S.T.B., J.C.D., The Simple Convalidation of Marriage, VI-135 pp., 1937.

103. BRUNINI, REV. JOSEPH BERNARD, J.C.D., The Clerical Obligations of Canons 139 and 142, X-121 pp., 1937.

104. CONNOR, REV. MAURICE, A.B., J.C.D., The Administrative Removal of Pastors, VIII-159 pp., 1937.

105. GUILFOYLE, REV. MERLIN JOSEPH, J.C.D., Custom, XI-144 pp., 1937.

106. HUGHES, REV. JAMES AUSTIN, A.B., A.M., J.C.D., Witnesses in Criminal Trials of Clerics, IX-140 pp., 1937.

107. JANSEN, REV. RAYMOND J., A.B., S.T.L., J.C.D., Canonical Provisions for Catechetical Instruction, VII-153 pp., 1937.

108. KEALY, REV. JOHN JAMES, A.B., J.C.D., The Introductory Libellus in Church Court Procedure, XI-121 pp., 1937.

109. McMANUS, REV. JAMES EDWARD, C.SS.R., J.C.D., The Administration of Temporal Goods in Religious Institutes, XVI-196 pp., 1937.

110. MORIARTY, REV. EUGENE JAMES, J.C.D., Oaths in Ecclesiastical Courts, X-115 pp., 1937.
111. RAINER, REV. ELIGIUS GEORGE, C.SS.R., J.C.D., Suspension of Clerics, XVII-249 pp., 1937.
112. REILLY, REV. THOMAS F., C.SS.R., J.C.D., Visitation of Religious, VI-195 pp., 1938.
113. MORIARTY, REV. FRANCIS E., C.SS.R., J.C.D., The Extraordinary Absolution from Censures, XV-334 pp., 1938.
114. CONNOLLY, REV. NICHOLAS P., J.C.D., The Canonical Erection of Parishes, X-132 pp., 1938.
115. DONOVAN, REV. JAMES JOSEPH, J.C.D., The Pastor's Obligation in Prenuptial Investigation, XII-322 pp., 1938.
116. HARRIGAN, REV. ROBERT J., M.A., S.T.B., J.C.D., The Radical Sanation of Invalid Marriages, VIII-208 pp., 1938.
117. BOFFA, REV. CONRAD HUMBERT, J.C.D., Canonical Provisions for Catholic Schools, VII-211 pp., 1939.
118. PARSONS, REV. ANSCAR JOHN, O.M.Cap., J.C.D., Canonical Elections, XII-236 pp., 1939.
119. REILLY, REV. EDWARD MICHAEL, A.B., J.C.D., The General Norms of Dispensation, XII-156 pp., 1939.
120. RYAN, REV. GERALD ALOYSIUS, A.B., J.C.D., Principles of Episcopal Jurisdiction, XII-172 pp., 1939.
121. BURTON, REV. FRANCIS JAMES, C.S.C., A.B., J.C.D., A Commentary on Canon 1125, X-222 pp., 1940.
122. MIASKIEWICZ, REV. FRANCIS SIGISMUND, J.C.D., Supplied Jurisdiction According to Canon 209, XII-340 pp., 1940.
123. RICE, REV. PATRICK WILLIAM, A.B., J.C.D., Proof of Death in Prenuptial Investigation, VIII-156 pp., 1940.
124. ANGLIN, REV. THOMAS FRANCIS, M.S., J.C.D., The Eucharistic Fast, VIII-183 pp., 1941.
125. COLEMAN, REV. JOHN JEROME, J.C.D., The Minister of Confirmation, VI-153 pp., 1941.
126. DOWNS, REV. JOHN EMMANUEL, A.B., J.C.D., The Concept of Clerical Immunity, XI-163 pp., 1941.
127. ESSWEIN, REV. ANTHONY ALBERT, J.C.D., Extrajudicial Penal Powers of Ecclesiastical Superiors, X-144 pp., 1941.
128. FARRELL, REV. BENJAMIN FRANCIS, M.A., S.T.L., J.C.D., The Rights and Duties of the Local Ordinary Regarding Congregations of Women Religious of Pontifical Approval, V-195 pp., 1941.
129. FEENEY, REV. THOMAS JOHN, A.B., S.T.L., J.C.D., Restitutio in Integrum, VI-169 pp., 1941.
130. FINDLAY, REV. STEPHEN WILLIAM, O.S.B., A.B., J.C.D., Canonical Norms Governing the Deposition and Degradation of Clerics, XVII-279 pp., 1941.

131. GOODWINE, REV. JOHN, A.B., S.T.L., J.C.D., The Right of the Church to Acquire Property, VIII-119 pp., 1941.

132. HESTON, REV. EDWARD LOUIS, C.S.C., Ph.D., S.T.D., J.C.D., The Alienation of Church Property in the United States, XII-222 pp., 1941.

133. HOGAN, REV. JAMES JOHN, A.B., S.T.L., J.C.D., Judicial Advocates and Procurators, XIII-200 pp., 1941.

134. KEALY, REV. THOMAS M., A.B., Litt.B., J.C.D., Dowry of Women Religious, IX-152 pp., 1941.

135. KEENE, REV. MICHAEL JAMES, O.S.B., J.C.D., Religious Ordinaries and Canon 198, V-164 pp., 1942.

136. KERIN, REV. CHARLES A., S.S., M.A., S.T.B., J.C.D., The Privation of Christian Burial, XVI-279 pp., 1941.

137. LOUIS, REV. WILLIAM FRANCIS, M.A., J.C.D., Diocesan Archives, X-101 pp., 1941.

138. McDEVITT, REV. GILBERT JOSEPH, A.B., J.C.D., Legitimacy and Legitimation, X-247 pp., 1941.

139. McDONOUGH, REV. THOMAS JOSEPH, A.B., J.C.D., Apostolic Administrators, X-217 pp., 1941.

140. MEIER, REV. CARL ANTHONY, A.B., J.C.D., Penal Administrative Procedure Against Negligent Pastors, XI-240 pp., 1941.

141. SCHMIDT, REV. JOHN ROGG, A.B., J.C.D., The Principles of Authentic Interpretation in Canon 17 of the Code of Canon Law, XII-331 pp., 1941.

142. SLAFKOSKY, REV. ANDREW LEONARD, A.B., J.C.D., The Canonical Episcopal Visitation of the Diocese, X-197 pp., 1941.

143. SWOBODA, REV. INNOCENT ROBERT, O.F.M., J.C.D., Ignorance in Relation to the Imputability of Delicts, IX-271 pp., 1941.

144. DUBÉ, REV. ARTHUR JOSEPH, A.B., J.C.D., The General Principles for the Reckoning of Time in Canon Law, VIII-299 pp., 1941.

145. McBRIDE, REV. JAMES T., A.B., J.C.D., Incardination and Excardination of Seculars, XX-585 pp., 1941.

146. KRÓL, REV. JOHN T., J.C.D., The Defendant in Ecclesiastical Trials, XII-207 pp., 1942.

147. COMYNS, REV. JOSEPH J., C.SS.R., A.B., J.C.D., Papal and Episcopal Administration of Church Property, XIV-155 pp., 1942.

148. BARRY, REV. GARRETT FRANCIS, O.M.I., J.C.D., Violation of the Cloister, XII-260 pp., 1942.

149. BOLDUC, REV. GATIEN, C.S.V., A.B., S.T.L., J.C.D., Les Études dans les Religions Cléricales, VIII-155 pp., 1942.

150. BOYLE, REV. DAVID JOHN, M.A., J.C.D., The Juridic Effects of Moral Certitude on Pre-Nuptial Guarantees, XII-188 pp., 1942.

151. CANAVAN, REV. WALTER JOSEPH, M.A., Litt.D., J.C.D., The Profession of Faith, XII-143 pp., 1942.

152. DESROCHERS, REV. BRUNO, A.B., Ph.L., S.T.B., J.C.D., Le Premier Concile Plénier de Québec et le Code de Droit Canonique, XIV-186 pp., 1942.

153. DILLON, REV. ROBERT EDWARD, A.B., J.C.D., Common Law Marriage, X-148 pp., 1942.

154. DODWELL, REV. EDWARD JOHN, Ph.D., S.T.B., J.C.D., The Time and Place for the Celebration of Marriage, X-156 pp., 1942.

155. DONNELLAN, REV. THOMAS ANDREW, A.B., J.C.D., The Obligation of the Missa pro Populo, VII-131 pp., 1942.

156. ELTZ, REV. LOUIS ANTHONY, A.B., J.C.D., Cooperation in Crime, XII-208 pp., 1942.

157. GASS, REV. SYLVESTER FRANCIS, M.A., J.C.D., Ecclesiastical Pensions, XI-206 pp., 1942.

158. GUINIVEN, REV. JOHN JOSEPH, C.SS.R., J.C.D., The Precept of Hearing Mass, XIV-188 pp., 1942.

159. GULCZYNSKI, REV. JOHN THEOPHILUS, J.C.D., The Desecration and Violation of Churches, X-126 pp., 1942.

160. HAMMILL, REV. JOHN LEO, M.A., J.C.D., The Obligations of the Traveler According to Canon 14, VIII-204 pp., 1942.

161. HAYDT, REV. JOHN JOSEPH, A.B., J.C.D., Reserved Benefices, XI-148 pp., 1942.

162. HUSER, REV. ROGER JOHN, O.F.M., A.B., J.C.D., The Crime of Abortion in Canon Law, XII-187 pp., 1942.

163. KEARNEY, REV. FRANCIS PATRICK, A.B., S.T.L., J.C.D., The Principles of Canon 1127, X-162 pp., 1942.

164. LINAHEN, REV. LEO JAMES, S.T.L., J.C.D., De Absolutione Complicis in Peccato Turpi, V-114 pp., 1942.

165. McCLOSKEY, REV. JOSEPH ALOYSIUS, A.B., J.C.D., The Subject of Ecclesiastical Law According to Canon 12, XVII-246 pp., 1942.

166. O'NEILL, REV. FRANCIS JOSEPH, C.SS.R., J.C.D., The Dismissal of Religious in Temporary Vows, XIII-220 pp., 1942.

167. PRINCE, REV. JOHN EDWARD, A.B., S.T.B., J.C.D., The Diocesan Chancellor, X-136 pp., 1942.

168. RIESNER, REV. ALBERT JOSEPH, C.SS.R., J.C.D., Apostates and Fugitives from Religious Institutes, IX-168 pp., 1942.

169. STENGER, REV. JOSEPH BERNARD, J.C.D., The Mortgaging of Church Property, 186 pp., 1942.

170. WALDRON, REV. JOSEPH FRANCIS, A.B., J.C.D., The Minister of Baptism, XII-197 pp., 1942.

171. WILLETT, REV. ROBERT ALBERT, J.C.D., The Probative Value of Documents in Ecclesiastical Trials, X-124 pp., 1942.

172. WOEBER, REV. EDWARD MARTIN, M.A., J.C.D., The Interpellations, XII-161 pp., 1942.

173. BENKO, REV. MATTHEW ALOYSIUS, O.S.B., M.A., J.C.D., The Abbot *Nullius*, XVI-148 pp., 1943.

174. CHRIST, REV. JOSEPH JAMES, M.A., S.T.L., J.C.D., Dispensation from Vindicative Penalties, XIV-285 pp., 1943.

175. CLANCY, REV. PATRICK M. J., O.P., A.B., S.T.Lr., J.C.D., The Local Religious Superior, X-229 pp., 1943.

176. CLARKE, REV. THOMAS JAMES, J.C.D., Parish Societies, XII-147 pp., 1943.

177. CONNOLLY, REV. JOHN PATRICK, S.T.L., J.C.D., Synodal Examiners and Parish Priest Consultors, X-223 pp., 1943.

178. DRUMM, REV. WILLIAM MARTIN, A.B., J.C.D., Hospital Chaplains, XII-175 pp., 1943.

179. FLANAGAN, REV. BERNARD JOSEPH, A.B., S.T.L., J.C.D., The Canonical Erection of Religious Houses, X-147 pp., 1943.

180. KELLEHER, REV. STEPHEN JOSEPH, A.B., S.T.B., J.C.D., Discussions with Non-Catholics: Canonical Legislation, X-93 pp., 1943.

181. LEWIS, REV. GORDIAN, C.P., J.C.D., Chapters in Religious Institutes, XII-169 pp., 1943.

182. MARX, REV. ADOLPH, J.C.D., The Declaration of Nullity of Marriages Contracted Outside the Church, X-151 pp., 1943.

183. MATULENAS, REV. RAYMOND ANTHONY, O.S.B., A.B., J.C.D., Communication, a Source of Privileges, XII-225 pp., 1943.

184. O'LEARY, REV. CHARLES GERARD, C.SS.R., J.C.D., Religious Dismissed After Perpetual Profession, X-213 pp., 1943.

185. POWER, REV. CORNELIUS MICHAEL, J.C.D., The Blessing of Cemeteries, XII-231 pp., 1943.

186. SHUHLER, REV. RALPH VINCENT, O.S.A., J.C.D., Privileges of Religious to Absolve and Dispense, XII-195 pp., 1943.

187. ZIOLKOWSKI, REV. THADDEUS STANISLAUS, A.B., J.C.D., The Consecration and Blessing of Churches, XII-151 pp., 1943.

188. HENEGHAN, REV. JOHN JOSEPH, S.T.D., J.C.D., The Marriages of Unworthy Catholics: Canons 1065 and 1066, XVI-213 pp., 1944.

189. CARROLL, REV. COLEMAN FRANCIS, M.A., S.T.L., J.C.L., Charitable Institutions.

190. CIESLUK, REV. JOSEPH EDWARD, PH.B., S.T.L., J.C.L., National Parishes in the United States.

191. COBURN, REV. VINCENT PAUL, A.B., J.C.D., Marriages of Conscience, XII-172 pp., 1944.

192. CONNORS, REV. CHARLES PAUL, C.S.SP., A.B., J.C.D., Extra-Judicial Procurators in the Code of Canon Law, X-94 pp., 1944.

193. COYLE, REV. PAUL RAYMOND, A.B., J.C.D., Judicial Exceptions, X-142 pp., 1944.

194. FAIR, REV. BARTHOLOMEW FRANCIS, A.B., S.T.L., J.C.D., The Impediment of Abduction, XII-122 pp., 1944.

195. GALLAGHER, REV. THOMAS RAPHAEL, O.P., A.B., S.T.Lr., J.C.D., The Examination of the Qualities of the Ordinand, X-166 pp., 1944.

196. GANNON, REV. JOHN MARK, S.T.L., J.C.D., The Interstices Required for the Promotion to Orders, XII-100 pp., 1944.

197. GOLDSMITH, REV. J. WILLIAM, B.C.S., S.T.L., J.C.D., The Competence of Church and State Over Marriages—Disputed Points, X-128 pp., 1944.

198. GOODWINE, REV. JOSEPH GERARD, A.B., S.T.B., J.C.D., The Reception of Converts, XIV-326 pp., 1944.

199. KOWALSKI, REV. ROMUALD EUGENE, O.F.M., A.B., J.C.D., Sustenance of Religious Houses of Regulars, X-174 pp., 1944.

200. McCOY, REV. ALAN EDWARD, O.F.M., J.C.D., Force and Fear in Relation to Delictual Imputability and Penal Responsibility, XII-160 pp., 1944.

201. McDEVITT, REV. VINCENT JOHN, PH.B., S.T.L., J.C.L., Perjury.

202. MARTIN, REV. THOMAS OWEN, PH.D., S.T.D., J.C.D., Adverse Possession, Prescription and Limitation of Actions: The Canonical "Praescriptio," XX-208 pp., 1944.

203. MIKLOSOVIC, REV. PAUL JOHN, A.B., J.C.L., Attempted Marriages and Their Consequent Juridic Effects.

204. MUNDY, REV. THOMAS MAURICE, A.B., S.T.L., J.C.D., The Union of Parishes, X-164 pp., 1944.

205. O'DEA, REV. JOHN COYLE, A.B., J.C.D., The Matrimonial Impediment of Nonage, VIII-126 pp., 1944.

206. OLALIA, REV. ALEXANDER AYSON, S.T.L., J.C.D., A Comparative Study of the Christian Constitution of States and the Constitution of the Philippine Commonwealth, XII-136 pp., 1944.

207. POISSON, REV. PIERRE-MARIE, C.S.C., A.B., PH.L., TH.L., J.C.L., Droits Patrimoniaux des Maisons et des Eglises Religieuscs.

208. STADALNIKAS, REV. CASIMIR JOSEPH, M.I.C., J.C.D., Reservation of Censures, X-141 pp., 1944.

209. SULLIVAN, REV. EUGENE HENRY, S.T.L., J.C.D., Proof of the Reception of the Sacraments, X-165 pp., 1944.

210. VAUGHAN, REV. WILLIAM EDWARD, J.C.D., Constitutions for Diocesan Courts, X-210 pp., 1944.

211. PARO, REV. GINO, S.T.D., J.C.L., The Right of Apostolic Legation.

212. BALZER, REV. RALPH FRANCIS, C.P., J.C.D., The Computation of Time in a Canonical Novitiate, X-227 pp., 1945.

213. DOUGHERTY, REV. JOHN WHELAN, A.B., S.T.L., J.C.L., De Inquisitione Speciali.

214. DZIOB, REV. MICHAEL WALTER, J.C.L., The Sacred Congregation for the Oriental Church.

215. EIDENSCHINK, REV. JOHN ALBERT, O.S.B., B.A., J.C.D., The Election of Bishops in the Letters of Pope Gregory the Great, VIII-200 pp., 1945.

216. GILL, REV. NICHOLAS, C.P., J.C.L., The Spiritual Prefect in Clerical Religious Houses of Study.

217. HYNES, REV. HARRY GERARD, S.T.L., J.C.D., The Privileges of Cardinals, XII-183 pp., 1945.

218. McDEVITT, REV. GERALD VINCENT, S.T.L., J.C.D., The Renunciation of an Ecclesiastical Office, XIV-179 pp., 1945.

219. MANNING, REV. JOSEPH LEROY, J.C.D., The Free Conferral of Offices, VII-116 pp., 1945.

220. MEYER, REV. LOUIS G., O.S.B., A.B., S.T.B., J.C.D., Alms-gathering by Religious, XII-163 pp., 1945.

221. O'DONNELL, REV. CLETUS FRANCIS, M.A., J.C.L., The Marriage of Minors.

222. PRUNSKIS, REV. JOSEPH, J.C.D., Comparative Law, Ecclesiastical and Civil, in Lithuanian Concordat, X-161 pp., 1945.

223. SWEENEY, REV. FRANCIS PATRICK, C.SS.R., J.C.D., The Reduction of Clerics to the Lay State, X-199 pp., 1945.

224. VOGELPOHL, REV. HENRY JOHN, J.C.L., The Simple Impediments to Holy Orders.

225. BROCKHAUS, REV. THOMAS AQUINAS, O.S.B., J.C.L., Religious who are known as *Conversi*.

226. GRIESE, REV. ORVILLE NICHOLAS, S.T.D., J.C.L., Marriage and the Procreation of Offspring.

227. BOUDREAUX, REV. WARREN LOUIS, J.C.L., The *"ab acatholicis nati"* of Canon 1099, § 2.

228. BOWE, REV. THOMAS JOSEPH, A.B., J.C.L., Religious Superioresses.

229. DIEDERICHS, REV. MICHAEL FERDINAND, S.C.J., J.C.L., The Jurisdiction of the Latin Ordinaries over their Oriental Subjects.

230. DINGMAN, REV. MAURICE JOHN, A.B., S.T.L., J.C.L., The Plaintiff in Contentious Trials.

231. FRISON, REV. BASIL, C.M.F., M.Mus., J.C.L., The Retroactivity of Law.

232. GALVIN, REV. WILLIAM ANTHONY, M.A., J.C.L., The Administrative Transfer of Pastors.

233. GORACY, REV. JOSEPH C., J.C.L., The Diriment Matrimonial Impediment of Major Orders.

234. HALE, REV. JOSEPH FRANCIS, M.A., S.T.L., J.C.L., The Pastor of Burial.

235. HENRY, REV. JOSEPH ARTHUR, A.B., J.C.L., The Mass and Holy Communion: Interritual Law.

236. LINENBERGER, REV. HERBERT, C.PP.S., J.C.L., The False Denunciation of an Innocent Confessor.

237. LOWRY, REV. JAMES MARTIN, A.B., J.C.L., Dispensation from Private Vows.

238. LYNCH, REV. GEORGE EDWARD, A.B., S.T.L., J.C.L., Coadjutors and Auxiliaries of Bishops.

239. LYNCH, REV. TIMOTHY, M.S.SS.T., J.C.L., Contracts between Bishops and Religious Congregations.

240. McCLUNN, REV. JUSTIN DAVID, A.B., S.T.L., J.C.L., Administrative Recourse.

241. McGARVEY, REV. THOMAS JOSEPH, A.B., S.T.L., J.C.L., Bination.

242. McGRATH, REV. JAMES, A.B., J.C.L., The Privilege of the Canon.

243. MARBACH, REV. JOSEPH FRANCIS, A.B., J.C.L., Marriage Legislation for the Catholics of the Oriental Rites in the United States and Canada.

CPSIA information can be obtained at www.ICGtesting.com
Printed in the USA
BVOW01*0350250315

393163BV00001B/8/P